# Trumping the Media

# Trumping the Media

## Politics and Democracy in the Post-Truth Era

**MICHAEL MARIO ALBRECHT**

BLOOMSBURY ACADEMIC
NEW YORK • LONDON • OXFORD • NEW DELHI • SYDNEY

BLOOMSBURY ACADEMIC
Bloomsbury Publishing Inc
1385 Broadway, New York, NY 10018, USA
50 Bedford Square, London, WC1B 3DP, UK
29 Earlsfort Terrace, Dublin 2, Ireland

BLOOMSBURY, BLOOMSBURY ACADEMIC and the Diana logo
are trademarks of Bloomsbury Publishing Plc

First published in the United States of America 2023
Paperback edition published 2024

Copyright © Michael Mario Albrecht, 2023, 2024

For legal purposes the Acknowledgments on pp. vi–vii constitute an extension of this copyright page.

Cover image: Donald Trump's Twitter page, July 2019 © PjrStudio / Alamy

All rights reserved. No part of this publication may be reproduced or transmitted in any form or by any means, electronic or mechanical, including photocopying, recording, or any information storage or retrieval system, without prior permission in writing from the publishers.

Bloomsbury Publishing Inc does not have any control over, or responsibility for, any third-party websites referred to or in this book. All internet addresses given in this book were correct at the time of going to press. The author and publisher regret any inconvenience caused if addresses have changed or sites have ceased to exist, but can accept no responsibility for any such changes.

Library of Congress Cataloging-in-Publication Data
Names: Albrecht, Michael Mario, author.
Title: Trumping the media : politics and democracy in the post-truth era / Michael Mario Albrecht.
Other titles: Politics and democracy in the post-truth era
Description: New York, NY : Bloomsbury Academic, 2022. | Includes bibliographical references and index. | Summary: "Examines the rise of Donald Trump through the lens of new media landscapes and cultural shifts that have emerged since the 1980s, when Trump came to prominence"– Provided by publisher.
Identifiers: LCCN 2022008934 (print) | LCCN 2022008935 (ebook) | ISBN 9781501364860 (hb) | ISBN 9781501398063 (pb) | ISBN 9781501364846 (epdf) | ISBN 9781501364853 (ebook) | ISBN 9781501364839
Subjects: LCSH: Trump, Donald, 1946–In mass media. | Mass media–Political aspects–United States. | Press and politics–United States. | Deception–Political aspects–United States.
Classification: LCC E912 .A38 2022 (print) | LCC E912 (ebook) | DDC 302.230973–dc23/eng/20220511
LC record available at https://lccn.loc.gov/2022008934
LC ebook record available at https://lccn.loc.gov/2022008935

| ISBN: | HB: | 978-1-5013-6486-0 |
|---|---|---|
| | PB: | 978-1-5013-9806-3 |
| | ePDF: | 978-1-5013-6484-6 |
| | eBook: | 978-1-5013-6485-3 |

Typeset by Integra Software Services Pvt. Ltd.

To find out more about our authors and books visit www.bloomsbury.com and sign up for our newsletters.

# Contents

Acknowledgments  vi

Introduction  1

1 Politics and Electronic Media  13
2 Conservative Talk Radio and Shock Jocks  39
3 Reality TV, Professional Wrestling, and Entertainment as Reality  63
4 The President Is Tweeting  89
5 4chan, Reddit, Far-Right Politics, and Insurrection  113
6 The Press as "Enemy of the People": A Crisis of Epistemic Authority  141
7 Post-Truth, Fake News, and Postmodernism  167

Conclusion  195

References  206
Index  212

# Acknowledgments

The days leading up to the election of Donald J. Trump in 2016 were bizarre for me personally. On October 31, I hit the milestone of turning forty. A few days later, my favorite sports team, the Chicago Cubs, snapped a 108-year drought and won the World Series, just after midnight on November 3. The general election between Trump and Hillary Clinton went down on November 8, and the media called the election for Trump before midnight. That was a lot to process in a nine-day span.

Along with many progressives, liberals, and even some conservatives, I awoke on November 9, 2016, in a state of shock and disbelief. I spent that day with my students, trying to assure them that everything was going to be OK—though I was frightened that was not, in fact, the case. Even before the election, I recognized the significance of Trump as a political and media force and was already in the process of developing a January-term topics course called Donald Trump: Media & Politics. That course—which I believe to be the first course in the United States focused solely on the forty-fifth president—took on added meaning as Trump was inaugurated halfway through the course. As a class, we watched the inauguration on January 20th from our respective abodes because it was Sunday (though there were many comments on the discussion board). Then on Monday, I took the class to the St. Petersburg iteration of the Women's March—part of the largest single-day protest in US history. The course was a success, the march was cathartic, and I began to think about Trump as an object of study. I would like to thank my former colleagues in the communication discipline of Eckerd College—James Janack and Kristina Wenzel Egan—for their support and encouragement as I developed and taught my Trump course in the 2017 and 2018 winter terms.

As I embarked upon my Trump research, I presented papers about the president at several conferences. The comments and discussions that emerged from those panels were extraordinarily generative and provided fodder for many of the ideas that ended up in this book. I presented papers about Trump and the media at the Popular Culture Association (PCA) conferences in Seattle (2016), San Diego (2017), and Indianapolis (2018); the National Communication Association (NCA) conventions in Dallas (2017) and Salt Lake City (2018); as well as the Mid-Atlantic Popular and American Culture Association (MAPACA) conference in Pittsburgh (2019). The 2017 Media, Communication, and Film Studies Programs at Liberal Arts Colleges Symposium in Waterville, Maine, provided a space for me to discuss the challenges of teaching about Donald Trump in the classroom with some amazing teachers and scholars.

The 2017 PCA conference was especially fruitful, as it encouraged an acquisition editor for Bloomsbury Academic's Media Studies division to contact me about the possibility of turning my work on Trump into a manuscript. The seeds having been planted, I contacted Bloomsbury in 2018 and have worked with Katie Gallof, the editor, since then. I would like to thank Katie for her hard work and her belief in this project; t has been a delight to work with her and all of the members of the responsive, professional, and talented team at Bloomsbury. I would also like to thank the reviewers who provided enthusiastic encouragement and provocative suggestions at both the proposal and full-draft stages.

When you tell people that you are writing a book about Donald Trump, nearly everyone responds with their thoughts and offers a take on the subject. Those with whom I have conversed about Trump or who have provided guidance about the book include Matthew Ascah, Brandi Askin, Joey and Zac Burchfield, Summer Cunningham, Analisa and Jeff DeGrave, Alison Dozier, Megan Foley, Chuck Goehring, Leslie Hahner, Dave Himmelfarb, Holly Willson Holladay, Jessie Fly, Abe Kahn, Kembrew McLeod, Jennifer Musial, Tom Oates, Gerni Oster, Christina Petersen, Kevin Reiling, John Roberts, Jessica Thorn, Courtney Walker, K.C Wolfe, and the members of the Potato Society, especially the late Erin Kitzinger. I appreciate all of your sage advice and lively discussions. I would especially like to thank Karen Pitcher Christiansen, David Heineman, Paul Johnson, Sangeet Kumar, and Zack Stegler for reading drafts of my chapters during the editing phase. Their insight and sharp commentary have proven to be invaluable as I worked through this book. (Also, one of the aforementioned people suggested *Trumping the Media* for a title, and I am grateful—though not sure exactly who to thank.)

My grandmother, Ann Marcanti, and my parents, Bruce and Nancy Albrecht, have also provided ideas and support throughout the process. (I hope my grandmother loses her wager about Trump.) Thanks to everyone who listened to my rambling about the former president over the years or who tolerated me when I loudly and somewhat drunkenly assured everyone at the 2016 election watch party that he would lose the election—even late on election night when the inevitable was obvious. The Trump era and its aftermath have been challenging and frightening for many people and I am glad to have had such a strong support network and a Boodles to help me navigate this moment in history.

# Introduction

On January 8, 2021, Twitter banned Donald J. Trump from its platform, ending his direct line of communication to his supporters, detractors, and the mainstream media less than two weeks before his presidential term ended. The Twitter ban came in the wake of the occupation of the US Capitol building on January 6, in which Trump supporters broke into the Capitol building and incited chaos for several hours. The insurrection at the Capitol building came in the aftermath of a rally that Trump had on the National Mall, in which he encouraged his supporters to "stop the steal" and to march on the Capitol building. "The steal" to which Trump was referring was the results of the November 2020 election, which Trump lost to Joe Biden but which he refused to concede. Inside the Capitol, members of Congress were voting to certify the electoral votes from the election—an official action, but a *pro forma* one. Trump was furious that the members of Congress had certified the election for his opponent, Joe Biden, calling the outcome an "egregious assault on our democracy." He then encouraged his opponents to walk to the Capitol, where "we are going to cheer on our brave senators and congressmen and women... and we are probably not going to be cheering so much for some of them—because you will never take back our country with weakness."[1]

Trump did not, in fact, accompany the rally-goers to the Capitol; while they breached the building, Trump watched the cable television coverage unfold and did nothing to encourage his supporters to stop their actions and withdraw from the Capitol as mayhem ensued for several hours. For the next two days, Trump continued to tweet in displeasure of Congress certifying the election results and in support of his followers until Twitter made the decision that his tweets might incite violence. In their memo explaining the decision, Twitter stated that Trump's tweets "are likely to inspire others to replicate the violent acts that took place on January 6, 2021, and that there are multiple indicators that they are being received and understood as encouragement to do so."[2] Since his rise to prominence in the political field, Trump used

Twitter as a central mechanism through which he communicated directly to a large audience, bypassing the traditional gatekeepers of mainstream media. Moreover, Trump's tweets became news in and of themselves; mainstream media would cover them as news, amplifying their volume and expanding their potential audience. Trump's connection to Twitter was so deeply intertwined that many had referred to him as the "Twitter President," and his removal from the platform created an uncanny absence from the media environment.[3] Trump had dominated the news for so long by inserting himself through his use of social media that his absence was keenly felt across myriad media.

While Twitter was the most consistent way that Trump engaged through contemporary media, he was also able to rely upon skills and discourses from other media to construct the dominant media figure that characterized his campaign and presidency. In *Trumping the Media*, I argue that Trump was quite adept at adopting and manipulating a variety of media and consistently used his ability to navigate contemporary media to his advantage. Moreover, because of his ability to navigate contemporary mediated environments, he was able to circumvent existing media establishments and produce a version of truth that he himself constructed. In addition to the "Twitter President," some pundits also labeled Trump the "reality TV President."[4] Trump was the star of the NBC reality television show *The Apprentice* (2004–17), which increased his popularity and his recognizability before he began his foray into politics. It also taught him the tropes of a genre more interested in entertainment and shock value than in providing the unvarnished truth. It also helped him hone a character that he had been crafting since his rise to fame in the 1980s. Throughout his political career, he performed a combative, boorish masculinity that developed alongside the rise of conservative talk radio in the 1980s and 1990s. His political positions reflected far-right movements that percolated in the swampy depths of the internet on Reddit and 4chan, bringing discourses of the alt-right into mainstream politics. Trump's success at performing in the contemporary media environment and selecting content from various media speaks to changes in the media environment that have transpired over the last several decades. I situate Trump within particular media discourses and show how he was able to use these media to his advantage in his rise to the apex of US politics and his ability to maintain a rabidly devoted political following.

From the time he started his presidential campaign in the summer of 2015, mainstream media could not get enough of Donald Trump, and though many pundits did not think his presidential candidacy was serious, it received tremendous coverage across a variety of media. During the 2016 presidential campaign, the major cable news channels would broadcast his rallies in their entirety, giving Trump a decided advantage in "earned media" over his opponents. The tracking firm mediaQuant estimated that Trump received approximately $5 billion in earned media from the generous media coverage by mainstream media in the 2016 presidential election.⁵ Late in 2016, CNN's president admitted that it was a "mistake" to air so many Trump speeches in their entirety, and that Trump "delivered on PR and delivered on ratings."⁶ This sentiment is echoed by CBS's chairman Les Moonves, who claimed that Donald Trump running for president "might not be good for America, but it's damn good for CBS."⁷ Large media companies were enamored of Trump's rallies and Twitter use from the beginning, and largely failed in their capacity as gatekeepers, preferring to make money by providing direct access to Trump as a new media behemoth

Because of his ability to perform across multiple media platforms and to hold the attention of the mainstream media, Trump was able to suck the oxygen from other candidates and to become the center of the media environment during the 2016 presidential election and indeed throughout his four-year presidency. Trump was a marketable commodity, and because of the for-profit nature of many news outlets, they were eager to boost his candidacy. This aligns with a traditional political economic critique of corporate news, which holds that when news becomes a for-profit enterprise, it forsakes journalistic ethics in order to seek the highest profits. As media scholar Robert McChesney explains, the owners of news media outlets maintain a "constant drumbeat for profit, their concern with minimizing costs and enhancing revenues, invariably influences the manner in which news is collected and reported."⁸ Writing in 2003, McChesney is quite prescient about the corporate media's thirst for a candidate like Trump, who would be able to drive ratings and would subsequently be able to maximize profits.

While McChesney was correct about the mainstream corporate media's lust for cash, he is unable to foresee the potential for politicization that would emerge through these corporate media. The media environment changed with the advent and omnipresence of social media in the world of contemporary politics. McChesney argues that "journalism, which, in theory, should inspire political involvement, tends to strip politics of meaning and promote a broad depoliticization. It is arguably better at generating ignorance and apathy than informed and passionately engaged citizens."⁹ The mediated environment that brought Trump to power and which ultimately saw him oversee an insurrection on the Capitol was one in which journalism itself was highly politicized. Trump's followers would refer to mainstream journalists as the "lügenpresse," a term borrowed from Nazi Germany, meaning "lying press" as a show of fidelity to their leader.¹⁰ The very outlets from which people accessed their news were polarized and politicized, and they were consuming different versions of the truth that comported with their political affiliations. Many of the alternative truths found their roots in alternative media that were devoid of the gatekeeping function of traditional journalistic media, and many of these ideas that would never previously have made it past the journalistic gatekeepers were able to find their way into mainstream discourses.

Because of his direct access to a mainstream audience with decidedly little gatekeeping by established media, Trump was able to construct a version of truth that held purchase only among his political followers. From the beginning, the press had difficulty coming to terms with a politician with a relationship to a singular truth that was markedly different from other politicians. All politicians stretch the truth, omit, or embellish in order to maintain their political standing, but they do so within the constraints of the establishment press who "hold their feet to the fire" by asking them pointed questions that they answer, even if somewhat obliquely. Trump refused to play the media's game by dismissing the mainstream media as untrustworthy and producing his own version of the truth, often out of whole cloth. Trump's disregard for objective truth and empirical reality led to journalist Salena Zito's aphorism that would be often repeated in relation to Trump's relationship to the truth. She noted that when the soon-to-be president makes counterfactual statements, "the press takes him literally, but not seriously; his supporters take him seriously, but not literally."[11] This turn of phrase became widely used by pundits to describe the popularity of Trump and his ultimate success in the November 2016 election. My goal in this book is to take Trump seriously as well as the myriad discourses that surround, support, and maintain the campaign and presidency of Donald J. Trump.

In an effort to take the forty-fifth president seriously, my goal throughout this book is not to decipher what is actually true about Donald Trump but rather to interrogate the complex and often contradictory ways in which scholars, journalists, pundits, and bloggers write and think about Trump. I am less interested in Trump as a unique individual, and instead focus on Trump as a nodal point at which myriad discourses about truth, reality, and contemporary media intersect. In other words, I am less interested in who Trump really is or what Trumpism really means than in the ways in which scholars, journalists, bloggers, and other cultural producers write about Trump and think about Trumpism. As a set of complex and often contradictory discourses, Trumpism circulates as a media construction, and the novel ways in which Trump circulates as political marker reconfigures the terrain of politics in the twenty-first century.

Many of the ideas in the book are not necessarily novel ideas. For example, numerous scholars, pundits, and journalists have made the point that reality television provides a useful framework for conceptualizing Donald Trump. My goal in the book is not to make the same claims that have been made by others but rather to gather and cull the ideas of others and put different versions of the argument in conversation with one another. In many ways, mine is a meta-analysis in which I construct narratives about Trump and his relationships to truth, reality, and contemporary media from already existing discourses. As such, I often take as my source material existing discourses from editorials, think pieces, commentaries, and existing scholarship, recombining and rethinking existing bits of discourse in order to tell a particular narrative and tell a different story.

Donald Trump is a fascinating figure in US politics and contemporary popular media because he dominated the media landscape throughout his initial candidacy and his term as president. Trump broke presidential norms and expectations so often that the term "unprecedented" seems meaningless in discourses about Trump. The last year of his presidency was particularly chaotic as Trump oversaw a global pandemic, the worst in 100 years, and he became a source of disinformation about the pandemic rather than a trusted leader guiding a country through one of its darkest periods. Moreover, the pandemic came during an election year, and Trump consistently looked to protect his political standing in the face of the pandemic, flaunted the recommendations of his own medical experts, and ultimately contracted Covid-19 during the height of campaign season. After a short stay in Walter Reed hospital, Trump tweeted: "Don't be afraid of Covid. Don't let it dominate your life."[12] This was at a point in time when hundreds of Americans were dying every day from the virus, no vaccine was on the horizon, and officials were desperately trying to contain the spread of the virus.

For Trump, to admit that the virus was a problem was to admit a personal failing, and his followers showed their dedication to Trump by eschewing the use of face masks and downplaying the seriousness of the virus that would ultimately claim 400,000 American lives during the last year of Trump's presidency.[13] Several days after Trump was released from the hospital after his stint with Covid-19, Twitter flagged the president for claiming that he was consequently immune from the virus after having experienced it. Trump Tweeted: "A total and complete sign off from White House Doctors yesterday. That means I can't get it (immune), and can't give it. Very nice to know." Twitter subsequently tagged the tweet with the addendum: "This Tweet violated the Twitter Rules about spreading misleading and potentially harmful information related to COVID-19."[14] Twitter was waging an epistemological battle against Trump over the ways in which "truth" could be produced and dispersed across its platform.

For most of Trump's political career, Twitter had been happy to let Trump tweet whatever he wanted without repercussion, even if Trump's version of the truth often consisted of myriad lies and derivations from official versions of the truth. Twitter felt that its only responsibility was to be a platform for free speech, and that it should give particularly wide berth to public figures because of their position in society. Twitter reserves the right to remove users from their platform for violating its terms of service but makes an exception on the grounds of "public interest" for elected officials. According to Twitter's policies, they "limit exceptions to one critical type of public-interest content—Tweets from elected and government officials—given the significant public interest in knowing and being able to discuss their actions and statements."[15] When Twitter began to flag Trump's tweets as being potentially misleading and harmful, they were pushing against the years during which Trump had taken advantage of the platform's "public interest" loophole through which Trump was able to produce his own truth, his followers were able to retweet without consequence, and mainstream news media were able to cover his tweeting habits as news.

The first tweets that Twitter flagged as potentially misleading by Trump were not about the coronavirus but were instead about Trump's insistence that mail-in ballots were unreliable.[16] Already in May 2020, Trump was preparing his followers for an election that would be tightly contested and priming them to be suspicious of mail-in ballots. When Trump ultimately lost the election by a thin margin in several crucial states, he immediately claimed that the election had been rigged and that mail-in ballots were to blame for his loss. According to Trump, he had been the legitimate winner of the 2020 presidential election, but a constellation of nefarious forces had conspired to insert Joe Biden into the highest office in the land. Mainstream media have taken to calling this the "big lie," perpetrated by Trump, and the schism between those who adhere to the version of reality in which Trump won the 2020 presidential election in 2020 and those who refuse the "big lie" is the dominant political schism in 2021.

The term "big lie" comes from political theorist Hannah Arendt, who suggests that authoritarian regimes create a world in which the government perpetually lies until its population can no longer differentiate between facts and fiction. Under such a regime the population will ultimately fall prey to a big lie that tears "a hole in the fabric of factuality"—lies that are so big that they "require a complete rearrangement of the whole factual texture—the making of another reality."[17] Writing for the *New York Times*, historian Timothy Snyder suggests that for most of his presidency, Trump's inability to exploit a "big lie" is what kept his administration from teetering into actual fascism. For him, "as he was unable to enforce some truly big lie, some fantasy that created an alternative reality where people could live and die, his pre-fascism fell short of the thing itself."[18] However, when Trump began to tout the big lie in the wake of the November 2020 election, and when it escalated to the point of an insurrection by January 2021, the big lie had fulfilled its purpose of reconfiguring the lived reality of many people. Snyder goes on to argue, "The claim that Trump was denied a win by fraud is a big lie not just because it mauls logic, misdescribes the present and demands belief in a conspiracy. It is a big lie, fundamentally, because it reverses the moral field of American politics and the basic structure of American history."[19] Trump was successfully able to mobilize his base through the big lie because he had primed the pump by insisting upon a candidacy and presidency that rested upon epistemological uncertainty.

Part of this epistemological uncertainty stemmed from a move away from monopolistic control of news media on the part of a few gatekeepers. From the Second World War until the 1980s, most of the national news media were controlled by three major television stations, and a handful of "papers of record," all of which worked to ensure that politics remained contained within a fairly narrow window of acceptability. Conterminously, for those thirty-five years, US politics had bought into the ideals of liberal democracy with a moderate social democratic social net undergirding free-market capitalism dominated by white men. The political space between the two major political parties was relatively narrow, and discourses outside of the mainstream were treated by the establishment media as radical and not treated as serious news. As news was televised on the major broadcast networks, it hewed toward coverage that appealed to the widest possible audience, thereby excluding opinions that were beyond the political pale. Writing about broadcast television in the 1960s and 1970s, television scholar Jason Mittell notes that "television journalism typically tries to present perspectives matching and reinforcing the presumed consensus values and assumptions of its audience."[20] Neither Donald Trump as a person nor his extreme political positions would have survived in a political and media climate built upon pillars of consensus.

The media consensus represented a relative political consensus that stemmed from the New Deal and prevailed in the years after the Second World War through the beginning of the 1960s because of the economic prosperity that the United States saw during this period. This era has particular resonance for Trump's politics because according to sociologist John Campell, when idealizing the past, "Trump seemed to refer to the 1950s and 1960s—America's postwar Golden Age. This was probably the time most Trump supporters assumed he had in mind when he talked about making America great again."[21] The various social movements of the 1960s and 1970s saw a moment in which people of color, women, and LGBTQ folks gained increased rights and visibility, and established social norms about sex and authority were challenged. The backlash to these advances created a schism in society between those who embraced these seemingly radical changes and those who longed for the country as it was before these cultural changes transpired.

This schism has only deepened today as one party, the Democrats, has largely embraced the diversity of these cultural changes, while the Republican Party has become increasingly the party of white America. Political scientist Alan Abramowitz notes that "compared with American society in the mid-twentieth century, the early twenty-first century version is much more racially and ethnically diverse, more dependent on government benefits, more sexually liberated, more religiously diverse, and more secular. It is also much more divided and more bitterly divided along party lines."[22] Before Donald Trump popularized a red ballcap emblazoned with his "Make American Great" slogan on it, a segment of the US population had already been prepared to long for an erstwhile era when the country was a better place to live. Further, when Trump used racial overtones to hammer his point home, his audience was already primed to understand that the "great" American to which the hat referred was one imbued with white patriarchal values. Moreover, a sector of the media environment that accompanied the rise of Donald Trump from the 1980s to the 2010s abetted the polarization of the American public and created an audience with a sympathetic ear for the racialized nostalgia inherent in the desire to make America great again.

Trump's "Make America Great Again" logo was not even an original; it was rebooted from Ronald Regan's 1980 campaign, which was also a reactionary push against the cultural changes of the 1960s and 1970s. The election of Reagan in 1980 saw a shift toward ideological solidification of political parties; in the 1970s there were still many moderate Democrats and liberal Republicans. It also represented a lurch rightward—a shift in the "Overton window" of acceptable political discourses on the conservative side of the spectrum. Journalist Derek Robertson defines the "Overton window" as "the range of ideas outside which lie political exile or pariahdom."[23] Beginning with the election of Ronald Reagan in the 1980s, the frame of acceptability for nationally successful conservative politics has continued to move rightward; concomitantly, various new media have emerged to challenge the dominance of the three-channel broadcast media that persisted in the postwar era. In order for the political landscape to accept a figure like Donald Trump, the media landscape had to change, and it did with the introduction of cable television, the rise of right-wing talk radio, and eventually the meteoric rise of the internet.

The shifts in the Overton window have been so great as to have challenged the very premise of democratic liberalism itself. Faith in the electoral democratic system and the peaceful transition of power have always been central to discourses of US politics, and mainstream media have traditionally pushed anything beyond that as unthinkable and beyond the pale. What distinguished the United States in the popular imagination from horrible totalitarian states like Nazi Germany and Stalinist USSR—as well as smaller dictatorships, juntas, and the like—was its commitment to the ideals of liberal democracy and the peaceful transfer of power. That a defeated president would fail to admit defeat and would persuade a considerable percentage of the population to believe his big lie demonstrates that not only Trump's uncanny ability as a politician and a manipulator of media but also the Overton window had already been shifted considerably to allow for the emergence of a figure like Trump. Trump had support from a variety of media that allowed him to bypass those traditional media that would traditionally have served as gatekeepers and stopped the rise of Trump before it escalated. However, by the time Trump descended the escalator of his hotel and announced his run for presidency in 2016, he was already a product of and an adept influencer of a mediated political system that had radically changed in the preceding thirty-five years.

## Chapter Descriptions

In *Trumping the Media*, I work to tell the story of how Trump has engaged and inhabited different media environments in order to achieve power and popularity and ultimately to be elected and to serve as the president of the United States. In Chapter 1, "Politics and Electronic Media," I offer a brief survey of the relationship between politics and entertainment as they have intertwined and coexisted since the first commercial radio broadcast in 1920. Chapter 2 is "Conservative Talk Radio and Shock Jocks," in which I outline the rise of conservative talk radio in the 1980s and the ways in which the genre created an immediate audience for Trump. Further, Trump's public persona of boorish masculinity reflects the shock jocks that emerged in the 1980s alongside of conservative talk-show hosts. More than any other medium, conservative talk radio helped to foster the rightward swing of US conservatism and its polarizing tactics.

Donald Trump's level of stardom grew in the decade of the 2000s as he rode the reality television craze to a hit show and a resurrection of a career that had seemingly been reduced to tabloid fodder. In Chapter 3, "Reality TV, Professional Wrestling, and Entertainment as Reality," I look at Trump's performance as a politician through the lens of reality television. I am particularly interested in the ways in which the genre sculpts the notions truth and reality and the ways that Trump applies the lessons about the malleability of truth and instability of reality to his career in politics. Trump began using Twitter to promote *The Apprentice*, and the microblogging platform ultimately became the lifeblood through which his entire political existence flowed. In Chapter 4, "The President Is Tweeting," I show the ways in which Trump was able to use the platform to circumvent traditional media to communicate directly with his followers and to create news out of whole cloth. Without any gatekeepers to hold him back, he was able to offer a meta-commentary on his own candidacy, precedency, and the media coverage thereof. When Trump was ultimately banned from Twitter, much of the oxygen left his media performance, and he was no longer able to insert himself into every moment of the news cycle.

The internet was founded on utopian dreams in which every voice could be heard, and no one's would be censored. Unfortunately, this ultra-libertarian stance on free speech allows not only for robust discourse to be debated within the public sphere but also for ideas that most would find highly objectionable to coexist within the same space. In Chapter 5, "4chan, Reddit, Far-Right Politics, and Insurrection," I show that far-right white supremacist groups rallied around the campaign of Donald Trump and were able to use sites such as Reddit and 4chan to distribute a more palatable version of their hateful discourse. Ultimately, the discourses circulating through these sites allowed for a shift in the Overton window such that these white supremacist discourses found their way into mainstream discourses and ultimately found the ear of the president himself. Trump subsequently developed a constellation of various right-wing militia groups and conspiracy theorists who transformed Trump from just another political figure to one that threatened the very structures that undergird the liberal democracy that has prevailed in the United States since its founding.

One of the structures that serve as a foundation for liberal democracy is the notion of a free press that operates independently from the government and ideally independently from commercial interests. While the history of journalism is replete with many occasions when the press failed to live up to these ideals, the Trump presidency caused some journalists and scholars of journalism to question the validity and efficacy of such bedrock journalistic ideals as the "watchdog function" and the press's role as the "fourth estate." In Chapter 6, "The Press as 'Enemy of the People': A Crisis of Epistemic Authority," I look at the ways in which journalists and journalism studies scholars have tackled the role of the press as the profession wrestles with the problems that emerge when a president shows a rabid disdain for journalism and the institutional norms that structure the profession.

One particular point of friction is the discrepancy between the journalistic ideal of finding and reporting objective truth and Trump's complete disregard for objective facts and empirically verifiable reality. In the final chapter,

"Post-Truth, Fake News, and Postmodernism," I examine the notion of truth and look at the ways in which postmodern scholars have interrogated the notion. I situate Donald Trump within these discourses, specifically his complicated relationship to truth. The mainstream media were able to normalize Trump's rampant disregard for facts; only when Trump forwarded the "big lie" and was able to mobilize his followers to violence toward revered institutions did media institutions ultimately rein him in to a certain extent. Even with his insistence that the 2020 election was rigged and that he should rightly have been sworn in for a second term, the majority of his devout followers continued to adhere to his version of the truth and to maintain avid support for him. To quote Arendt, he had torn a "hole in the fabric of factuality," and the consequences of his particular relationship to truth will extend beyond the scope of this book and will affect US media and politics for the considerable future.

## Notes

1. Maggie Haberman, "You Will Never Take Back Country with Weakness," *The New York Times*, January 6, 2021, https://www.nytimes.com/2021/01/06/us/politics/trump-speech-capitol.html
2. Twitter Inc., "Permanent Suspension of @realDonaldTrump," *Twitter*, January 8, 2021, https://blog.twitter.com/en_us/topics/company/2020/suspension.html
3. Lisa Gitelman, "How Will History Remember the Twitter President?," *CNN*, January 20, 2021, https://www.cnn.com/2021/01/20/opinions/fate-of-trumps-tweets-matters-for-history-gitelman/index.html
4. Jeff Nesbit, "Donald Trump Is the First True Reality TV President," *Time*, December 9, 2016, https://time.com/4596770/donald-trump-reality-tv/
5. Emily Stewart, "Donald Trump Rode $5 Billion in Free Media to the White House," *The Street*, November 20, 2016, https://www.thestreet.com/politics/donald-trump-rode-5-billion-in-free-media-to-the-white-house-13896916
6. Paulina Firozi, "CNN President: Airing so Many Full Trump Rallies Was a 'Mistake'," *The Hill*, October 14, 2016, https://thehill.com/blogs/ballot-box/presidential-races/301147-cnn-president-airing-so-many-full-trump-rallies-was-a
7. Eliza Collins, "Les Moonves: Trump's Run Is 'Damn Good for CBS'," *Politico*, February 19, 2016, https://www.politico.com/blogs/on-media/2016/02/les-moonves-trump-cbs-220001
8. Robert McChesney, "The Problem of Journalism: A Political Economic Contribution to an Explanation of the Crisis in Contemporary US Journalism," *Journalism Studies* 4, no. 3 (2003): 306.
9. McChesney, 304.

10  Rick Noack, "The Ugly History of 'Lügenpresse', a Nazi Slur Shouted at a Trump Rally," *The Washington Post*, October 24, 2016, https://www.washingtonpost.com/news/worldviews/wp/2016/10/24/the-ugly-history-of-luegenpresse-a-nazi-slur-shouted-at-a-trump-rally/

11  Salena Zito, "Taking Trump Seriously, Not Literally," *The Atlantic*, September 23, 2016, https://www.theatlantic.com/politics/archive/2016/09/trump-makes-his-case-in-pittsburgh/501335/

12  German Lopez, "If Trump Has Learned Anything from Not Getting COVID-19, He's Not Showing It," *Vox*, October 5, 2020, https://www.vox.com/future-perfect/2020/10/4/21501511/trump-covid-19-coronavirus-tweet-leaving-walter-reed-hospital

13  Adam Gellar and Janie Har, "US Virus Deaths Top 400K as Trump Leaves Office," *Associated Press*, January 19, 2021, https://apnews.com/article/donald-trump-pandemics-public-health-coronavirus-pandemic,f6e976f34a6971c889ca8a4c5e1c0068

14  Kanishka Singh and Bhargav Acharya, "Twitter Flags Trump Tweet for Violating Its Rules on COVID-19 Information," *Reuters*, October 11, 2020, https://www.reuters.com/article/us-usa-election-trump-twitter/twitter-flags-trump-tweet-for-violating-its-rules-on-covid-19-information-idUSKBN26W0TI

15  Twitter, Inc., "About Public-Interest Exceptions on Twitter: Defining the Public Interest," *Twitter*, https://help.twitter.com/en/rules-and-policies/public-interest

16  Barbara Ortutay and Dino Hazell, "In a First, Twitter Adds Fact-Check Warnings to Trump Tweets," *Associated Press*, May 26, 2020, https://apnews.com/article/virus-outbreak-donald-trump-ap-top-news-politics-entertainment-700c52aab0869253625b80255a397f19

17  Hannah Arendt, "Truth and Politics," in *Between Past and Future: Eight Exercises in Political Thought* (New York: Penguin Books, 1968), 253.

18  Timothy Snyder, "The American Abyss," *The New York Times*, January 9, 2001, https://www.nytimes.com/2021/01/09/magazine/trump-coup.html

19  Ibid.

20  Jason Mittell, *Television and American Culture* (New York: Oxford University Press, 2010), 132.

21  John L. Campbell, *American Discontent: The Rise of Donald Trump and Decline of the Golden Age* (New York: Oxford University Press, 2018), 21.

22  Alan I. Abramowitz, *The Great Alignment: Race, Party Transformation, and the Rise of Donald Trump* (New Haven, CT: Yale University Press, 2018), 12.

23  Derek Robertson, "How an Obscure Conservative Theory Became the Trump Era's Go-To Nerd Phrase," *Politico*, February 25, 2018, https://www.politico.com/magazine/story/2018/02/25/overton-window-explained-definition-meaning-217010

# 1

# Politics and Electronic Media

Politics and electronic media have been deeply intertwined at least since KDKA in Pittsburgh broadcast the first commercial radio signal in 1920 on the night of the presidential election, so that their listeners could learn of the election results. As media have transformed to include television, satellite syndication, the World Wide Web, and eventually social media, politicians have embraced new media to various degrees. Popular entertainment has also followed the development of electronic media since the first broadcast, though the sphere of "serious" news and politics and the unserious sphere of popular entertainment have often remained separate. The ascendency of Donald Trump to the presidency reflects an erasure of any barriers between popular entertainment and politics. As political scientist Mehnaaz Momen articulates, "at some point, most clearly evident in the era of Trump, we discover that politics and entertainment have largely become indistinguishable from each other."[1] Trump has lived his life as a celebrity, won the election as a celebrity, and governed as a celebrity; for him, the entertainment value always takes priority over the underlying politics of any situation.

Trump, of course, is not the first politician to use electronic media to their advantage, nor is he the first person to blur the lines between the spheres of politics and entertainment. However, Trump is able to inhabit the role of celebrity so completely and to absorb the logic of different media that he is able to perfect what many others were only able to attempt. To take a turn of phrase from the world of comedy, Trump commits fully to the bit; as such, when other politicians try to dip their toe into the world of entertainment, they come across as disingenuous or stiff. Because Trump has lived his life immersed in the world of celebrity entertainment, he is able to bring that world into politics and use his skills effectively against his opponents.

In *Audience of One*, journalist James Poniewozik parallels Trump's rise to the highest reaches of entertainment and politics with the rise of television itself. For Poniewozik, Trump has spent so much of his life on television that the celebrity and the medium are indistinguishable. He describes Trump as "a man who, through a four-decades-long TV performance, achieved symbiosis with the medium. Its impulses were his impulses; its appetites were his appetites; its mentality was his."[2] He goes on to say that "because Trump so thoroughly fused himself with the pop culture of the last forty years, because he was both an omnipresence on TV and a compulsive devourer of TV, his story is its story, and vice versa."[3] I agree with Poniewozik that Trump was indeed a product of TV, but that is only part of the story; he was also able to master other media, either directly or indirectly, and was able to use an entire arsenal of the available mediascape to his advantage to win the presidency. He drew on his experiences on talk radio to develop skills in boorish masculinity that he used to develop a perceived kinship with the white working-class constituents. He also used his radio skills on the television when he used the friendly media space of Fox News for his own weekly call-in show, where he would only appear via phone. Trump was also able to master the medium of Twitter and was thus more able to relate to his constituents through social media than other candidates. He also used the medium to wink toward the more explicitly racist and misogynist trolls who occupied darker spaces on the internet, and found a considerable allyship with the alt-right, though at times he had to disavow any connections in that direction, often reluctantly. Thus, while television is one medium through which Trump derives his power, he uses the entire mediascape at his disposal to fuse entertainment and politics.

In this chapter, I offer a brief history of the century of electronic media that led up to Trump's presidency and select some moments when new media challenged the way that politics was practiced or when entertainment media and politics crossed paths. This history will focus on the period from the 1980s onward, when Donald Trump joins the story, to show how he used the rise of entertainment media from the 1980s onward to forward his professional career and eventually his political career. As political media and entertainment media become more completely enmeshed in the twenty-first century, the notion of a serious and sacrosanct truth from the world of politics begins to blend with a more subjective version of truth from the world of entertainment, and the political conditions are ripe for a politician with a fungible notion of truth to thrive.

## Radio and Television

After that initial broadcast from KDKA in 1920, Warren Harding won the presidential election, but he would not live to be the first president to broadcast over the airwaves; his successor, Calvin Coolidge, would claim that honor in 1923 after Harding's untimely death earlier that year. Franklin

Roosevelt was the president who is best known for using the radio to increase his political popularity. Many of his supporters saw his "fireside chats" as a steady, calming voice of a leader in the face of the tragedies of the Great Depression and the Second World War. As radio historian Susan Douglas explains, Roosevelt "understood the intimacy radio afforded, with its emphasis on listening and the power of the human voice to convey familiarity and affinity... He brilliantly exploited the affordances of this medium, and just as the radio networks were establishing their own news divisions that would now compete with the press."[4] The majority of the newspaper editorial boards opposed Roosevelt in the 1936 and 1940 elections, but Roosevelt was able to circumvent the established gatekeepers of the time and appeal directly to the people, foreshadowing the strategy that Trump would take with social media in his 2016 run. Radio would eventually establish itself to be a staple for news and politics by the 1940s, earning its bona fides through its coverage of the Second World War, and the networks that established themselves on radio after the war made the move to television once that medium exploded after the war.

Roosevelt was actually the first president to appear on television, doing so at the 1939 World's Fair, but the broadcast did not expand beyond the greater New York area, as television had not yet been perfected and was in very few homes at the time. After the war, Harry Truman gave the first ever televised speech from the White House in 1947, though still few Americans owned televisions. It did portend a future when American presidential politics would be deeply intertwined with the medium of television. By the 1952 election cycle, television was in the majority of American homes, and was a key part of the race. The Republican vice-presidential candidate Richard M. Nixon found himself embroiled in the first of what would become many corruption scandals in his career. Dwight Eisenhower, the presidential nominee, was under pressure to replace Nixon on the ticket with someone with a cleaner record. In order to save his political career, Nixon took to the airwaves and gave a televised speech, with his wife next to him for support, denying that he had taken any illegal funds and explaining their humble financial situation to the entire country. He noted that his wife "doesn't have a mink coat, but she does have a respectable Republican cloth coat. And I always tell her that she'd look good in anything."[5] The coup de grace of the speech was when he mentioned that one gift that he did accept was a "little cocker spaniel in a crate that he sent all the way from Texas. Black-and-white spotted. And our little girl—Tricia, the six-year-old named it Checkers. And you know the kids love that dog, and I just want to say this right now, that regardless of what they say about it, we're going to keep it."[6] Nixon went on to keep his slot on Eisenhower's ticket and to remain in American politics for the next two decades. The "Checkers speech," as it would come to be known, laid the blueprint for how politicians could use television as a public relations tool, and how they could use it to present themselves as part of a family unit and use their family as props to construct that image.

An apocryphal tale alleges that just as television helped to save Nixon's career in 1952, it almost ruined his career in 1960, when many credit Nixon's inability to understand the medium as the reason for him losing the first-ever televised presidential debate against John F. Kennedy. For those who watched the debate, Nixon appeared to be sweaty and shifty compared to his more youthful opponent, who seemed nonplussed in front of the cameras. Famously, polling suggested that a majority of people who listened to the debate on the radio felt that Nixon had won, while for those who watched the event on television, a majority felt that Kennedy had won. Even though communication scholars David Vancil and Sue Pendell debunked the myth that the debate swayed voters differently depending on the medium, the legend persists.[7] In *Understanding Media*, media scholar Marshall McLuhan famously argues that part of the reason for this discrepancy was because Kennedy looked right for TV. The audience who thought he won the debate was not necessarily asking the question of whether he would make the best president, but whether he would make the best TV personality. McLuhan writes that "anybody who looks as if he might be a teacher, a doctor, a businessman, or any of a dozen other things all at the same time is right for TV."[8] In other words, Kennedy won because he generically fit well into the space of "TV personality," whereas people watched Nixon with his sweaty brow and five-o'-clock shadow and thought "there's something about this guy that isn't right," in McLuhan's words.[9] For McLuhan presenting oneself as if one were the type of person who should be on television was essential for survival on the medium. Donald Trump built his empire out of presenting himself as a great builder, presenting himself as a ridiculously wealthy man, and presenting himself as the kind of person who is famous for being on television. As James Poniewozik explains,

> he understood, early in his career, that there was much more upside in *playing* a businessman than in *being* a businessman. By performing yourself to match the mental cartoons people generate when they hear the words "wealth" and "success" and "luxury," you come to represent those things. And thus, anything you're selling—an apartment, a bottle of water, a political platform—becomes imbued with those things.[10]

Trump used the medium of television to construct his image and then used a variety of media to expand upon the capabilities that television had to offer.

The tumult of the 1960s unfolded as audiences mourned the death of a president on television, watched a seemingly unwinnable war take place in their living rooms, and see a culture and generational divide transpire on the medium that was now in nearly every home in the United States. By 1968, Nixon was running for president again, and the country seemed to be tearing at the seams. Desperate not to seem stiff and out-of-touch as the country had perceived him in 1960, Nixon went on one of the country's hippest comedy shows, *Rowan & Martin's Laugh-In* (1967–73) and delivered the memorable catch phrase "sock it to me" for a bemused television audience. The brief appearance is memorable because it represents a moment when television's political sphere crossed into the entertainment sphere, a trend that would accelerate as the decades progressed. If the debate with Kennedy demonstrated that televisual details that enhanced entertainment—shaving, shirt color, makeup—were important for politicians, Nixon's one-liner was a step further into the terrain of televised entertainment.

In 1975, *Saturday Night Live* (1975–) went on the air, and it has been mixing entertainment and politics since its inception. In 1975 and 1976, comedian Chevy Chase did an impersonation of President Gerald Ford that portrayed him "as a bumbling idiot who staggered from one crisis to the next."[11] Chase's portrayal always included at least one pratfall, which came to stand in for Ford and his presidency. The portrayal referred to a moment when Ford slipped and fell down the stairs to Air Force One; much of its humor derived from irony because Ford was one of the most athletic presidents, having been a star football player for the University of Michigan. While comics satirizing politicians is nothing new, what was new was the way that Ford used the media technologies to "talk back" to Chase and *Saturday Night Live*. At a fundraiser in 1976, Ford riffed on Chase's impersonation of him, and even borrowed Chase's catchphrase, ending his speech by declaring: "I'm Gerald Ford, and You're Not."[12] To show that they were good sports, the Ford administration sent their press secretary Ron Nessen to host the show. Nessen played opposite Chase's "fake" Ford and told Chase that "that's why I want to host this show, to demonstrate that this administration has a sense of humor. You may remember in 1968, Nixon said, 'Sock it to me' on *Laugh-In*, and it may have made the difference in the election."[13] The show even got the "real" Gerald Ford to tape the show's cold-open catchphrase "Live from New York, It's Saturday Night" from the Oval Office. Here, Ford set a precedent for the "real" world of politics to interact with the "fake" world of entertainment in ways that would become increasingly complicated over the next four decades. Even though Ford would not fare as well in 1976 as Nixon had in 1968, the tradition of politicians interacting with their impersonators on *Saturday Night Live* has continued throughout the decade, and the lines between the ostensible reality of "real" news and politics and the "fake" world of entertainment have become increasingly muddled. Since Ford's appearance on *SNL* a bona fide movie star and a tabloid celebrity-cum-reality television star have ascended to the highest office in the United States.

Donald Trump has made several appearances on *Saturday Night Live*, including hosting the show as he was running for president in 2016. However, his first media appearance came on the front page of *The New York Times* in 1973, when he was accused of racial discrimination in an article titled "Major Landlord Accused of Anti-Black Bias in City."[14] A 1976 picture in *The Times* features Trump and a Cadillac with DJT vanity license plates.[15] By the end of the decade, Trump had achieved a bit of notoriety in the New York City market, but had yet to achieve national fame. Trump made his first appearance on national television on *The Today Show* with Tom Brokaw in 1980, as Trump had just broken ground on Trump Tower in Manhattan.[16] With his first national appearance only three months before Reagan's decisive victory over Jimmy Carter, Donald Trump's rise to prominence is nearly coterminous with that of Ronald Reagan, the president who stands in as synecdoche for the 1980s. By the end of the decade, Trump would be a household name, and would blend in with the ethos of the era.

## Ronald Reagan and the 1980s

Donald Trump was not the first entertainment figure to become president; that was Ronald Reagan, who had a long career on television and film as a movie star who was quite famous, but who did not star in any particularly acclaimed movies. His most memorable role was that of Notre Dame quarterback George Gipp in 1940's *Knute Rockne, All American*, where he received his nickname "The Gipper." He was also known for playing alongside a chimp in *Bedtime for Bonzo* (1951). Despite his less-than-Oscar-worthy screen roles, Reagan became a household name for his advertising deals, his role as the head of the Screen Actors Guild, and for hosting the televised anthology series *General Electric Theater* (1953–62). By the 1960s, he had become active in conservative politics, and he gave a memorable speech in support of Barry Goldwater at the 1964 Republican National Convention called "A Time for Choosing." Reagan was then elected governor of California in 1966, flirted with a presidential run in 1968, was reelected as governor in 1970, ran in earnest for president in 1976, and finally won the office in 1980. So, while Reagan was indeed from the entertainment industry, he differed from Donald Trump because he had nearly twenty years of political experience behind him when he took office as president. Moreover, he had further political experience as head of the Screen Actors Guild and as a spokesperson for the General Electric company before he took office as governor of California.

Reagan's two greatest political gifts were his ability to spin a compelling yarn, regardless of the actual facts, and his unyielding optimism. One of Reagan's early jobs was as a radio announcer in Iowa for Chicago Cubs' baseball games. There was no satellite transmission at the time, so Reagan would transcribe the telegraphed bare bones of the game and would fill in the color. In an often-told anecdote, at one point during a game, the telegraph signal went out, and Reagan had to stall for the audience. According to the tale, he gave the audience a wonderful description of a long at-bat with myriad fly balls in which the batter called time out many times and the pitcher stepped off the mound and shook off signs from the catcher. When the signal came back, it turns out that the batter had popped out on the first pitch.[17] Whether the story is true is less relevant than that it explains Reagan's uncanny ability to insert a well-crafted narrative that provides entertainment and satisfies an audience without necessarily heeding the actual facts of the situation. In fact, Reagan was famous for telling stories, which he ascribed to himself, that had actually happened in movies that he played in. For example, Reagan had a favorite anecdote about being captain in a plane in the Second World War and telling the gunner that "we'll ride it down together." Reagan never did serve in the Second World War due to poor eyesight, but it was the plot of 1944's *A Wing and a Prayer*, a movie that Reagan didn't even act in.[18] As media scholar Susan Jeffords explains, for Regan, "The success of the story, especially a story in which he could figure as a hero, was more important than any facts involving the events themselves."[19] Reagan's avuncular charm and persistent optimism allowed him to use his Hollywood bona fides to confuse facts with fiction to construct a world the way he wanted it to be—the way it ought to be—rather than the way it really was. It is unsurprising that Donald Trump lifted his "Make America Great Again" slogan from The Gipper, as it exudes the optimism without content that characterized the fortieth president as much as the slogan for his 1984 reelection campaign, "It's Morning in America," suggesting that Reagan was well on his way to making America great again.

The 1980s brought with it new strategies for televised news. Throughout the 1960s and 1970s, the networks separated their news and entertainment divisions, not expecting their news divisions to make a profit but rather having them be subsidized by the entertainment wings of the networks. As such, news and politics were under no obligation to be entertaining, as the goal was to create the ostensible best news possible rather than to garner the most viewers and consequently to attract the most advertisers. Because of increasing competition and pressure from shareholders, news divisions became expected to run a profit for their networks. As such, the broadcasts carried with them an expectation of entertainment, and politicians were rewarded for using the entertainment capabilities of electronic media to their advantage. One of the reasons that the networks changed their business models was the introduction of cable television, which first started broadcasting to select locations in the 1970s but started to reach a much larger audience in the 1980s. As the audience for cable television grew, the oligopolistic control of the big three networks shrunk, and they could no longer afford to subsidize their news channels.

One cable channel in particular challenged the news model that the big three networks had offered for decades. CNN went on the air in 1980 and offered news twenty-four hours a day, as opposed to the thirty-minute news block offered by the networks of ABC, NBC, and CBS. Because it had nearly unlimited time to focus on the news, CNN could offer a decidedly different product from the major networks. As historians Kevin Kruse and Julian Zelizer argue, "CNN's ultimate goal was to beat the networks in terms of the speed and depth of its coverage. It aimed both to break news before the 'big three' but also to handle a broader range of stories, from human-interest tales to coverage of weather catastrophes."[20] Because the big networks were reluctant to cut into their regularly scheduled network programs for news that was breaking during the day, CNN was often the only station during the 1980s that would broadcast live breaking news. However, the increased liveness of the news dramatically changed the way that it was constructed. If the networks only needed to produce a half-hour program every night, they had nearly a full day to report, fact-check, synthesize, analyze, and editorialize the news before it was broadcast. If edits, fact-checks, and analysis were done on the fly, a different version of newsworthiness was produced, with different expectations for truth, facts, and editorial content. Moreover, CNN was from the beginning a commercial enterprise; its job was to gain subscriptions for cable subscriptions and for its advertisers. As such, the news it presented often slanted toward the sensational as it always had an eye on the numbers. Standards of newsworthiness and involvement in the market demonstrated a shift in the way that cable television constructed the news away from its broadcast forebearers, and these shifts continue in contemporary media culture as entertainment value is valued across the board in news broadcast, and standards of truth and editorialization have shifted as processes of news collection and editorialization have.

Another feature of Reagan's 1980s was that of deregulation of media industries. The growth of cable television, which allowed CNN to flourish during the 1980s, actually began in the 1970s, "when the FCC relaxed the rules that had contained cable's expansion, the industry began a growth spurt that continued a growth spurt that continued through the end of the twentieth century."[21] Deregulation in the 1980s also allowed for individuals to own satellite transponders, and consequently to get their television directly from the satellites. Satellite technology had allowed for greater possibility in live programs and for televised programs in syndication. In short, several technological and regulatory changes allowed for there to be a larger range of content offered on television.

One of the ways in which television expanded was with a new format—entertainment news. *Entertainment Tonight* (1981–) debuted in 1981 and *Lifestyles of the Rich and Famous* (1984–95) debuted in 1984; these two shows featured only celebrities, the gossip surrounding them, and the trappings of capitalism that they could afford. Featuring the catchphrase "champagne wishes and caviar dreams," *Lifestyles of the Rich and Famous* signified the excess of 1980s capitalism. It promised to take the viewer "behind the scenes" to reveal the exorbitant luxuries in which the glamorous people of the 1980s spent their lives. Donald Trump was a frequent subject of the show's fascination, as he was the perfect fit for the type of celebrity who enjoyed the glitz and glamor that accompanied wealth. The opening credit montage for the show even featured a shot of Trump walking down the hallway with Michael Jackson, the pair lending celebrity bone fides to the show.[22] As James Poniewozik explains, for Trump, wealth "was not just something performers had, it was a performance in itself."[23] Trump took the ethos of *Lifestyles of the Rich and Famous* and converted it into a decades-long plan for celebrity success. Regardless of his actual financial situation—even as he went through a very public bankruptcy—Trump presented himself as the apotheosis of a wealthy person. Trump became such a synecdoche for a rich person that he appeared as himself in over a dozen cameo roles in film and television. Most of these appearances occurred before Trump had his own television show and served to remind the public that Trump was a celebrity rich person who could stand in for one when the script called for a rich person. Many have even speculated that Trump is not nearly as wealthy as he lets on, and that the glitz and gilding is just a veneer to maintain the illusion of Trump as an ideal of a rich person.[24] Regardless of whether Trump is indeed a billionaire, Trump has gone to great lengths to avoid making his tax returns public, which leaves his actual net worth a mystery. For him and the logic of *Lifestyles of the Rich and Famous*, his actual wealth is inconsequential as long as he continues to play the part of the wealthy person and to maintain the patina of glamor.

The 1980s was the decade that brought Trump into the national media scene, and in many ways was the decade that defined Trump. Reaganomics and an ideological shift from the 1960s' mentality of collective good to the 1980s' ideology of individual excess, combined with a pithy one-liner from an Oliver Stone movie, have often characterized the 1980s as "the decade of greed," and Donald Trump was a poster child for that characterization. In fact, by the end of the decade, Trump's brand had become so alluring that he considered running for president for the first time. There was an effort in New Hampshire in 1987 to draft Trump for the Republican ticket to run as a successor to Ronald Reagan in 1988. Although Trump told the crowd that he had no intention of running for president, he gave a speech that presaged his nativist, "America First" ideals that would become a central component of his victorious campaign twenty-eight years later.[25] While Trump has proven to be flexible in terms of political parties and ideologies in the decades between his first potential campaign speech and his ultimate presidential victory, his certainty that US business was getting "killed" by overseas competitors has remained constant.

Another regulatory change that happened in the 1980s was the repeal of the Fairness Doctrine in 1987. The Fairness Doctrine's basic tenet was "that broadcasters had the obligation to address all sides of public controversy during the course of their broadcasting" and that "the public had a right to hear opposing viewpoints, and broadcast stations, as trustees of the airwaves, were obligated to treat controversial topics fairly."[26] In practice, this often meant that if a broadcast television or radio station gave a liberal point of view airtime, they were obliged to give a conservative point of view equal airtime. Similarly, if a television or radio station broadcast an entire show dedicated to a conservative or liberal side, they had an obligation to give equal time to the other side. When the Fairness Doctrine was repealed under Reagan, it opened the door for radio stations to devote entire stations to one side of the political spectrum. By the end of the decade, Rush Limbaugh had taken advantage of new satellite syndication capabilities as well as the deregulatory atmosphere exemplified by the repeal of the Fairness Doctrine to use A.M. radio to become a major voice in the conservative movement. By the 1990s, entire stations were devoted entirely to conservative politics, and talk radio changed the way that politics transpired during the decade. In the next chapter, I examine talk radio and the ways in which Donald Trump learned from conservative talk radio and used those lessons as he embarked upon a career in politics.

## The Nineties, the Internet, and Politics as Entertainment

The 1992 presidential campaign was remarkable for the ways in which the participants engaged popular culture in novel ways. Running for re-election on a ticket with President George H. W. Bush, the sitting vice president,

Dan Quayle, attacked a fictional TV personality for her not representing family values. *Murphy Brown* (1988–98, 2018) was a successful sitcom, and the titular newswoman had decided to have a child on her own. The vice president attacked her supposed brave decision to have a child alone and suggested that the only viable model for moral childrearing involved the nuclear family. For him, she was "a character who supposedly epitomizes today's high-paid, professional women—mocking the importance of fathers, by bearing a child alone, and calling it just another 'lifestyle choice.'"[27] The vice president's attacks happened while the show was on hiatus for the summer, but when it returned in the fall, it responded to Quayle as if he were a character in the show, blurring the distinction between the real-life vice president and the fictional diegesis of the show. Writing in 1996, communication scholars William Benoit and Kerby Anderson suggest that this incident was especially deserving of scholarly attention because the lines between fantasy and reality had been crossed in the political realm. They assert that "Quayle chose to criticize Hollywood generally and a popular fictional character specifically. Murphy Brown replied to an attack from a politician on a fictional television show. These artifacts conjoined to blur the traditional lines between fantasy and reality."[28] The Murphy Brown incident was one of the early instances that disrupted the ostensible firm distinction between the reality of politics and the fantasy of entertainment. That distinction would have to be thoroughly blurred to imagine a pathway for Donald Trump to become a serious candidate for president.

The star of the 1992 election cycle was a young Baby Boomer from Arkansas who also used entertainment to distinguish himself from previous politicians; perhaps the most famous instance of this was when Bill Clinton appeared on the Arsenio Hall show playing an Elvis Presley song on the saxophone and donning Ray Ban sunglasses. This was an exponential leap forward from Richard Nixon's cameo on *Laugh In*, and its entertainment value emerged for different reasons. In the case of Nixon, the reason for the catch phrase's hilarity was the dissonance between Nixon's staid humorless persona and his awkward attempt to take him out of his comfort zone. Nixon was obviously most comfortable playing the part of the politician, and the conceit of the joke that he was willing to play along with the gag, even though it was not his thing. On the other hand, Clinton seemed to relish in the moment of playing the sax on the late-night host's show. For him, he was showing that he was meant to be an entertainer, and the politics game was just a manifestation of that; in a perfect world, Clinton would rather be playing sax for a living, but he would have to settle for the show business of politics. Clinton reprised his saxophone performance at the inaugural ball in 1993 and at several moments during his presidency.

At another moment in Clinton's presidency in 1994, Clinton appeared on an MTV town hall and was asked about his preferred style of underpants—boxers or briefs. After being briefly taken aback, Clinton responded that he sometimes wore both styles but that he usually wore briefs. That an audience member would feel comfortable enough asking the president of the United States about his favorite style of underwear is testament of how far popular entertainment had infiltrated the realm of politics. In 1998, Clinton became embroiled in a scandal that found him having an affair with a young intern. The ensuing impeachment saga featured graphic descriptions of the president's sex life and would further tear down the barriers between popular entertainment and serious presidential politics, and the 1990s would prove to be a critical decade for the dissolution of the spheres of the political and popular entertainment.

In 1993, the first web browser, Mosaic, allowed anyone with access to a personal computer to have access to the World Wide Web. By 1995, Microsoft was bundling a web browser with its new version of Windows, and the exponential rise of the internet in the late 1990s was on its way. While the internet had been available for several decades, the World Wide Web, with its graphic interface, coupled with easy access through dial-up modems through services such as Microsoft Network and America Online, brought the internet to a much wider audience. Donald Trump registered for his first website, Trump.com, in 1997, and the first evidence of the site is from 1998; it's unclear when the site went live.[29] Most of his early websites were advertisements for his businesses and properties, though a 2000 website shows a video of Trump. He would not really emerge as a player on the internet until the rise of Twitter in the late 2000s, though he did have success with a branded computer game for Windows—Donald Trump's Real Estate Tycoon (2002).

Though the internet had not become a central part of presidential campaigns, the 1996 campaigns actually did feature some rudimentary websites. In fact, as of 2020, the Dole/Kemp and Clinton/Gore websites from 1996 were still maintained as relics from a different age of the World Wide Web.[30] The 2000s would see campaigns increasingly rely upon the internet for fundraising, advertising, and for making connections with voters. By the time Trump ran for president in 2016, the internet was such a huge part of the campaign that many believe that international provocateurs or even bots may have swung the election in Trump's favor by using disinformation campaigns on the internet. The simplistic form of the Dole/Kemp website seems remarkably quaint in comparison to the sophisticated campaign tactics that pervade in contemporary presidential politics.

Perhaps the most important media development of 1996 was the addition of two new cable news channels: MSNBC and Fox News. While it would be several years before MSNBC would find an audience, Fox News became a player almost immediately as it provided a conservative alternative to the three major broadcast news stations and CNN. Purporting to be "fair and balanced," the network was the brainchild of two conservative players: media mogul Rupert Murdoch and long time political operative Roger Ailes. Murdoch and Ailes saw the success that conservative talk radio had in constituting an audience for conservative listeners and wanted to bring that audience onto cable television. From its inception, Fox News was just as interested in image and entertainment as it was in presenting the world, and it proved to be fertile ground for any political scandal or gossip, no matter how sordid. Much to the good fortune of the network, within a year of it going on the air, Bill Clinton was embroiled in a sex scandal with an intern, which was fuel for the conservative outrage machine and perfect fodder for the burgeoning network. By the early 2000s, Fox News would be the top-rated cable news network in the country and would eventually become the top-rated cable network of any kind. When Donald Trump ran for president in 2016, Fox News at times served as an arm of his campaign, and several of the pundits on the channel gave Trump advice both on the air and in private during his presidency.

By 1998 Bill Clinton's sexual dalliances had resulted in his impeachment, and the country's trust in government was exceedingly low. Perhaps consequentially, the 1998 midterms saw Jesse Ventura elected governor of Minnesota. Jesse "The Body" was a former professional wrestler with little political experience (he had been a one-term mayor of a small suburb in Minnesota) who ran as an outsider and employed a populist rhetoric that frightened the establishment Republicans and Democrats alike. Ventura's 1998 campaign is perhaps the most analogous campaign to Donald Trump's 2016 campaign as both defied existent political commonsense and relied upon their positions as entertainment celebrities to win election. Further connecting the two figures, Donald Trump has a long history with the world of professional wrestling, and scholars and pundits have compared his approach to politics to the way a professional wrestler approaches the spectacle that is professional wrestling. Ventura even interviewed Trump before Wrestlemania XX in 2004.[31] Writing about Jesse Ventura, rhetorical scholar James Janack suggests that politicians can deploy a Bakhtinian performance of the carnivalesque to position themselves as outsiders in relation to other candidates. For him, "when considered in the context of contemporary politics, there is an analogous relationship between the carnivalesque spirit of opposition to the dominant culture and outsiderism's professed opposition to contemporary political culture... Voters embrace an outsider partly to protest 'politics as usual,' just as people have embraced carnival partly to protest against official institutions."[32] From the minute he rode down the escalators in Trump

Tower, Trump's campaign relied upon the carnivalesque as its central driving mechanism. He was more outlandish than all of the other candidates, which, in turn, allowed him more airtime and print coverage, and he would simply up the ante on the carnival if another candidate vied for more media attention. Once he was in the presidential office, he defied many of the norms that constitute "politics as usual," and continued to fuel the fire for a carnivalesque media atmosphere that he consistently adds more fuel to sustain.

Professional wrestling as a spectacle is itself an excursion into the carnivalesque in which many of the usual rules of society are turned on their heads. Donald Trump has hosted wrestling events at his hotels, and has even participated in the extravaganzas, at one point winning the privilege of shaving the head of WWE's CEO Steve McMahon with the help of wrestling star "Stone Cold" Steve Austin.[33] Had McMahon won the tag-team bout, his prize would have been the honor of shaving Trump's famous golden locks; of course, the results of disputes in the arena of professional wrestling are preordained, and Trump's hair was never actually in danger. Donald Trump spent enough time hosting and participating in wrestling events that he has been inducted into the WWE hall of fame. Writing in the heat of the 2016 election journalist Jeremy Gordon notes that

> for a while, it became trendy to insist that the 2016 presidential election, with all its puffed chests and talk of penis size, seemed more like a wrestling pay-per-view event than a dignified clash of political minds. In politics, as in wrestling, the ultimate goal is simply to get the crowd on your side. And like all the best wrestling villains—or "heels"—Donald Trump is a vivacious, magnetic speaker unafraid to be rude to his opponents.[34]

Trump used the skills that he gleaned from his time spent with WWE to his advantage on the campaign trail, and followed in the footsteps of professional wrestler Ventura, who paved the way for an outsider to use the logic of the carnivalesque to his advantage on the campaign trail and beyond. Minnesota journalist Hannah Jones compared the two political figures and maintains that while both have very different political ideologies, "both of them are also their own best advocates when it comes to trumpeting their intelligence, strength, and political capability. And both of them have a strange love-hate relationship with the media, which they crave for the notoriety and decry for any dents in their reputations."[35] Ventura also formed the Reform Party for his 1998 run, and they were seeking a candidate to run for president in 2000.

In 2000, Trump was considering another run for president, and this time he was taking it more seriously than he had in 1988. The relative success of Ross Perot in the 1992 and 1996 election cycles coupled with the astonishing victory of Jesse Ventura for governor in 1998 increased the expectations for third-party candidates in the 2000 election cycle. Some of Ventura's supporters encouraged Trump to enter the race, and Trump actually did for a short while, competing in some of the primaries and winning the California primary before eventually bowing out to eventual nominee Pat Buchanan, whom Trump ironically critiqued for being too nativist, racist, and homophobic.[36] Though the campaign was brief, Trump was already trying out lines that he would rehash and perfect in his 2016 run. At a 2000 event, he opined that "in business and in life, people want to hear straight talk. We're tired of being bullshitted by these moron politicians."[37] Trump was perfecting his outsider persona, which he would use to great effect in 2018. The third-party influence would also have great effect in the 2000 election as the candidacies of Pat Buchanan and Green Party candidate Ralph Nader likely tipped the scales of the election in favor of George W. Bush.

## The New Millennium

Among the "journalists" covering the 2000 election were a group of comedians from *The Daily Show* (1996–), newly revamped with host Jon Stewart. Though ostensibly part of a comedy troupe for a basic cable show, *Daily Show* correspondents were able to get access to the candidates and even to the national conventions. The show eventually won a Peabody Award for its "Indecision 2000" coverage, further blurring the line between its role as a "fake news" comedy program and part of journalistic news proper. Cultural studies scholar Amber Day notes that *The Daily Show* works to demonstrate the constructed nature of 'real" news by demonstrating the ways in which the boundary between real news and fake news can be easily traversed. When correspondents from the show go into the conventions or when "real" news footage is used on the set of the show, then *The Daily Show* works to show that it is constructed. As Day argues, "it is precisely the importation of the 'real' or nonfictional into the mimetic frame of the program that can serve to call attention to the way in which the 'real' is itself constructed."[38] The show started to show the tactics by which the 'real" journalists worked to produce the air of trustworthiness necessary for journalistic integrity, and subsequently the show worked to weaken the traditional news media's ethos of respectability. Day argues that "it is through this act of pointing out the artificiality of real newscasts, press conferences, and other forms of public discussion that, for many of its fans, this 'fake' news show actually comes closer to embodying the characteristics—like authenticity and truth—that we would normally associate with the 'real.'"[39] When Trump starts attacking establishment journalism as "fake news," the ground for this is already fertile as "fake news" satire has troubled the notion of real news throughout the 2000s.

Jon Stewart's protégé Stephen Colbert further troubled the notion of political reality through satire when he launched his own program that aired after *The Daily Show*. While *The Daily Show* parodied a traditional nightly news program, *The Colbert Report* (2005–14) riffed on the pundit-based news programs that had come to thrive in the era of cable news. Colbert played a version of himself who was a bloviating know-it-all who bowed to conservative dogma and failed to see nuance in political arguments. Though his program started a decade before Trump's campaign, he already served as a parody for the Trump candidacy, for Colbert's candidacy had no compunction about making up facts if those facts helped him make his argument. As media studies scholar Geoffrey Baym contends, Colbert "invokes the postmodern argument that objective reality is inaccessible and that facts themselves are social constructs, more the products of human institutions and practices than reflective of any a priori reality."[40] He cites a particular interview against an antiwar activist who showed statistics that at the time the majority of Americans had turned against the Iraq War. Colbert retorts: "I don't accept your statistics. Even if it's true I don't accept them. A majority of Americans thought Hitler was a great guy. That's a fact. I just made up that fact, but that doesn't keep it from being a fact."[41] Colbert's satirical deconstruction of facts comports with Kellyanne Conway's notion of "alternative facts," or indeed the way facts have been deployed throughout the Trump campaign and administration. Trump was not the first politician or pundit to traffic in alternative facts; thus, when Colbert rendered a performance ad absurdum of a pundit insisting upon the fungibility of facts it reads as a lampoon in the 2000s. However, in the era of Trump, the actual president performs the absurdist understanding of facts, and the logic of the jester has been usurped by a "real" politician—or at least a politician trained in the production of reality on television.

In 2000 reality television broke in the United States. *Survivor* (2000–) and *Big Brother* (2000–) were the big summer hits, and *Survivor*'s finale drew the second biggest audience of the year, after the Super Bowl.[42] The 2000s saw network and cable television channels producing a deluge of reality television content that changed the landscape of television in the decade. Television producers loved reality TV because of its relative cost efficiency. The first season of *Survivor* was filmed on location in a remote location in Borneo and featured a one-million-dollar prize to the winner. Yet because it did not have to hire writers and did not have to use known actors in the production, it was still much cheaper to produce than scripted television. Further, it could bypass the writing and acting unions that protected those groups from exploitation from the producers—the characters on *Survivor* were not protected by television unions.

By the middle of the 2000s, a sub-genre of reality television was emerging dubbed "celebreality," which took the reality television format and added washed-up or D-list celebrities to the mix to add a different atmosphere to the show. VH-1 is credited with developing both the style of reality television and the portmanteau for cable television, but *Survivor*'s producer Mark Burnett saw the possibility of bringing celebreality to network television with Donald Trump, who at the time was a washed-up media star from the 1980s or 1990s.[43] Trump initially did not want to do *The Apprentice*, because he was worried the show might make him look bad; one of Trump's biggest insecurities is being perceived as less rich or important than he presents himself. Burnett had to assure Trump that he would frame the show as a comeback success story and always portray Trump in the absolute best light, as a shrewd businessman who has a keen eye for the finest talent and the finest things money can buy. In a voiceover for the show's pilot, Trump explains, "I was seriously in trouble. I was billions of dollars in debt. But I fought back, and I won, big league."[44] Producers on the show admit that there was a vast difference between the way that they portrayed Trump and his lifestyle in Trump Tower and the actual conditions in which he was living and doing business. Patrick Keefe explains that "*The Apprentice* portrayed Trump not as a skeezy hustler who huddles with local mobsters but as a plutocrat with impeccable business instincts and unparalleled wealth—a titan who always seemed to be climbing out of helicopters or into limousines." He goes on to cite a producer on the show who asserts, "Most of us knew he was a fake. He had just gone through I don't know how many bankruptcies. We walked through the offices and saw chipped furniture. We saw a crumbling empire at every turn. Our job was to make it seem otherwise."[45] The discrepancy between the portrayal of Trump and the actual conditions reflects the logic of reality television in which "reality" is the product of performances, editing, and suspended disbelief on the part of the audience. Trump was not the first politician to bring the logic of reality television to politics but he so absorbed the logic of reality television that when he ran for president, any distinction between Trump the reality star and Trump the politician was moot. In Chapter 3, I examine more specifically the ways in which Trump utilizes the logic of reality television in his life and his politics.

The rise of reality TV is followed shortly by the rise of Web 2.0, which was a term for a variety of internet technologies that made it possible for internet users not only to be consumers of content but also to be producers. Cheap and widespread access to broadband internet provided the infrastructure for the proliferation of an assortment of social networking, blogs, and microblogs to proliferate that allowed for a larger number of people to participate in the production of content than in the early days of the World Wide Web. In addition to myriad blogs from the professional level to the amateur level, MySpace launched in 2003, Facebook in 2004, YouTube in 2005, and Twitter in 2006. Social networking was such a phenomenon that *Time* magazine selected "You" as its "Person of the Year" in 2006 and featured a reflective cover to emphasize the point. In the cover article, Lev Grossman wrote that "for seizing the reins of the global media, for founding and framing the new digital democracy, for working for nothing and beating the pros at their own game, *Time*'s Person of the Year for 2006 is you."[46] This utopian moment in the mid-2000s allowed Grossman to muse that "his is an opportunity to build a new kind of international understanding, not politician to politician, great man to great man, but citizen to citizen, person to person. It's a chance for people to look at a computer screen and really, genuinely wonder who's out there looking back at them."[47] While this utopianism seems naïve in retrospect, it speaks to the hopefulness of a moment of transition when web technologies were replacing traditional gatekeepers and challenging the reality on offer by the dominant media. As such, the rise of Web 2.0 comports with the rise of reality television in that they both reconfigured the relationship between the constructed frontstage of entertainment media that was produced entirely by media producers and the "real" backstage that was invisible in traditional media.

Changes in internet technology changed the terrain of presidential politics in the 2000s. In the 2004 election cycle, Howard Dean rose to the top of the Democratic field before the Iowa caucuses by relying upon small donors that he solicited from the internet and grassroots organizing through the website meetup.com. Dean's campaign motivated the left wing of the Democratic Party, which had for over a decade been dominated by moderate establishment candidates. When Dean finished a disappointing third in the caucuses, he gave a rousing speech, promising to fight on, subsequently listing the names of the states in which he was going to fight, and finally the White House. He capped it off with a boisterous "heeyeah" that was soon to be fodder for late-night comics and to be dubbed the "Dean Scream," which would prove to be disastrous for his campaign. Writing fifteen years in retrospect, journalist Mark Murray argues that the Dean Scream "was one of the very first viral moments in American politics and a forerunner of how politics is played today."[48] Though the scream predates YouTube or Facebook, it was shared through email and became synonymous with the candidate. It was one of the first instances in which a short soundbite was shared widely using internet technology and had a major impact on a political campaign.

Two years later, Virginia senator George Allen was caught on camera referring to an intern from the opposing campaign as "Macaca" at a campaign rally. Before Web 2.0 technologies were fully institutionalized, candidates did not have to worry that what they said on the campaign trail might be picked up by a small camera and broadcast onto the personal devices of millions of people. In fact, many candidates tailored what they would say on the campaign trail to the crowd to which they were speaking; this was no longer possible because every word that a candidate uttered had the possibility of being picked up and immediately broadcast through Web 2.0 technologies. George Allen was forced to apologize for his comments and ultimately lost a senate seat that was supposed to be an easy win for the Republicans. Further, Allen had his eye on higher political office, and he saw victory in the senatorial election as a stepping-stone to the presidential election two years later. With one offhand comment in the era of Web 2.0, Allen's senatorial and presidential aspirations were dashed. Politicians, journalists, and pundits saw the power of the new technologies and the way they might reconfigure existing power structures in political campaigns.

Allen's political career was taken down by what was then known as the "blogosphere," which was a collection of blogs—websites updated more frequently than traditional journalistic sites with various degrees of journalistic credibility, integrity, and ethics—which usually rely upon commentary rather than primary-source journalism. The blogosphere preceded social media and came head-to-head with establishment media during the 2004 campaign. Long time CBS anchor Dan Rather reported that President George W. Bush had "shirked his duties" while serving in the National Guard and "received favorable treatment" because of his powerful father.[49] The documents that Rather produced to back up his story were made public and "the authenticity of the documents was challenged by a conservative blogger and former Air Force officer. Thanks to the expertise of several bloggers who compared fonts and confirmed the suspicion of forgery, this news quickly spread all over the blogosphere."[50] Because of the work done by bloggers, Rather was forced to retract his story and resign from his post at CBS. The power of the blogosphere in the early 2000s foreshadowed the ability of alternative media with less clout than establishment behemoths like those working for CBS News to find a foothold in the national media conversation. Subsequent politicians would find different strategies for harnessing the power of these alternative media from the blogosphere to the proliferation of social media, which exploded in the 2010s.

When he ran for president in 2008, Barack Obama was a decided underdog to the favorite Hillary Clinton for the Democratic nomination. Obama relied upon the strategies that Howard Dean had begun to employ in 2004 and developed a base of small donors that he contacted through the internet, which now included Facebook and Twitter, for his financial support. While Hillary Clinton continued to rely mainly upon larger donations from a smaller number of people, Obama developed a broader donor base by raising money in smaller denominations. Moreover, because he was making use of social media technologies, he was able to form a more personal relationship with his voting base through the new technologies. Following the 2008 election, David Carr describes "a network of supporters who used a distributed model of phone banking to organize and get out the vote, helped raise a record-breaking $600 million, and created all manner of media clips that were viewed millions of times. It was an online movement that begot offline behavior, including producing youth voter turnout that may have supplied the margin of victory."[51] For Carr, the remarkable thing about the Obama campaign was that he was able to mobilize people offline by the work his campaign did online; social media could translate into viable political action. By 2016, when Trump won the presidency, social media was a part of every campaign, but Obama in 2008 was the first to really take advantage of its value as an organizing tool.

The 2008 election also brought Sarah Palin onto the national entertainment and political stage when John McCain selected her to be his running mate. The governor of Alaska, Palin, provided a stark contrast to her septuagenarian running mate with her folksy charm, relative youth, and conventional good looks. The self-identifying "hockey mom" introduced herself to the national media in her speech at the 2008 Republican National Convention when asked the question in the form of a joke: "What's the difference between a 'hockey mom' and a pit bull? Lipstick!"[52] With quips like those at the convention, Palin became not only the second woman to be nominated by a major party for the vice-presidency but also a national media sensation.

For those on the far right, Palin provided a burst of fresh populist energy because she was not afraid to "go rogue" and to espouse far-right political discourse with a twinkle in her eye. For those on the left, she represented the anti-intellectual stream in Republican politics, as exemplified by her inability to name a publication that she regularly read in an interview with CBS News' Katie Couric. During the interview, Palin first attempts to dodge the question, but Couric persists, and Palin answers: "All of them, any of them that have been in front of me all these years."[53] In an interview with ABC News' Charlie Gibson, Palin boasts about that international bona fides that she had accrued simply because of Alaska's proximity to Russia. When Gibson pushes the issue, asking her why proximity to Russia made her well-suited to succeed in international affairs, despite no previous experience with international diplomacy, Palin retorts: "They're our next-door neighbors and you can actually see Russia from land here in Alaska, from an island in Alaska."[54] The reaction to the series of interviews characterized Palin as an intellectually uncurious lightweight. However, comic Tina Fey's sendup of Palin on *Saturday Night Live* cemented Palin's legacy in the public imagination.

On the 2008 season premiere of *SNL*, which immediately followed Palin's interviews with Couric and Gibson, Fey's Palin debates failed 2008 presidential candidate Hillary Clinton, played by Amy Poehler. Clinton's considerable experience in the sphere of foreign policy is juxtaposed with Palin's inexperience as Clinton asserts, "I believe that diplomacy should be the cornerstone of *any* foreign policy," and Palin retorts, "And I can see Russia from my house."[55] Fey's impersonation of Palin gained considerable traction on YouTube (then a very new phenomenon) and her caricature became indistinguishable from the "real" Palin in the eyes of much of the public. A 2011 article from the fact-checking cite Snopes had to debunk the claim that Palin herself had really uttered the phrase "I can see Russia from my house."[56] Media scholar Nickie Michaud Wild maintains that Fey's impersonation of Palin had usurped the real Palin in the public imagination that the mainstream political press began to offer punditry based on Fey rather than Palin herself. Wild avers that "journalists used the Palin satire as a substitute for their own analysis, often just referring to it as if it alone contained the very points they were trying to make. Journalists began to write about satirical commentary, as if those delivering it had become opinion leaders to them."[57]

Whether Fey's sendup of Palin had lasting political consequences is questionable; McCain's presidential campaign followed the coattails of a wildly unpopular George W. Bush, and the market crashes of fall 2008 came at the height of the campaign season and portended the worst recession since the Great Depression of the 1930s. Regardless of its immediate political effects, Sarah Palin's campaign foreshadowed the ability of a charismatic, nonintellectual populist to excite the far right and to draw heavily upon her televisual persona rather than her political experience. After losing the 2008 election, Palin resigned from the governorship and subsequently starred in a short-lived reality television series, *Sarah Palin's Alaska* (2010). Despite a great deal of speculation, especially during the 2012 election cycle, Palin has yet to reenter the political arena. In 2016, she dutifully endorsed Donald Trump, leading journalists and pundits to compare the two politicians. Journalist Don Goneya asserts that "Donald Trump's rise can be seen as a natural extension of the kind of politics that Palin herself embraced after her unsuccessful run for vice president—combining populism, rage, and celebrity."[58] Trump was able to amplify all of these qualities through his deft use of social media, which allowed him to maintain a continuous presence in public discourse throughout the Obama administration and during his subsequent campaign and presidency.

## Social Media

In May 2009, less than four months after Obama had been in office, Donald Trump sent his first tweet: "Be sure to tune in and watch Donald Trump on Late Night with David Letterman as he presents the Top Ten List tonight!"[59] His first tweet for an appearance on Letterman, on which he would promote *The Celebrity Apprentice*, does not resemble the personalized and bombastic tweets that would come to characterize Trump's account. This tweet feels like it was created by a public relations person, and most of Trump's early tweets are in a similar vein, unaware of the massive power that Twitter allows between a celebrity personality and their fans. By the end of Obama's first term, however, Trump solidified himself as one of the most vocal critics of Obama and members of the "birther" movement, a movement that insists that Obama was not born in the United States and subsequently was an illegitimate president. In a 2012 tweet, Trump writes: "Let's take a closer look at that birth certificate. @BarackObama was described as being 'born in Kenya'" and includes a link to the conspiracy website WorldNetDaily.[60] Trump had turned Twitter into one of his key political weapons, and in Chapter 4, I specifically look at the way in which he utilized Twitter for political ends and to mobilize his public.

Social media show the potential for political outsiders to use the media for their own political gains. As someone with no political experience, and someone who started with almost no political allies or endorsement, Donald Trump is the embodiment of relying upon the discourse of an outsider as well as the media situated outside of the establishment to develop his political power. When a politician looks for supporters outside of the political mainstream, they often find folks who are on the very edges of society and outside of the Overton window of what is politically acceptable. Beginning when Donald Trump developed his political base with unsubstantiated conspiracy theories about Barack Obama's country of origin, Trump courted people on the far margins of political society. Challenging the ethnic origin of the country's first Black president has racist undertones, and by loudly suggesting that Obama might be an illegitimate president, Trump was loudly blowing racist dog whistles and attracting many with their siren call. Ever since his "birther" phase, Trump has flirted with members of the far right or the alt-right, as they have worked on rebranding themselves to be less off-putting. Many on the alt-right use media sites such as 4Chan and Reddit to organize. These sites that allow nearly any kind of speech on their sites, no matter how hateful, are where many racist and misogynist memes find their origin. While Donald Trump himself does not directly interact with 4Chan and Reddit, these sites show great support for him and often represent a politics that is quite outside of that which is acceptable in mainstream politics. Moreover, Trump and his supporters, including members of his family, have retweeted and reposted memes and posts from these sites including sites that are from avowed white supremacists. While always maintaining some degree of plausible deniability, Trump has worked to avoid completely disavowing members of his base who might identify with the white supremacists.

The increased visibility of white supremacists has coincided with increased visibility of conspiracy groups, the most prominent of which is QAnon. QAnon is a group whose origins started on 8chan, a successor to 4chan, whose core belief is that "a group of Satan-worshiping elites who run a child sex ring are trying to control our politics and media."[61] Followers of this moment believe that Donald Trump was chosen to combat these evil forces, and he is a savior figure in the movement. During the insurgency at the Capitol on January 6, 2021, members of QAnon were highly visible alongside white supremacist groups like the Proud Boys and revolutionary fronts like the Boogaloo Boys. All of these groups use the darker corners of the internet for their organization and existence, though they have used their increased notoriety and visibility to receive attention on mainstream media. The presidency of Donald Trump mobilized forces on the dark web and ultimately brought them out into the open through his tacit and explicit endorsement of white supremacist ideals and his refusal to disavow groups that might have otherwise remained on the fringe. Perhaps the insurrection that bookended Trump's presidency was unsurprising considering the rise in visibility of these types of groups and Trump's refusal to disavow them.

## Notes

1. Mehnaaz Momen, *Political Satire, Postmodern Reality, and the Trump Presidency: Who Are We Laughing At* (Landham, MD: Lexington Books, 2019), 1.
2. James Poniewozik, *Audience of One: Donald Trump, Television, and the Fracturing of America* (New York: Liveright Publishing, 2019), xvi.
3. Poniewozik, xvii.
4. Susan Douglas, "Breaking the Rules of Political Communication," in *Trump and the Media,* eds. Pablo J. Boczkowski and Zizi Papacharissi (Cambridge, MA: The MIT Press, 2018), 135.
5. Rick Perlstein, *Nixonland: The Rise of a President and the Fracturing of America* (New York: Scribner Books, 2008), 39.
6. Perlstein, 40.

7   David L. Vancil and Sue D. Pendell, "The Myth of Viewer-Listener Disagreement in the First Kennedy-Nixon Debate," *Central States Speech Journal*, 38, no. 1 (1987): 16–27.
8   Marshall McLuhan, *Understanding Media: The Extensions of Man* (Cambridge, MA: The MIT Press, 2001), 330.
9   McLuhan, *Understanding Media*, 330.
10  Poniewozik, 38.
11  Kevin M. Kruse and Julian E. Zelizer, *Fault Lines: A History of the United States since 1974* (New York: W. W. Norton & Company, 2019), 37.
12  Josh Compton, "Live from DC: *Saturday Night Live* Political Parody References in Presidential Rhetoric," *Comedy Studies* 7, no. 1 (2016): 65.
13  Kathryn Cramer Brownell, "The *Saturday Night Live* Episode That Changed American Politics," *Time*, April 15, 2016, https://time.com/4292027/gerald-ford-saturday-night-live/
14  David W. Dunlop, "1973: Meet Donald Trump," *The New York Times*, July 30, 2015, https://www.nytimes.com/times-insider/2015/07/30/1973-meet-donald-trump/
15  Ibid.
16  Poniewozik, 21–2.
17  Rick Perlstein, *The Invisible Bridge: The Fall of Nixon and the Rise of Reagan* (New York: Simon and Schuster, 2014), 249.
18  Susan Jeffords, *Hard Bodies: Hollywood Masculinity in the Regan Era* (New Brunswick, NJ: Rutgers University Press, 1994), 4.
19  Jeffords, 5.
20  Kruse and Zelizer, 140.
21  Sarah Banet-Weiser, Cynthia Chris, and Anthony Freitas, "Introduction," in *Cable Visions: Television beyond Broadcasting*, eds. Sarah Banet-Weiser, Cynthia Chris, and Anthony Freitas (New York: New York University Press, 2007), 19.
22  "*Lifestyle of the Rich and Famous* Intro," *YouTube*, December 31, 2016, https://www.youtube.com/watch?v=C4N9OA6MYYM.
23  Poniewozik, 41.
24  Tina Nguyen, "Is Donald Trump Not Really a Rich Person," *Vanity Fair*, May 31, 2016, https://www.vanityfair.com/news/2016/05/donald-trump-net-worth
25  Michael Kruse, "The True Story of Donald Trump's First Campaign Speech—In 1987," *Politico*, https://www.politico.com/magazine/story/2016/02/donald-trump-first-campaign-speech-new-hampshire-1987-213595
26  Susan Douglas, *Listening in: Radio and the American Imagination, from Amos "n" Andy and Edward R. Murrow to Wolfman Jack and Howard Stern* (New York: Times Books, 2002), 298, 299.
27  William L. Benoit and K. Kerby Anderson, "Blending Politics and Entertainment: Dan Quayle versus Murphy Brown," *Southern Journal of Communication* 62, no. 1 (1996): 75.

28 Benoit and Anderson, 73.
29 Adrienne LaFrance, "Donald Trump's Lost 1990s Websites," *The Atlantic*, February 13, 2017, https://www.theatlantic.com/technology/archive/2017/02/trump-1990s-websites/516432/
30 "Dole Kemp Online Campaign," accessed June 28, 2020, http://www.dolekemp96.org/
31 Aaron Oster, "Donald Trump and the WWE: How the Road to the White House Began at WWE," *Rolling Stone*, February 1, 2016, https://www.rollingstone.com/politics/politics-news/donald-trump-and-wwe-how-the-road-to-the-white-house-began-at-wrestlemania-35697/
32 James Janack, "The Rhetoric of 'The Body': Jesse Venture and Bakhtin's Carnival," *Communication Studies* 57, no. 2 (2006): 197–214.
33 Oster.
34 Jeremy Gordon, "Is Everything Wrestling?" *New York Times Magazine*, May 27, 2016, https://www.nytimes.com/2016/05/27/magazine/is-everything-wrestling.html
35 Hannah Jones, "How Fair Is It to Compare Donald Trump to Jesse Venture?" *City Pages*, November 5, 2018, http://www.citypages.com/news/how-fair-is-it-to-compare-donald-trump-to-jesse-ventura/499452251
36 Tom Squitieri, "A Look Back at Trump's First Run," *The Hill*, October 7, 2015, https://thehill.com/blogs/pundits-blog/presidential-campaign/256159-a-look-back-at-trumps-first-run
37 Ibid.
38 Amber Day, "And Now... the News? Mimesis and the Real in *The Daily Show*," in *Satire TV: Politics and Comedy in the Post-Network Era*, eds. Jonathan Gray, Jeffrey P. Jones, and Ethan Thompson (New York: New York University Press, 2009), 86.
39 Ibid.
40 Geoffrey Baym, "Stephen Colbert's Parody of the Postmodern," in *Satire TV: Politics and Comedy in the Post-Network Era*, eds. Jonathan Gray, Jeffrey P. Jones, and Ethan Thompson (New York: New York University Press, 2009), 135.
41 Baym, 135–6.
42 Steve Johnson, "*Survivor* Finale Posts Ratings Even Larger than Show's Hype," *Chicago Tribune*, August 25, 2000, https://www.chicagotribune.com/news/ct-xpm-2000-08-25-0008250272-story.html
43 Brian Stetler, "With 'Celebreality,' VH-1 Attracts Ratings and Chagrin," *The New York Times*, August 30, 2009, https://www.nytimes.com/2009/08/31/business/media/31cable.html
44 Patrick Radden Keefe, "How Mark Burnett Resurrected Donald Trump as an Icon of American Success," *The New Yorker*, December 27, 2018, https://www.newyorker.com/magazine/2019/01/07/how-mark-burnett-resurrected-donald-trump-as-an-icon-of-american-success

45  Ibid.
46  Lev Grossman, "You—Yes, You—Are *Time*'s Person of the Year," *Time*, December 25, 2006, http://content.time.com/time/magazine/article/0,9171,1570810,00.html
47  Ibid.
48  Mark Murry, "As Dean's 'Scream" Turns 15, It's Impact on Politics Lives On," *NBC News*, January 17, 2019, https://www.nbcnews.com/politics/meet-the-press/howard-dean-s-scream-turns-15-its-impact-american-politics-n959916
49  Jim Rutenberg, "Familiar Role for Rather and His Critics," *The New York Times*, September 17, 2004,
50  Viviane Serfaty, "Passionate Intensity: Political Blogs and the American Journalistic Tradition," *Journal of American Studies* 45, no. 2 (2011): 305.
51  David Carr, "How Obama Tapped into Social Networks' Power," *The New York Times*, November 9, 2008, https://www.nytimes.com/2008/11/10/business/media/10carr.html
52  Brendan Scott, "She's a 'Pitt Bull with Lipstick'," *The New York Post*, September 4, 2008, https://nypost.com/2008/09/04/shes-a-pit-bull-with-lipstick/
53  m35nyntk545, "Sarah Palin Can't Name a Newspaper She Reads," *YouTube*, https://www.youtube.com/watch?v=xRkWebP2Q0Y
54  ABC News, "Excerpts: Charlie Gibson Interviews Sarah Palin," *ABC News*, September 11, 2008, https://abcnews.go.com/Politics/Vote2008/story?id=5782924&page=1
55  Don Roy King, "SNL Transcripts: Michael Phelps: 09/13/08: A Non-Partisan Message from Sarah Palin & Hillary Clinton," *SNL Transcripts Tonight*, October 8, 2008, https://snltranscripts.jt.org/08/08apalin.phtml
56  David Mikkelson, "Did Sarah Palin Say 'I Can See Russia from My House?'" *Snopes*, January 29, 2011, https://www.snopes.com/fact-check/sarah-palin-russia-house/
57  Nickie Michaud Wild, "Dumb vs. Fake: Representations of Bush and Palin on *Saturday Night Live* and Their Effects on the Journalistic Public Sphere," *Journal of Broadcasting & Electronic Media* 59, no. 2 (2015): 495.
58  Don Gonyea, "How Sarah Palin Paved the Way for Donald Trump," *NPR*, January 23, 2016, https://www.npr.org/2016/01/23/464068087/how-sarah-palin-paved-the-way-for-donald-trump
59  Peter Oborne and Tom Roberts, *How Trump Thinks: His Tweets and the Birth of a New Political Language* (London: Head of Zeus Books, 2017), 3.
60  Oborne and Roberts, 63.
61  Kevin Roose, "What Is QAnon, the Viral Pro-Trump Conspiracy Theory?" *The New York Times*, March 4, 2021, https://www.nytimes.com/article/what-is-qanon.html

# 2

# Conservative Talk Radio and Shock Jocks

At his State of the Union address in 2020, Donald Trump presented radio personality Rush Limbaugh with the Presidential Medal of Freedom, the highest civilian honor that a person can receive. Many viewed Trump's decision to bestow Limbaugh with the honor as a slap in the face to the opposition party by selecting such a controversial figure without any warning; Trump was "owning the libs," in the parlance of the conservatives. However, Trump was also paying a debt to talk radio, which emerged as a dominant form of popular media in the late 1980s and has paved the way for a brash style of white masculinity that resonated with millions of listeners and which Trump took up as his political persona. Conservative talk radio emerged at a particular historical and political moment when white men felt as if they were losing political power due to the advances of feminism and the civil rights movement. These white men felt as if they had found a space where they could air their grievances, and figures like Rush Limbaugh provided both a sympathetic ear and an angry voice that spoke to the fears that circulated in discourses about white masculinity at the end of the twentieth and beginning of the twenty-first centuries. Like Limbaugh, Donald Trump spoke to the perceived grievances of white men as they felt a country that was once theirs had become feminized and multiculturized through culture and politics. Talk radio was one bastion of white male authority where the desire to make America great again resonated soundly. Donald Trump used strategies that he learned from talk radio to construct part of the multifaceted self that ultimately became a successful politician and president.

## Shock Jocks and Insult Comedy

Limbaugh was the most popular and most influential of a handful of political talk radio hosts including Sean Hannity, Mark Levin, and Michael Savage. Some, like Hannity, have gone on to even more successful television programs on Fox News, and the cable channel and talk radio have maintained a close relationship. The obverse to the political talk radio, which rose to prominence at the same time, were the shock jocks, the most popular of which is Howard Stern (though he no longer is on terrestrial radio). Both the political talk radio hosts, led by Limbaugh, and the shock jocks, led by Stern, rose to prominence in the late 1980s, and became cultural institutions by the 1990s. Radio personalities often blurred the lines between the political jocks and the shock jocks, as Limbaugh often featured adolescent antics on his program, and shock jocks like Don Imus had serious political candidates on his radio program, and even eventually landed a show on MSNBC. What unites all of these broadcast personalities is a boorish masculinity that challenges the political and cultural gains that women have made as a result of the second-wave feminist movement. Writing at the turn of the twenty-first century, communication scholar Susan Douglas highlights "talk radio's central role in efforts to restore masculine prerogatives to where they were before they women's movement." For her, "talk radio is as much—maybe even more—about gender politics at the end of the century as it is about party politics."[1] The gender politics that proliferate on talk radio see men as having their position of power threatened by women, particularly those who identify as feminists. The hosts and callers perform a version of masculinity that evokes a time before second-wave feminism made mainstream media politically correct and aligns with the masculinity on offer in the persona of Donald Trump.

Rush Limbaugh takes particular umbrage with feminism. He coined the term "feminazi" and is famous for quipping that "feminism was created so that unattractive ugly broads could have access to the mainstream."[2] In 2012, Limbaugh made a considerable amount of national news, and lost a considerable number of sponsorships, by calling a Georgetown law student a "slut" and a "prostitute" for advocating for government-sponsored birth control in front of Congress. Limbaugh opined, "It makes her a slut, right? It makes her a prostitute. She wants to be paid to have sex. She's having so much sex she can't afford the contraception." The next day, he offered no apology, but doubled down on his misogynist remarks, stating that he would "buy all of the women at Georgetown University as much aspirin to put between their knees as they want."[3] This kind of anti-feminist banter proliferated on Rush

Limbaugh's radio program, which operated as a kind of safe space for men who felt a nostalgia for a time when their power went unchallenged. For Limbaugh and his listeners, feminism represented an existential threat to a way of life that they saw as quickly receding into the dustbins of history. As masculinity scholar Jackson Katz notes, conservative talk radio jocks "speak with an old-school masculine authority that recalls an idealized past, when (white) men were in control in the public and private spheres and no one was in a position to actively challenge their power."[4] When Donald Trump encourages his fans to Make America Great Again, millions of men already know what he is talking about because the likes of Rush Limbaugh have already primed them through talk radio to envision a world that has been taken away from them through feminism. Moreover, they have already imagined a kind of utopic community where they can all hang out without the eavesdropping ears of those who threaten to take it away.

One strategy that Donald Trump has borrowed from talk radio was his propensity to insult the groups or individuals who were his real or perceived political enemies. During the campaign, Hillary Clinton became "Lyin' Hillary," Marco Rubio became "Little Marco," and *The New York Times* became "The Failing *New York Times*." He saves some of his most vitriolic attacks for women, calling Hillary Clinton a "nasty woman" during one debate. In another, Trump took a question posed by moderator Megyn Kelly, prompting him to claim that she had "blood coming out of her eyes, blood coming out of her 'wherever,'" insinuating that she must have been menstruating to have asked him such a question.[5] American studies scholar Oscar Winberg suggests that what he defines as "insult politics" is inseparable from the overall political strategy of Donald Trump. For Winberg, "the insult politics of Donald Trump . . . was inseparable from his candidacy from the beginning," from the moment he threw his hat in the ring and labeled Mexicans as criminals.[6] Winberg then draws a direct line between political talk radio hosts and Trump, demonstrating that these broadcast provocateurs' use of insult commentary to provoke paved the lane for Trump's disparaging discourse. The folks on talk radio (as well as Fox News and on the internet) could engage in insult politics without repercussions because they were outside of the serious field of politics. Presidents, senators, and congresspersons were still expected to act with a certain level of decorum. While the political media still wielded a great deal of power in terms of shaping the debate by creating an echo chamber of conservative ideas, their brand of insult politics was still relegated to the sidelines. Winberg argues, "Trump, who became a political figure on the air of Fox News and a variety of conservative talk radio shows, has erased the difference between the rhetoric of the echo chamber and national politics."[7]

After the campaign, Trump continued to perform his insult politics through tweets and press conferences; he continued to unleash his harshest insults in the direction of women. Just as the talk radio audience luxuriates in a space that is predominantly free from women's voices and ideas, Trump seems to pine for a time when women could not challenge his authority, and his inclination is to insult them.

One way in which Trump's insult politics manifests is in the vein of something like an insult comic. At the debate when he was challenged by Megyn Kelly, she mentioned times when he had referred to women as "fat pigs, dogs, slobs, and disgusting animals." Before Kelly could finish her question, Trump unleashed a zinger: "only Rosie O'Donnell." After applause from the audience, Kelly finally finishes her question, and Trump responds saying, "I think that the problem with this country is being politically correct. I've been challenged by so many people, and I don't frankly have time for total political correctness... And frankly, what I say, and oftentimes it's fun, it's kidding. We have a good time."[8] Here, Trump reverses the charges against him back onto Kelly; it's not his fault if she can't take a joke—she's just being too politically correct. Political correctness has been a canard of conservative talk radio hosts and comics for decades, and Trump disavows his position as a politician and claims himself to be a mere comic to avoid the charges of misogyny.

Cultural critic Emily Nussbaum suggests that Trump's ability to perform as an insult comic is one of the reasons that he prevailed in the 2016 election. She maintains that "Trump was a hot comic, a classic Howard Stern guest. He was the insult comic, the stadium act, the ratings-obsessed headliner who shouted down hecklers. His rallies boiled with rage and laughter, which were hard to tell apart."[9] One irony about Trump is that he rarely or never laughs in public. Writing about Trump on the campaign trail, Leslie Savan notes that "we don't know what he does behind closed doors, but before the cameras, the candidate hasn't emitted deep, jocular bursts of air in nearly a year and a half."[10] Nevertheless, Trump is able to evoke laughter in his audiences, and as Nussbaum notes, the difference between laughter and rage is difficult to discern. She also interestingly points to Howard Stern, a talk radio host, as an example of the type of humor that Trump is aiming for. Stern is less known for his political talk (though he did run for governor of New York on the Libertarian ticket in 1994); however, he is an exemplar of the boorish masculinity that has come to define talk radio. Nussbaum writes about the gender trap in the kind of humor that Trump and Stern lay down, noting that it presents an obstacle for the decent listener. By protesting the humor or claiming that what they are saying is not funny or not even a joke, the listener is revealing themselves to be priggish, square, or politically correct. Nussbaum uses the metaphor of a finger trap to describe the situation.

You are placed loosely within the joke, which is so playful, so light—why protest? It's only when you pull back—show that you're hurt, or get angry, or try to argue that the joke is a lie, or, worse, deny that the joke is funny—that the joke tightens. If you object, you're a censor. If you show pain, you're a weakling.

By this type of bullying and by accumulating large crowds to enforce it, men like Trump and Stern are able to wield great deals of power by using jokes that are "only meant in fun."

## Trump and Stern

If Trump blurred any distinction between an insult politician, insult comic, and talk radio show, the line between entertainment and politics on talk radio had already been dissolved many years ago. Shock jocks like Howard Stern have their roots in the 1970s with "topless radio" and the 1980s with the "morning zoo" format.[11] Stern established himself as the king of the morning zoo format in New York City and eventually became syndicated nationally. Stern's rise to national prominence was nearly concomitant with Rush Limbaugh's rise to national prominence in the late 1980s. Like Limbaugh, he pined for a world that has passed him by. Susan Douglas argues that Stern "was especially determined to defy the liberal sensibilities about race, gender, physical disabilities, and sexual orientation that had emerged from the social movements of the 1960s and 1970s."[12] Communication scholar Zack Stiegler notes a tendency for political talk show hosts to transition from shock jocks and morning zoo crews to the political side, with the common factor of the groups being the ability to create a community of like-minded listeners who bond around the idea of controversy.[13] Limbaugh, Stern, and their ilk would not have gained their popularity or their notoriety without crossing lines of decency and developing adoring fans who found community in these guys "telling it like it is" regardless of what the social norms of the times were. Stiegler argues that in more recent times, what shocks over the airways is less often crude sex talk but is rather crossing the lines of political correctness in terms of racial, sexual, or homophobic speech. He maintains that "what shocks in talk radio today tends not to be sex, bawdy comedy routines, or foul language, but hate speech," and he refers to Limbaugh referring to Sandra Fluke as a slut and a prostitute and Don Imus referring to the Rutgers women's basketball team as "nappy headed hos."[14] As an insult comic, Donald Trump can be the ultimate shock jock as he can use both locker room material and the more contemporary hate speech material. His adoring audiences love him for "keeping it real," "telling it like it is," and for flaunting the confines of political correctness.

Trump actually considered hosting a talk radio show during his presidency. There was an irony to this because Trump had discontinued the traditional presidential weekly radio address, which had its roots in the Franklin Roosevelt presidency, and had been a relatively consistent part of every administration since Reagan's.[15] In March 2020, Trump met with his advisers about a two-hour show in which listeners would call up and he would answer questions about the coronavirus. Apparently, the only reason that this did not become a reality was because Trump did not want to compete with Rush Limbaugh.[16] Trump either did not want to step on Limbaugh's toes or did not want to have to worry about getting trounced in the ratings by the reigning king of political talk radio. In any case, Trump understands that his schtick would translate well onto talk radio, and he reveres the power that Limbaugh had in that arena.

Trump did have previous experience on talk radio. In fact, Trump used to frequent Howard Stern's radio show, where between 1993 and 2015, he appeared as a guest at least thirty-nine times.[17] In a 1997 interview, shortly after the death of Princess Diana, the radio shock jock Stern interviewed Trump and asked him on-air, "You could have gotten her, right? You could have nailed her." Trump responded, "I think I could have." In a later interview he tells Stern, "I think she's magnificent. Lady Di was truly a woman of great beauty." Stern asks, "Would you have slept with her?" Trump replies, "Without Hesitation. She had the height, she had the beauty, she had the skin—the whole thing." He added, "She was crazy, but these are minor details." In another exchange, Stern suggests that Trump, a known germophobe, should get all of his potential sexual partners STD tests before engaging in sexual activity. The two joke about requiring Lady Di to get STD tests, with Trump playing out the scenario: "Go back over to my Lexus, because I have a new doctor, we wanna give you a little checkup."[18] Here, Trump is calling back to his first appearance on Stern's show, when he admitted to his germophobia and bragged or joked about having all of his (ostensibly myriad) sexual partners tested for AIDS before he would sleep with them. Perhaps the most revolting part of the scenario that is bandied about by the two grown men is the strange doctor waiting in the Lexus, presumably to examine the unsuspecting woman's genitals. The fact that HIV cannot be detected through a gynecological exam seems unimportant to the story; its import is in the way that the two casually discuss requiring a woman to undergo a humiliating test with a strange person in a car. Further, the underlying assumption behind the scenario is that women will do nearly anything for the opportunity to sleep with Donald Trump.

In a 2007 interview, when Trump was sixty-one years old, he recounted how attracted he was to Britney Spears when she was "saying she was a virgin" and was so "cute and wholesome and nice." Trump was so enamored of Spears that he "wasn't even afraid of those germs."[19] These stories are among the many tales of Trump being lecherous toward women, tendencies that Stern typically encourages on his program. However, Trump has yet to pay a political price for his misogyny and Stern is still paid handsomely for his role as a shock jock. Of course, nothing is revelatory in noting that Donald Trump and Howard Stern are churlish pigs with very little respect for women. Numerous instances bear witness to the two men disrespecting women, treating them as objects, and generally luxuriating in the puerile and the prurient. Even the fact that the two were riffing about the recently deceased and much beloved former Princess of Wales is hardly noteworthy, except that it confirms that no person or topic is off-limits for their irreverence. What is interesting about Trump and Stern is that they were using the platform of talk radio, which proved to be a powerful avenue through which anti-establishment conservative ideas circulated into the mainstream of political discourse. As political journalist Steve Richards notes "the arguments that proved to be potent for Donald Trump began with the 'shock jocks' who were allowed to broadcast their provocative views in the US. They were the embryonic Trumps. They set the scene for him, and they made the unsayable more than sayable."[20] According to this logic, talk radio became a place where unconventional conservative ideas could simmer with a receptive audience that was a somewhat "safe space" for the implied and explicit white male supremacy discourses that could circulate under the guise of an opposition to political correctness. Boorish "locker room talk" could circulate with more explicit political content that resonated with a predominantly white male audience who felt aggrieved by a society in which such locker room talk and the privilege behind it no longer went unquestioned.

Richards goes further to contend that "when Trump declared, of Mexican immigrants 'they're bringing drugs, they're bringing crime they're rapists, and some, I assume, are good people,' he was echoing the language of the shock jocks. He was a presidential shock jock. It was when shock jocks began to acquire a following that shameless populism became part of the debate."[21] One could similarly argue that when Trump mocked a disabled reporter and bragged to Billy Bush about grabbing unsuspecting women by the genitals, he was simply engaging in the same kind of banter that was par for the course on shows such as Stern's. In fact, when Trump noted that "a woman who is very flat-chested is hard to be a 'ten,'" he did so on the *Howard Stern Show* (1986–).[22] That quote was featured ad nauseam in numerous attack ads against Trump in the 2016 campaign. Yet, Trump still won, and he won because he was able to win a larger percentage of the ostensibly aggrieved white men who felt that Trump spoke for them. The attack ads were ineffective in that population because Trump's misogyny was exactly the reason they admired him, and degrading women simply confirmed that he was "one of the guys" who did not care about the norms of political correctness. Moreover, they had been primed for exactly this reaction by over two decades of talk radio programs they admired that version of masculinity and hoped that the election of Donald Trump would allow boorish masculinity to once again circulate without repercussions in Trump's America.

## Entertainment over Truth

The success of right-wing talk radio had as much to do with its entertainment value as it had to do with its political salience. Limbaugh and Stern had more in common then they might have liked to admit, and Trump intuited that success in emulating a talk radio format as a politician would rely first and foremost on his ability to entertain. Historical journalist Brian Rosenwald maintains that what separated Limbaugh and other talk radio hosts from traditional conservative commentators was their ability to entertain, even as their desire to entertain might place them at odds with the conservative establishment or conservative values. He holds that "Limbaugh and his ilk cared about politics and policy, but, as we have seen, conservative political hosts knew how to amuse audiences, and they recognized that politics had to come second behind keeping listeners glued to their radios."[23] Trump brought this state of mind to the campaign trail. He was not a traditional conservative by any measure, but he could maintain an audience, even if that audience just tuned in to hate-watch him. Rosenwald notes that "one quality that candidate Trump shared with the most successful conservative media personalities: he was always captivating, even to those who paid attention only to wince and seethe."[24] People wanted to find out what Trump was going to say next, and Trump never failed to up the ante by continuing to cross the boundaries of acceptable norms, or to eschew political correctness, much to the delights of his crowds who felt like he was saying what they were feeling but could never articulate.

Liberal talk radio has never had the large crowds that conservatives have enjoyed. While NPR serves a niche market, and a group of liberals in the 2000s tried to emulate the success of conservative hosts like Rush Limbaugh with the ill-fated Air America, liberal talk radio has never had the widespread success of conservative radio. Some have argued in a McLuhanite manner that the medium is more conducive to loud slogans and angry demagoguery than it is to thoughtful, reasoned arguments, and that liberals tend to prefer the latter type of style to make their argument. This position is outlined by political scholar William Mayer, though he does not necessarily agree with the claim. Mayer writes that a "widely proffered explanation for the conservative character of talk radio is that the medium demands broad slogans and uncomplicated simple-minded discussion of the issues, a task at which conservatives, it is argued, are very good. Liberals, by contrast, have a more nuanced view of the world not easily reducible to simple catch-phrases and quick solutions."[25] Like Mayer, I am skeptical of the claim that the medium is inherently better suited to the style that radio jocks like Limbaugh employ; the hosts on NPR seem to use the medium quite deftly for long-form pieces that require the speaker and the audience to engage in a thoughtful communicative act. Even Limbaugh, despite his bluster, develops arguments and themes over weeks and months that only regular listeners are able to digest fully. Like most media phenomena, the near monopoly by conservatives on political talk radio is the result of the complex interplay of several cultural, political, and economic forces. This, of course, did not stop Rush Limbaugh from opining that a liberal could not do his job "for the simple reason that liberals don't laugh about things. I have a sense of humor."[26]

While the medium of radio may not be inherently suited for the loud antics and demagogic sloganeering of Rush Limbaugh, he and others like him showed that the format could be successful, and Donald Trump, either consciously or intuitively, saw that as a pathway to politics. As Rosenwald argues, Trump was the ideal candidate for the political world unleashed by talk radio and its progeny. His pugnacious style—constantly lashing out at liberals, the GOP establishment, and the mainstream media—was exactly what talk radio had offered for almost three decades.[27] Trump understands that the content of a speech is immaterial as long as it is entertaining and as long as it creates a sense of community among the crowd, and it piques an emotional response against the other side. Like talk radio, the point is to entertain and to create a community that defines themselves as underdog crusaders against a mainstream establishment. Even once Rush Limbaugh became the king of right-wing media and Donald Trump ascended to the presidency, they needed their crowds to feel as if they were champions for the underdogs who were not getting a fair shake in the contemporary media environment. This is the reason that Trump continued to have political rallies even after he won the presidency; his rallies allowed him to play the part of the king of the underdogs. Trump's political rallies served a similar function as to when Rush Limbaugh went on the air; he can feed off the raw energy of his constituents and strengthen his community of like-minded followers. Moreover, in the twenty-first-century media environment, those political rallies were carried and replayed on myriad media platforms, so the political energy and sense of community that they enabled and constructed flowed through multiple media channels.

The political energy that flowed through his community of followers shapes the truth of Donald Trump's politics. Trump is entirely unconcerned about the details of facts or the notion of truth as traditionally conceived; rather, he achieves his authenticity by his ability to command a crowd. Likewise, Limbaugh and the talk radio crowd are not constrained by the conventional truth of the media establishment or even conservatism as usually understood because they are able to forgo the gatekeepers who have traditionally maintained the boundaries of truth. Rosenwald notes the reciprocal relationship between media unmoored from gatekeepers and politicians who trust these media to inform their politics. He notes that when talk radio hosts "spotlighted salacious, often-unverified stories that make for great radio, they forced the mainstream media to address these same stories, thereby damaging journalists' capacity to serve as gatekeepers who determined newsworthiness."[28] He goes on to explain that "with the traditional media no longer an arbiter of truth, extremist politicians were free to make outlandish claims that no one could effectively dispute."[29] Rather than have a shared notion of truth that is built upon consensus around which policy and democratic norms could be maintained, truth became politicized and unconstrained by the traditional gatekeepers of establishment journalism. Listeners to talk radio and supporters of Trump engage an entirely different register of truth than those who engage mainstream media, and dialogue between the groups has become increasingly difficult without a common reality from which to begin a dialogue.

Out on the farther reaches of the consensual truth spectrum are those who travel in conspiracy theory like the talk radio host Alex Jones. Conspiracy theories have a long history in the United States, but talk radio provides a large platform for conspiracy theorists to operate and allows for them to circulate much more broadly than they might otherwise. A *New York Times* article from 2016 claimed that Jones's radio program was syndicated on 160 stations, and that clips from his website were viewed over a billion times on YouTube.[30] Jones is best known for peddling theories about major events—the moon landing, the Boston Marathon bombing, and the Sandy Hook Elementary School shooting—being "false flag" operations, actually taken on by the US government. Conspiracy theories do not need to operate within any parameters of acceptable truth or facts and can thus be wildly absurd and creative.[31] Donald Trump has been known to circulate in conspiratorial circles, most notably in his insistence that Barack Obama was born in Kenya and that vaccines can cause autism, both claims that Jones has forwarded on his show.[32]

While Alex Jones is too loose with the facts for most mainstream media or politics, Donald Trump not only appeared on Jones's show, but also emphatically thanked Jones and his audience once he was elected president for their help in getting him to the Oval Office.[33] Journalist Maggie Haberman writes that "when Donald Trump emerged from the haze of his surprise victory in the presidential election, one of his first calls was apparently to an early supporter, a controversial radio host and conspiracy theorist with a large following."[34] Most politicians would want nothing to do with a person who claimed that the horrific shootings at an elementary school were staged by child actors and nefarious government figures in an effort to take away the guns of average Americans and centralize the power of the central government. By 2019, Jones had even been banned from Facebook and Twitter for spreading his outrageous claims.[35] However, Trump felt no compunction about not only appearing on Jones's program but also for actively seeking the approval of Jones and that of his followers. The conspiratorial-minded talk radio audience is primed to believe versions of truth that veer from those condoned by establishment sources, and Trump used that to his advantage as he provided a version of truth that did not coincide with expert opinions, political pundits, or mainstream media outlets like *The New York Times*.

Communication scholars Van den Bulk and Hyzen suggest that Trump and Jones had a mutually beneficial relationship in the 2016 campaign, with Jones providing access to members of the extreme far right, and Trump offering a dint of mainstream respectability for Jones. They argue that their "mutual endorsement gave Trump access to Jones's Alt Right following and helped push Jones/Infowars and their counter-hegemonic message closer to the mainstream."[36] Importantly, Trump found a way to access the alt-right, which in 2016 was just starting to get mainstream media attention, but which would prove to be extraordinarily receptive to Trump's nationalist and racist tendencies. If appearing on Howard Stern allowed Trump to hone his boorish masculinity bone fides, appearing on Alex Jones's radio show demonstrated to members of the alt-right that Trump was indeed "one of them." No other political figure would dare to appear on a show as controversial as Jones's, and Trump made more than a tacit endorsement of them when after Jones told Trump that the vast majority of his audience was Trump supporters, Trump replied, "Your reputation is amazing. I will not let you down."[37]

For most of the mainstream media and political punditry, Alex Jones's reputation was anything but amazing; in his statement, Trump was aligning himself with those conspiratorially minded who could see the "real" truth, and not those "sheeple" who would follow whatever the mainstream media told them. Rhetorical scholar Jennifer Mercieca argues that "conspiracy theory was very good for Trump's political ambitions," and that in the heat of the presidential campaign, "Trump had advanced more than fifty different conspiracies within the year since he had launched his presidential campaign."[38] Many of those conspiracy theories came right from Alex Jones himself, and Mericieca notes that Jones even mentioned on the air how "surreal" it was to hear Trump repeat the content of his radio program on the campaign trail nearly unaltered.[39] Jones returned the favor by amplifying any theories that Trump was pushing, such as the scenario in which Hillary Clinton rigged and stole the primary election from Bernie Sanders in 2016 and that she was prepared to steal the general election in November.[40] The relationship between conspiratorial talk radio and the Trump campaign was mutually beneficial, and it allowed information and ideas to flow between a mainstream campaign and the outer reaches of the right-wing political universe.

Talk radio allowed a broader audience to hear content that was outside of the norms of mainstream media and Trump was able to bring that message to a broader audience. If Trump uttered something on the campaign trail, no matter how absurd, mainstream news sources would have to cover it because it came from a major presidential candidate. This allowed previously shadowy ideologies on the right to come out of those shadows and bring their ideas to the surface. Trump used the power of talk radio, which by the time of his campaign was deeply intertwined with social media and the internet, to allow conspiratorial ideas and marginalized ideologies to have sat alongside mainstream ideologies, thus expanding the Overton window for political acceptability.

## Race and Division

Numerous commentators have analyzed the increased polarization of the country as the two parties have become increasingly ideological and have moved away from more centrist positions. Historians Kevin Kruse and Julian Zelizer argue that the United States has always been divided along lines of politics, economics, race, and gender, but that after the Second World War, the country reached a certain détente in which it seemed to be united in its relative prosperity and its opposition to communism. However, the turbulent decade of the 1960s created fault lines, which have caused that era of relative tranquility to crumble, and the decades since have seen the country forgoing the postwar consensus and dividing itself along those fault lines. Kruse and Zeilzer further argue that "believing consensus was beyond reach, Americans sought to guarantee that different voices could be heard, and divergent views could be seen. Abandoning the search for common ground in political and economic life, they increasingly valued competition and even conflict. From the 1970s on, the United States would seem less and less united with each passing decade."[41] The political shifts of the 1960s were a double-edged sword for those interested in progressive change. On the one hand, they brought issues of racial, economic, and gendered inequality to the fore of politics and even made substantial legislative changes that changed people's lives for the better. On the other hand, those changes removed the veneer of unity by restructuring politics, culture, and everyday life in ways that were much more divisive.

As minorities and women achieved greater rights in the 1960s and 1970s, white men increasingly felt as if their rights had been taken away and as if they were losing their place and status in the United States. One obvious manifestation of this deep divide was in party politics where the Democrats became an increasingly multicultural party and the Republicans became almost exclusively the party of white Americans. Alan Abramowitz looks at the ways in which the parties have continued to align with ideological positions and that this led to an electorate increasingly polarized around race. He maintains that "the deep partisan divide that exists among the politically engaged segment of the American public as well as among political elites and activists is, fundamentally, a disagreement over the dramatic changes that have transformed American society and culture since the end of World War II, and that continue to have huge effects in the twenty-first century."[42] Rush Limbaugh has been one of the forces making the conservative movement increasingly inhospitable for people of color. When Barack Obama was running for president, Rush Limbaugh continually ran a clip called "Barack the Magic Ne**o," which was a parody song to the tune of "Puff the Magic Dragon."[43] The song became so popular in conservative circles that a CD including the song was sent by a member of the Republican National Committee to all of its members, and the member who sent it was forced to defend the song.[44] Limbaugh is also able to alienate non-white voters through serious policy efforts. In 2014, as a Republican Congress was working with Barack Obama to enact immigration reform, Limbaugh and other talk radio hosts worked to kill the legislation. According to Rosenwald, "Republicans believed that if they supported immigration reform, indeed any bipartisan action, enraged media personalities could trigger a serious primary challenge."[45] Rush Limbaugh and conservative talk radio worked to make the Republican Party inhospitable to people of color and consequently the party of white people, who valued the hegemony of white masculinity that reigned before the changes brought about by the 1960s and 1970s.

Donald Trump became the candidate for the erstwhile white man who promised to Make America Great Again by restoring whiteness to its central position of authority. In a country that was demographically shifting in such a way that white people would soon be a numerical minority, this exasperated the polarization that Kruse and Zelizer argue has been transpiring since the 1960s. In a widely circulated *Atlantic* article, journalist Ta-Nehisi Coates provocatively describes Trump as "The First White President," and argues that whiteness is what motivates his campaign and his politics. He avers that "it is often said that Trump has no real ideology, which is not true—his ideology is white supremacy, in all its truculent and sanctimonious power."[46] Coates tries to dispel a prominent assumption by pundits after the 2016 election that Trump won because he won over the "white working-class voter" and shows that the average salary of the Trump voter was higher than it was for the Clinton voter. Instead, the biggest predictor of whether someone would vote for Trump was not class but race. Trump and his supporters were invested in the authority of whiteness, and this whiteness is blinding at a Trump rally and in the exit polls after the election. Coates clarifies that "not every Trump voter is a white supremacist, just as not every white person in the Jim Crow South was a white supremacist. But every Trump voter felt it acceptable to hand the fate of the country over to one."[47] Like Limbaugh, Trump fought hard to demonstrate his investment in whiteness at his speeches and rallies.

While Trump has a long history of racism—from discriminatory housing practices, to vilifying the Central Park Five, to promoting birtherism—he used his speeches and rallies as a way of promoting whiteness while maintaining an air of humor or levity. Trump rallies are fun and entertaining, and he feeds off the crowd. One of the biggest applause lines he got during the 2016 cycle is when he would talk about the wall that he was going to build between the United States and Mexico, which was going to be big and beautiful, and that Mexico was going to pay for it. The latter part became a call and response as he would ask the crowd who would pay for the wall, and they would shout back "Mexico" with delight. Building a wall separating the United States from Mexico was not only politically divisive between Trump supporters and the Latinx community but also represents a physical manifestation of the nativism that Trump's investment in whiteness represents. When a crowd of white people delight in its potential construction, that investment in whiteness is confirmed. At times, the crowd's racism is more than just metaphorical. At a rally in 2019, Trump was attacking the foreign-born Muslim member of Congress Ilhan Omar when the crowd started chanting "send her back, send her back."[48] Trump presided over the crowd's chants, and it was clear that he felt that he presided over the white members of the country and those who had a vision of a country invested in whiteness, rather than one invested in a multicultural nation where a foreign-born Muslim woman could be a respected member of Congress. Trump's seemingly jocular references to violence against protesters led to a Black man being punched at one of his rallies in 2016. At several points during the campaign, he said that he would pay the legal fees for anyone who roughed up a protester, and with another protester he said, "I'd like to punch him in the face." This led up to a moment in a rally in Fayetteville, North Carolina when a protester who was being escorted out of the event was punched in the face by a rally-goer.[49] All of Trump's comments about violence at rallies were met with laughter, and in the moment, he was acting like a talk radio host, playing the crowd for the laugh, but the events primed the crowd for the violence that was enacted onto a Black body in the crowd. At a 2018 rally, Trump asks the crowd, if there is anything more fun than a Trump rally.[50] For those whose idea of humor derived in violence toward those who do not share Trump's idea of an idealized space that invests in whiteness, the answer to that question may indeed be that there is not indeed anything more fun.

Trump rallies represent a physical space where white Trump supporters can express their grievances about race. When she was writing about the appeal of political talk radio at the end of the 1990s, Susan Douglas suggests that "the anonymity it affords the listener—and many of the callers—make political talk especially compelling over this medium."[51] If the listeners and callers to Rush Limbaugh's show in the late 1990s felt the need to hide behind the relative anonymity of radio to express their investment in whiteness, by 2016 the success of Limbaugh, and the larger conservative media apparatus, had provided them with a leader that had allowed them to come out of the closet. If listeners liked Rush Limbaugh because he said things that no one else was saying, and they could chuckle along with him in their car alone, by 2017, the president of the United States was saying those things openly. Investment in white supremacy moved from the relative obscurity of the AM dial to the presidency.

In *The Twitter Presidency*, communication scholars Brian Ott and Greg Dickinson contend that Trump mobilized white rage through his rallies and other modes of discourse, and that this is his primary political currency rather than having any kind of coherent ideology. They contend that "white rage is the basis of Donald Trump's rhetorical style and, thus, widely evident in his general manner of communicating."[52] Ott and Dickinson borrow the notion of white rage from Carol Anderson, who uses it to describe the invisible kind of violence that is enacted upon Black people every time they make advances in US society. In *White Rage*, she maintains that "the trigger for white rage, inevitably, is black advancement. It is not the mere presence of black people that is the problem; rather it is blackness with ambition, with drive, with purpose, with aspirations, and with demands for full and equal citizenship."[53]

Anderson looks at the subsequent backlash against Black advancement after Reconstruction, the Great Migration, the civil rights movement, and the election of the first Black president. Trump was able to mobilize the white rage that seethed with the election of Barack Obama.

Radio has been an outlet for white rage since even before talk radio emerged when Limbaugh and his ilk came to power. In the 1930s and 1940s, Father Charles Coughlin, a Catholic priest, became quite prominent on the radio for his populist, anti-Semitic, and nativist discourses. He was able to capitalize on the white rage, which at the time was directed predominantly against Jews and communists, who were a threat to the good Christian values of the time. Historian Michael Kazin contends that "Coughlin spoke with conviction to people who were concerned about the world they were losing and afraid that 'big men'—liberal, secular, intellectual statists (and their wealthy friends) would cheat them out of whatever they could gain."[54] Coughlin's prominence faded at the beginning of the Second World War, and for Kazin this was because he adopted positions that were too anti-Sematic and too conservative for the public at the time. Fighting Hitler did make loud anti-Sematic positions less tenable, but the investment in whiteness and the concomitant feeling that something was being taken away from common folks by forces beyond their control remained. Anderson astutely shows the ways in which the changes that transpired between the Second World War and the 1980s worked to structure some of that deep-seated rage.

When his show came to prominence in the late 1980s, Rush Limbaugh worked to harness that white rage through the same medium that Father Coughlin did nearly half a century earlier; however, Limbaugh's racialized strategy is more complex than Coughlin's simplistic demagoguery. Limbaugh offers a complicated disavowal of race; he makes fun of racial minorities, as evidenced in the "Barack the Magic Ne**o" song that he often played, but claims that he is allowed to because he has moved past racial issues—so his comedy is all in good fun. If those liberals want to make a big deal about something being racist, that is because they are the real racists by always bringing up the notion of race to begin with. Cinema scholar Allison Perlman starts her analysis of Limbaugh by recounting a story of Limbaugh in 2011 pushing back against the mainstream media who were investigating accusations of sexual harassment against the Black presidential candidate Herman Cain. Limbaugh flipped the script and accused the liberal media of playing into racial stereotypes about overly sexualized Black men, adding, "what's next folks, a cartoon on MSNBC showing Herman Cain with huge lips eating a watermelon?"[55] Here, Limbaugh is able to call upon existing racial stereotypes while imagining that the liberals are the ones who are, in fact, indulging the racist fantasies. Perlman explains that Limbaugh "conflates racism with race consciousness and color blindness with racial progress. Although Limbaugh has been gleefully derisive toward other social movements of the 1960s, especially feminism and environmentalism, he has claimed the mantle of civil rights for conservatives."[56] Limbaugh's audience can rest easy knowing that the liberals are the real racists; when Limbaugh does it, he is only joking, and of course, liberals are unable to take a joke.

The final turn in the disavowal is to make being called a racist worse than actual racism. In a *Wall Street Journal* editorial, Joseph Epstein suggests that contemporary society should make the word taboo because "if you are politically on the left, racism is what you accuse people of who don't agree with you" and goes on to say that he "can think of no more devastating insult than being called a racist."[57] Attempting to remain color blind and to remove the notion of racism from mainstream discourse works to disavow the notion of whiteness. Limbaugh can enact racist stereotypes and sing about "Barack the Magic Ne\*\*o," but calling him a racist is off-limits because it makes manifest his whiteness. Ott and Dickenson maintain that whiteness needs to remain unseen, and when it is made visible, it mobilizes white rage. They claim that "whiteness functions invisibly, which is to say precognitively and apparently beyond critical engagement and symbolization. The effort to bring whiteness to the level of awareness, to make the precognitive cognitive or the nonsymbolic symbolic is met with violent resistance—that is to say with nearly inchoate rage."[58] Through their blustering style, boorish masculinity, and racially charged statements with just barely plausible deniability, Limbaugh and Trump call into being the white rage that simmers in a population that intensely feels the desire to make America great again, and becomes deeply enraged when called upon the racial anger that resides in that desire.

White rage fuels the apparent contradiction wherein Donald Trump espouses the most racist discourse of modern presidents and roils his audiences into a frenzy at his rallies and yet his constituents react viscerally to being labelled racists. A 2019 article in the *Atlantic* is titled "We're All Tired of Being Called Racists" as Elaina Plott asks Trump supporters to square their unfailing support for Trump with his consistent racist remarks. One rally-goer completely discarded any racism on the part of Trump, claiming that "insinuations of bigotry and racism were divisive tactics used by the liberal media to control minorities in this country. This is a president who serves minorities, because he loves minorities."[59] This perception of Trump does not comport with Ott and Dickerson, who claim that "Donald Trump is the walking, talking embodiment of white rage, which he enacts through his authoritarian management style, bullying manner, and hyperbolic, narcissistic, and demagogic discourse."[60] However, the seeming contradiction makes sense by taking Limbaugh, Epstein, and Trump at their word. Limbaugh has argued, "I don't have a racist bone in my body. I despise racism. Racism has nothing to do with me."[61] In his editorial, Epstein argues that "I should rather be called a coward, a cheat, a liar or anything else you happen to have in your personal arsenal of invective" than be called a racist.[62] Not to be outdone, Donald Trump has argued that he is "the least racist person anywhere in the world."[63] By assuring the public that they are not racist while simultaneously enacting white rage, these people give permission for Trump supporters to fully embrace their white rage and to take umbrage with those who might deign to call them racist for expressing those views or for endorsing a president who acts as the embodiment of that white rage.

## Fox News

In 1996, as conservative talk radio was making a name for itself on the AM dial, a new cable news station went on the air that purported to be "Fair and Balanced," as opposed to the existing news which ostensibly had a liberal bias. In 1996, the national news mostly consisted of the three network news channels' nightly half-hour broadcasts and CNN, which had been airing twenty-four-hour news since 1980. One of the axioms of Rush Limbaugh and other conservative news programs is that all these news outlets (plus the major national newspapers) delivered news from a decidedly liberal perspective. One of the selling points of Limbaugh was that he would provide the listener with real news that they could not get anywhere else. When Fox News launched in 1996, the conservative discourse of talk radio was able to expand its reach. As Brian Rosenwald argues, "Fox News gave talk fans the chance to watch the visual equivalent of their favorite radio programs. Over time Fox joined talk radio as a key building block in the foundation of the conservative echo chamber."[64] Roger Ailes, the mastermind behind Fox News, had been responsible for getting a televised version of Limbaugh's radio program on the air and conceived of Fox News as a televised equivalent of Limbaugh's show. Ailes had been interested in the relationship between conservative politics and media since he worked with the Nixon administration in the 1970s and was excited about the potential of a twenty-four-hour news channel.

By the early 2000s, Fox News had become the most popular news channel on television, and by the late 2010s, it was regularly the most watched channel on all of cable television.[65] Hosts from Fox News—such as Sean Hannity, Bill O'Reilly, Laura Ingraham, Glenn Beck—have had successful radio programs and vice versa. The network works in concert with talk radio to create a version of political truth that runs parallel to the news found from the traditional mainstream outlines. Together with online outlets, Fox News and talk radio reinforce the ideas on each platform and construct an echo chamber for discourses to circulate among their viewers and listeners.

As he was considering a political run, Donald Trump understood the power of Fox News, and used its morning show, *Fox and Friends* (1998–), like a radio call-in show. He started calling into the show in 2010 to talk about his show, *The Apprentice*, but also to opine about the news of the day and appreciated the friendly environment that he found on the show. By 2011, the show aired a news segment, "Mondays with Trump," in which Trump would regularly call into the show and give the Fox viewers some of the conservative takes that they wanted to hear while promoting his show.[66] As television critic James Poniewozic notes about Trump's run on *Fox and Friends*,

> Cable TV's mentality paralleled Trump's almost perfectly. It was antinarrative, a series of excitements and explosions without an arc, more like a movie trailer than a movie. Cable, like Trump, sought out conflict, rewarded provocation, framed life as a continual win-loss struggle, in which someone was always up and someone always down. What Fox took as a calculated strategy—the appeal to ugly, atavistic emotion—he took to by instinct.[67]

These traits that Poniewozic attributes to cable news can also apply to talk radio; when Trump is calling into *Fox and Friends*, he is just a talk radio call-in listener. Trump honed the skills that he would use on his campaign by doing stints on talk radio and by using Fox News, and as Poniewozic contends, his ability to play to the strengths of these media seems instinctual as Trump is able to slide easily between political news and entertainment, all while maintaining his Manichean sense of the world comprised of winners and losers.

In August 2016, *The New York Times* reported that Roger Ailes was helping Donald Trump prepare for his upcoming debates with Hillary Clinton.[68] While this would bring Trump's relationship with Fox News full circle, the pairing was never confirmed because Ailes had recently left Fox News in disgrace after years of persistent sexual assault toward multiple employees came to light. While the *New York Times* article did not go so far, other sources suggest that Ailes was aiding Trump throughout the campaign, even in the primaries.[69] This could imply that the tiff between Fox and Trump after the first debate, in which Trump thought the questions were unfair and which led to him boycotting a subsequent debate on Fox, was part of a larger scheme. In any case, the extent to which Ailes and Trump worked together might never be known because Ailes died shortly after Trump took office, and Trump is a notoriously unreliable source. Regardless of the level of involvement, their meetings suggest that the two men understood how to use Trump's unique media presence as a tool for winning the election and how to use the media on offer to maximize his particular tool set. Fox News was able to take the logic of talk radio to a much wider office, and Trump was able to capitalize upon the expanded office by using the tools that both required for success.

## Notes

1. Susan Douglas, *Listening in: Radio and the American Imagination, from Amos "n" Andy and Edward R. Murrow to Wolfman Jack and Howard Stern* (New York: Times Books), 289.
2. Steve Johnson, "Rush's Hour," *Chicago Tribune*, February 27, 1995, https://www.chicagotribune.com/news/ct-xpm-1995-02-27-9502270036-story.html
3. Maggie Fazeli Fard, "Sandra Fluke, Georgetown Student Called a 'Slut' by Rush Limbaugh, Speaks Out," *The Washington Post*, March 2, 2012, https://www.washingtonpost.com/blogs/the-buzz/post/rush-limbaugh-calls-georgetown-student-sandra-fluke-a-slut-for-advocating-contraception/2012/03/02/gIQAvjfSmR_blog.html
4. Jackson Katz, *Man Enough?: Donald Trump, Hillary Clinton, and the Politics of Presidential Masculinity* (Northampton, MA: Interlink Books, 2016), 124.
5. Jeremy W. Peters and Daniel Victor, "Megyn Kelly Says She Won't Be Cowed by Donald Trump," *New York Times*, August 10, 2015, https://www.nytimes.com/2015/08/11/us/megyn-kelly-says-she-wont-be-cowed-by-donald-trump.html
6. Oscar Winberg, "Insult Politics: Donald Trump, Right-Wing Populism, and Incendiary Language," *European Journal of American Studies* 22, no. 2 (2017): 1.
7. Winberg, 7.
8. "Transcript: Read the Full Text of the Primetime Republican Debate," *Time*, August 6, 2015, https://time.com/3988276/republican-debate-primetime-transcript-full-text/
9. Emily Nussbaum, "How Jokes Won the Election," *The New Yorker*, January 16, 2017, https://www.newyorker.com/magazine/2017/01/23/how-jokes-won-the-election
10. Leslie Savan, "Have You Ever Seen Trump Laugh?," *The Nation*, September 26, 2016, https://www.thenation.com/article/archive/have-you-ever-seen-donald-trump-laugh/
11. Zack Stiegler, "Michael Savage and the Political Transformation of Shock Jock," *Journal of Radio & Audio Media* 21, no. 2 (2014): 231.
12. Douglas, 304.

13 Stiegler, 233.
14 Ibid., 237.
15 Phillip Bump, "Trump Killed the Presidential Weekly Address, and No One Noticed," *The Washington Post*, July 12, 2019, https://www.washingtonpost.com/politics/2019/07/12/trump-killed-presidential-weekly-address-no-one-noticed/
16 Elaina Plott, "Trump Wanted a Radio Show, but He Didn't Want to Compete with Limbaugh," *The New York Times*, April 15, 2020, https://www.nytimes.com/2020/04/15/us/trump-radio-show-rush-limbaugh.html
17 "Donald Trump—The Howard Stern Interviews 1999–2015," *Factba.se*, accessed May 15, 2020, https://factba.se/topic/howard-stern-interviews.
18 Emily Heil, "In Newly Surfaced Howard Stern Interview, Trump Joked about Giving Princess Di an HIV Test," September 25, 2017, https://www.washingtonpost.com/news/reliable-source/wp/2017/09/25/in-newly-surfaced-howard-stern-interview-trump-joked-about-giving-princess-di-an-hiv-test/
19 Ibid.
20 Steve Richards, *The Rise of the Outsiders: How Mainstream Politics Lost Its Way* (London: Atlantic Books, 2017), 256.
21 Ibid.
22 Andrew Kaczynski and Nathan McDermott, "Donald Trump Said a Lot of Gross Things about Women on Donald Trump," *Buzzfeed*, February 24, 2016, https://www.buzzfeednews.com/article/andrewkaczynski/donald-trump-said-a-lot-of-gross-things-about-women-on-howar
23 Brian Rosenwald, *Talk Radio's America: How an Industry Took Over a Political Party That Took Over the United States* (Cambridge, MA: Harvard University Press, 2019), 118.
24 Rosenwald, 228.
25 William G. Mayer, "Why Talk Radio Is Conservative," *Public Interest* 156 (2004): 92–3.
26 Rosenwald, 33.
27 Ibid., 9.
28 Ibid., 5.
29 Ibid.
30 Liam Stack, "He Calls Hillary Clinton a 'Demon': Who Is Alex Jones?" *The New York Times*, October 13, 2016, https://www.nytimes.com/2016/10/14/us/politics/alex-jones.html
31 William Finnegan, "Donald Trump and the 'Amazing' Alex Jones," *The New Yorker*, June 23, 2016, https://www.newyorker.com/news/daily-comment/donald-trump-and-the-amazing-alex-jones
32 Bruce Y. Lee, "Alex Jones' Top 10 Health Claims and Why They Are Wrong," *Forbes*, August 16, 2018, https://www.forbes.com/sites/brucelee/2018/08/16/alex-jones-top-10-health-claims-and-why-they-are-wrong/#5c40800c3e7f

33  Maggie Haberman, "Alex Jones, Host and Conspiracy Theorist, Says Donald Trump Called to Thank Him," *The New York Times*, November 16, 2016, https://www.nytimes.com/2016/11/17/us/politics/alex-jones-trump-call.html
34  Ibid.
35  Kate Konger and Jack Nicas, "Twitter Bars Alex Jones and Infowars, Citing Harassment Issues," *The New York Times*, September 6, 2018, https://www.nytimes.com/2018/09/06/technology/twitter-alex-jones-infowars.html

Mike Isaac and Kevin Roose, "Facebook Bars Alex Jones, Louis Farrakhan and Others from Its Services," *The New York Times*, May 2, 2019, https://www.nytimes.com/2019/05/02/technology/facebook-alex-jones-louis-farrakhan-ban.html
36  H. Van Den Bulk and A. Hyzen, "Of Lizards and Ideological Entrepreneurs: Alex Jones and Infowars in the Relationship between Populist Nationalism and the Post-Global Media Ecology," *The International Communication Gazette* 82, no. 1 (2020): 50.
37  Ibid.
38  Jennifer Mercieca, *Demagogue for President: The Rhetorical Genius of Donald Trump* (College Station, TX: Texas A&M University Press, 2020), 119.
39  Mercieca, 123.
40  Ibid., 197.
41  Kevin M. Kruse and Julian E. Zelizer, *Fault Lines: A History of the United States since 1974* (New York: W. W. Norton & Company, 2019), 3.
42  Alan I. Abramowitz, *The Great Alignment: Race, Party Transformation, and the Rise of Donald Trump* (New Haven, CT: Yale University Press, 2018), x.
43  "Rush Limbaugh: Barack the Magic Negro," *YouTube*, accessed May 21, 2020, https://www.youtube.com/watch?v=5_FAJUFutyw
44  Rebecca Sinderbrand, "RNC Candidate Defends 'Barack the Magic Negro' Song," *CNN*, December 26, 2008, https://www.cnn.com/2008/POLITICS/12/26/rnc.obama.satire/
45  Rosenwald, 218.
46  Ta-Nehisi Coates, "The First White President," *The Atlantic*, October 15, 2017, https://www.theatlantic.com/magazine/archive/2017/10/the-first-white-president-ta-nehisi-coates/537909/
47  Ibid.
48  Jane Coaston, "The Trump Racism Spin Cycle," *Vox*, June 19, 2019, https://www.vox.com/policy-and-politics/2019/7/19/20699261/trump-conservatism-omar-racism-rally-send-her-back
49  Meghan Keneally, "A Look Back at Trump Comments Perceived by Some as Encouraging Violence," *ABC News*, October 19, 2018, https://abcnews.go.com/Politics/back-trump-comments-perceived-encouraging-violence/story?id=48415766
50  Emily Cochrane and Maggie Haberman, "Trump Hosts Fiery Rally on the Heels of a Whirlwind Week," *The New York Times*, March 10, 2018, https://www.nytimes.com/2018/03/10/us/politics/trump-rally-pittsburgh.html

51  Douglas, 311.
52  Brian Ott and Greg Dickenson, *The Twitter Presidency: Donald J. Trump and the Politics of White Rage* (New York: Routledge, 2019), 28, 29.
53  Carol Anderson, *White Rage: The Unspoken Truth of Our Racial Divide* (New York: Bloomsbury, 2016), 3.
54  Michael Kazin, *The Populist Persuasion: An American History* (Ithaca, NY: Cornell University Press, 1998), 133.
55  Allison Perlman, "Rush Limbaugh and the Problem of the Color Line," *Cinema Journal* 51, no. 4 (2012): 198.
56  Perlman, 199.
57  Joseph Epstein, "What Would We Do without the Word 'Racism'?" *Wall Street Journal*, August 2, 2019, https://www.wsj.com/articles/what-would-we-do-without-the-word-racism-11564782112
58  Ott and Dickenson, 32.
59  Elaina Plott, "'We're All Tired of Being Called Racists,'" *The Atlantic*, August 2, 2019, https://www.theatlantic.com/politics/archive/2019/08/trump-supporters-called-racists/595333/
60  Ott and Dickenson, 94.
61  Pearlman, 51.
62  Epstein.
63  David Jackson, "Trump Says He's the 'Least Racist Person in the World,' Sees Joe Biden as Democratic Debate Favorite," *USA Today*, July 30, 2019, https://www.usatoday.com/story/news/politics/2019/07/30/trump-claims-hes-least-racist-person-says-biden-democrat-favorite/1858853001/
64  Rosenwald, 101.
65  Nellie Andreeva and Ted Johnson, "Cable Ratings 2019: Fox News Tops Total Viewers, ESPN Wins 18–49 Demo as Entertainment Networks Slide," *Deadline*, December 27, 2019, https://deadline.com/2019/12/cable-ratings-2019-list-fox-news-total-viewers-espn-18-49-demo–1202817561/
66  James Poniewozik, *Audience of One: Donald Trump, Television, and the Fracturing of America* (New York: W.W. Norton & Company, 2019), 165.
67  Poniewozik, 169.
68  Maggie Haberman and Ashley Parker, "Roger Ailes Is Advising Donald Trump Ahead of Presidential Debates," *The New York Times*, August 12, 2016, https://www.nytimes.com/2016/08/17/us/politics/donald-trump-roger-ailes.html
69  David A. Graham, "Roger Ailes and Donald Trump: A Match Made for TV," *The Atlantic*, August 12, 2016, https://www.theatlantic.com/politics/archive/2016/08/roger-ailes-and-donald-trump-a-natural-match/496157/

# 3

# Reality TV, Professional Wrestling, and Entertainment as Reality

In December 2016, between the election and inauguration of Donald J. Trump, *Time* magazine ran a story with the headline: "Donald Trump Is the First True Reality TV President."[1] From 2004 to 2015, Trump hosted *The Apprentice* (2004–17) and its offshoot *The Celebrity Apprentice* (2008–15), and the two comprised one of the most successful reality television franchises of all time. In the *Time* piece, Jeff Nesbit offers a prediction for the Trump presidency: "It will look and feel a lot like a political reality TV show played out on a grand stage, with producers scripting the biggest fights behind the scenes while leaving plenty of room for unrehearsed, populist public drama."[2] Nesbit is providing a framework for thinking about how the logic of reality television operates. For him, the genre is meticulously scripted behind the scenes in ways that allow a seemingly natural and spontaneous performance to transpire in front of the cameras. While Nesbit's predictions may have overstated the ability of the Trump campaign to mastermind the backstage machinations of a quality political performance, his assertion does point toward the central structuring ambivalence of reality television. On the one hand, the genre purports to offer a glimpse into a reality that television had previously ignored; on the other hand, the nominal reality that the genre offers is entirely a construction. Reality television fans know that the reality they experience is not an unmediated glimpse into the lives of real people but is, in fact, scripted by producers, enhanced by editors, and performed by talent.

Many scholars have examined the genre of reality televisions since it rose to cultural prominence at the beginning of the twenty-first century. In the introduction to their edited collection *Reality TV*, television scholars Susan Murray and Laurie Ouellette maintain that reality television is defined by a "fusion of popular entertainment with a self-conscious claim to the discourse of the real."[3] As it fused to discourses of the real, the logic of reality television spread beyond the confines of popular entertainment and politics took on the logic of a reality television show. The front cover of Murray and Ouellette's collection is now eerily prescient, as it features an ad for NBC's *The Apprentice*, with an image of Donald Trump, and his catchphrase: "You're Fired." The rise of a bona fide reality television star to the presidency provides rich soil for scholars to connect reality television scholarship with contemporary politics. Rhetorical scholar Jennifer Dunn suggests that Trump's use of Twitter worked not only in ways to construct him as a "reality television President" but also in ways to constitute a society based on the logics of reality TV. She argues that

> Trump's tweets normalize his discourses as a reality TV president and further normalize reality television logics in society. The implications of this characterization for the presidency include the necessity of putting oneself in the starring role (often at the expense of the American people), needing to produce drama, defining protagonists and antagonists, and acting as the final judge for all people and ideas.[4]

While Trump himself worked to construct himself as a reality show television, the phenomenon of reality television had already primed an audience for a character like Trump to utilize its structure and logic for political gain. Specifically, Trump developed an insular epistemological ecosystem in which he could declare what was real and what was "fake news," and his adherents would follow, regardless of how seemingly outlandish his claims were. In order to interrogate this media logic, I look not only at the logic of reality television but also at the genre's close cousin, professional wrestling, and the concept of kayfabe, a term that pro wrestling borrowed from carnival workers that means "the illusion of realness."[5] Ultimately, I juxtapose reality television and Trump's reality TV presidency with an attempt at reality television in Russia, a country with a very different epistemological relationship to a fact-based truth.

## "I'm Not Here to Make Friends": A Logic of Reality TV

The germinal reality show *The Real World* (1992–present) promised to show "what happens when people stop getting polite and start getting real," and that basic promise continues to pervade reality television. Savvy viewers know that reality TV is not really real but is rather a version of reality, an instance of truth.

As theater scholar David Escoffery notes, "in the case of a reality show, we are given a representation (a TV program created for entertainment purposes) which purports to present 'the truth' (the unscripted, real activities of real people)."[6] At least since Nixon debated Kennedy with a five-o'clock shadow and sweat-glistening brow, politics has been a complicated negotiation between televised representation and reality, and Trump exacerbates that negotiation by providing little, if any, room between his mediated representation and his "true" self. For Trump, distinctions between his "real" life and his life as a televised celebrity often collapse. Cultural theorist Tom Syverson highlights Trump's years of preparation for his career in reality television and the seeming lack of difference between the Trump that appears on television and his "real life" persona. For him, "as Trump himself has shown, to be a successful reality television actor is to undertake a lifelong method-acting campaign."[7] Since he arrived on the television screen in the early 1980s, Trump has always seemed to be who he purports to be—even if that person might be obnoxious and unlikable—which makes him an appealing reality television star as well as an alluring politician.

By simultaneously serving as a mediated representation of reality and purporting to be an unmediated presentation of that reality, the genre of reality television challenges easy distinctions between an objective thing and a mediated representation of that thing. As Ouellette and Murray assert, "far from being the mind-numbing, deceitful, and simplistic genre that some critics claim it to be, reality TV provides a multilayered viewing experience that hinges on culturally and politically complex notions of what is real and what is not."[8] Trump's candidacy and subsequent presidency challenge the notion that political practices—debates, press conferences, speeches—reflect an underlying reality, while the media coverage of those events reflects an accurate portrayal of reality. If the savvy viewer understands that reality television is not, in fact, "real," they may still believe that politics and government are "real" in a more profound sense than reality television. On the one hand, government and politics are more "real" in the sense that the stakes are enormously higher for a presidential debate than they are for deciding whether to fire Andrew Dice Clay or Tom Green on *The Celebrity Apprentice*. On the other hand, politics are thoroughly mediated and structured as forms of entertainment with a goal of achieving high ratings and creating a residual buzz on social media. Most political candidates act in ways that nominally disavow the media apparatus that sustains their success and celebrity. They act as if what they are doing is "real" rather than engaging in a constructed media spectacle that closely resembles a reality television show.

Trump consistently acts as though he is a performer on a reality television show, and never lets on that perhaps there is more to the act than that. This type of performance necessitates an understanding of a certain version of reality, the terms of which are structured by its constructed-ness. Writing about the classic reality television show *Big Brother*, media scholar John Corner suggests that reality television offers the promise of the viewer being a fly-on-a-wall in an otherwise natural setting. "*Big Brother* operates its claims to the real within a fully managed artificiality, in which almost everything that might be deemed to be true about what people do and say is necessarily and obviously predicated on the larger contrivance of their being in front of the camera in the first place."[9] From his years as a notorious celebrity in printed and televised tabloids and his decade as the star of a successful reality television show, Trump has perfected the art of performing as a reality star. He is always playing a game according to the rules of reality television, while his opponents perform as more serious politicians. When his opponents do try to join him on the terms of reality television logic, they often seem clumsy, and sometimes fail spectacularly.

For Trump and his supporters, his 1987 coauthored memoir *The Art of the Deal* provides a window into the "real" Trump—a shrewd and cunning businessman who succeeds by negotiating better than his adversaries.[10] Trump's ethos is built on his reputation for being a smart dealmaker and a paragon of success in the business world. In the throes of Trump's general election campaign, Tony Schwartz, the coauthor of *The Art of the Deal*, gave an interview to *The New Yorker*'s Jane Mayer. In the interview, Schwartz contends that he sold out by writing the book and feels complicit in Trump's rise to power. Schwartz claims that he "put lipstick on a pig" and that he feels "a deep sense of remorse that I contributed to presenting Trump in a way that brought him wider attention and made him more appealing than he is."[11] Throughout the interview, Schwartz offers a supposedly inside look at the "real" Donald Trump, who is distinct and radically different from the Trump on offer in *The Art of the Deal*.

Erving Goffman's notion of a person's self having a frontstage and a backstage provides a useful framework for thinking about the gap between the Trump of *The Art of the Deal* and the Trump in Schwartz's inside analysis of the "real" Donald Trump. For Goffman, people perform a version of themselves to others, the "frontstage," while a different self exists that is not visible to others, the "backstage."[12] Celebrities such as Trump often maintain a public persona that is distinct from their private lives, and through memoirs or interviews, they try to provide their fans with a glimpse of their backstage life. People's affective relationship to celebrities often depends upon them feeling as if they know the "real" person behind the celebrity persona. An entire cottage industry of television shows, magazines, and websites exists to provide the public with access to the "backstage" of the celebrities they would like to know on a personal level. Part of the allure of Donald Trump has always been that the "frontstage" he presented through numerous appearances on television shows like *Lifestyles of the Rich and Famous* and through *The Art of the Deal* is nearly identical to the "backstage" persona that he projects throughout the media. In that version, Trump is a confident, successful, intelligent, capable, hegemonically masculine man who holds a deep appreciation for the "finer things" that accompany a lavish lifestyle and a love for "the game" inherent in high-stakes deal-making. The Schwartz interview shatters that façade by presenting Trump as a petty, insecure dullard who is only able to maintain his position of power through the sheer Machiavellian force of his willingness to lie at any cost. Ostensibly, Schwartz's characterization of Trump should have demonstrated that Trump's act was just that—an act. However, his followers never seemed to waver from their insistence that Trump was the figure of power, wealth, and strength that he projected, regardless of evidence to the contrary. Tom Syverson explains that "any fan of reality television will tell you: it doesn't matter what's staged and what's not. The program need only be compelling."[13] The reality television star version of Trump was more compelling to his fans than the "real" version of Trump exposed by Schwartz in his tell-all interview.

Reality show producer Mark Burnett was responsible for both *The Apprentice* and *Survivor* (2000–). In a spotlight about Burnett for *The New Yorker*, Patrick Keene explains that Trump was reluctant to do a reality show because he was worried that the producers would edit him to make him look bad. Keene quotes Burnett at a 2004 conference paraphrasing Trump saying, "I don't want to have cameras all over my office, dealing with contractors, politicians, mobsters, and everyone else I have to deal with in my business. You know, mobsters don't like, as they're talking to me, having cameras all over the room. It would play well on television, but it doesn't play well with them."[14] Burnett had to assure him that *The Apprentice* would make Trump look like a successful businessman who had a shrewd eye for deals, and who was a natural leader. Keefe maintains that "*The Apprentice* portrayed Trump not as a skeezy hustler who huddles with local mobsters but as a plutocrat with impeccable business instincts and unparalleled wealth—a titan who always seemed to be climbing out of helicopters or into limousines."[15] Reality television offered the frame that provided Trump the grandeur that he needed to rise on the national stage. Keefe also talked with Tony Schwartz, who takes some responsibility for Trump's meteoric rise, but who maintains that "*The Apprentice* was the single biggest factor in putting Trump in the national spotlight."[16] Trump's ascendency via reality television did not remove the sleazy taint from his persona; rather, it reframed the sleaze as a reality TV archetype synonymous with a Machiavellian version of success.

In his tell-all interview, Tony Schwartz presents Trump as a pathological liar. "He lied strategically. He had a complete lack of conscience about it." Mayer quotes him as saying, "since most people are 'constrained by the truth,' Trump's indifference towards it 'gave him a strange advantage.'"[17] Machiavellian ruthlessness and indifference to truth or ethics have long been strategies for reality television candidates. The first season of *Survivor* made reality TV a national phenomenon and featured Richard Hatch, who won the season by developing a strategic alliance for voting and being willing to turn on any of his cast-mates without consideration of their feelings or concern for their respect. Hatch embodies the "I didn't come here to make friends" trope of reality television, and the editing strategies of the show present him as indifferent to the feelings of others or even as sociopathic.

Television critic Emily VanDerWerff notes the similarities between Trump and Hatch in the early moments of the Trump campaign. According to VanDerWerff, Hatch

> generally seemed to get a huge kick out of behaving like a total asshole on TV. Hatch understood, on some intuitive level, that we wanted to see people give in to their own worst, most amoral impulses on our TV sets, and where he went, reality TV followed. Reality TV wasn't for the nice or pure of heart. It was for the nasty.[18]

Trump's detractors consistently identify the president as a nasty, calculating, quasi-sociopathic figure. A 2016 *Atlantic* article in the wake of the Tony Schwartz interview is simply titled "Donald Trump: Sociopath?"[19] In the case of both Trump and Hatch, the cool, calculated way that they can discard those who have previously helped them is polarizing. However, in both cases, these qualities are associated with their position as "businessmen" who are making effective decisions, even if those decisions are unpopular. In 2000, Hatch realized that the way to win the game of *Survivor* was to avoid making authentic friends and instead to create alliances that could be discarded once those people were no longer useful to him. Trump has used this strategy throughout his career, and in his *New Yorker* interview, Schwartz notes that Trump "had no close friends" and that "he'd like people when they were helpful and turn on them when they weren't. It wasn't personal. He's a transactional man—it was all about what you could do for him."[20] The same strategy that has sustained Trump's success for several decades allowed Richard Hatch to win *Survivor* and helped to launch reality television as a dominant media phenomenon in the twenty-first century.

Reality television also primed a viewing audience and voting public to embrace a character because he was nasty, ruthless, and potentially sociopathic, rather than despite those qualities. Regardless of one's political proclivities, Trump is "good television" in part because he embraces the qualities of the villain. He often uses vulgar or uncouth language, coins derisive nicknames for his opponents, and chastises political and personal opponents as "losers." Social scientists Sara Booker and Bradley Waite coined the term "humilitainment," which refers to the schadenfreude that viewers of reality television experience when participants or contestants experience deep embarrassment or humiliation on the air.[21] Civil libertarian John Whitehead suggests that humilitainment explains "why American TV watchers are so fixated on reality TV programming" as well as "how a candidate like Donald Trump with a reputation for being rude, egotistical and narcissistic could get elected."[22] Even those who are not fans of Donald Trump are often fascinated by the performer who is Donald Trump and the way he excoriates his opponents and brazenly defies the norms of politics, decorum, and often basic human decency.

One reality television tactic that Trump perfected was the ability to demand and maintain attention in a crowd of people clamoring for the attention of an easily distracted audience. Journalist Joy Lanzendorfer avers that "the secret to staying on TV is to act out, say outrageous things, and break the rules. Trump showed that politics now work that way, too."[23] Trump inhabits the reality TV trope of the bad guy and uses this persona to seize control of the media spotlight. She goes on to state that "like the brashest character on a reality competition, he banked on American respect for a maverick and eschewed rules of decorum. He might as well have been shouting that old reality TV chestnut, 'I'm not here to make friends.'"[24] One example of this was during the 2016 Republican primaries in which Trump appeared to be playing a different game than his opponents. While the other candidates ran traditional political campaigns, Trump questioned the stamina of "low energy" Jeb Bush and the veracity of "lying" Ted Cruz. He even embraced bizarre conspiracy theories, including one linking Senator Ted Cruz's father to Lee Harvey Oswald and the Kennedy assassination.[25] When desperate, other candidates tried to sink to the level of Trump, and often spectacularly failed. In one memorable moment, "little" Marco Rubio tried to belittle Trump by bringing attention to a long-held rumor that Trump has tiny hands, which served as a thinly veiled metaphor for his penis size. In a March 2016 debate, Trump noted that Rubio had "referred to my hands, if they are small, something else must be small. I guarantee you there is no problem. I guarantee."[26] By addressing the issue, Trump made Rubio seem petty and adolescent; only by years of honing his skills as a reality television "bad boy" who was "not there to make friends" could one embrace this kind of mudslinging and come out victorious.

Communication scholar Rachel Dubrofsky offers an astute analysis of Trump's presentation of self and his ability to defy conventional norms of politics. She notes that those who are most successful on reality TV are those who can perform as though the camera is capturing their "backstage" selves—that there is no distinction between the reality that is being filmed and that which would exist were the cameras not there. She emphasizes that "this is so regardless of how dislikeable the character or the behavior: Consistency, not likeability, is the barometer of authenticity."[27] Trump has an uncanny ability to always be on-brand on camera—he's consistently monstrous. She goes on to aver, "Trump presents as the same (monstrous, unpredictable, and dislikeable) person on his reality show, in his many public appearances prior to his bid for the presidency, during his campaign, and as president. He seemingly has no regard for the requirements of appropriate behavior in a given context."[28]

Dubrofsky maintains that Trump is only able to get away with his abhorrent behavior because of his status as a white man. She ultimately argues that Trump's monstrosity brings into sharp relief his whiteness and maleness, and his supporters come to see attacks on him as attacks on white patriarchal authority. She holds that "Trump is articulated in mainstream news as monstrous in relation to White (middle-class) norms, making whiteness evident."[29] She goes on to claim that "marking whiteness as monstrous functions strategically, facilitating an articulation of whiteness as disenfranchised, under attack, oppressed."[30] Dubrofsky is, of course, correct that Obama or Hillary Clinton could never break the norms that Trump is able to break. However, I suggest that Trump represents a broader shift in a mediascape that has been primed by a logic of reality TV to accept a broader swarth of monstrous behavior, if perhaps only from a famous white man. Trump was able to capitalize on a mediascape in which the very notion of reality has shifted as the line between reality television and "real" politics has blurred beyond distinction.

## Reality, Whatever That Means

Both Trump and reality television engage the notion of reality and blur distinctions between that which is real and that which is performed, constructed, or fake. The promise of reality television is that real people do real things, while it provides a version of reality and consequently destabilizes any attempt to capture a single version of reality. In a think piece for *The Atlantic*, Michael Hirschorn, the head of programming at VH-1 during the explosion of reality television on the channel in the 2000s, explains the difference between documentary filmmaking and reality television. Hirschorn maintains that "where documentaries must construct their narratives from found matter, reality TV can place real people in artificial surroundings designed for maximum emotional impact."[31] As American studies scholar Brian Edwards notes, media coverage of politics has traditionally inhabited the terrain of documentary filmmaking, but Trump takes advantage of his deep history in reality television and brings the logic of reality television to bear on contemporary mediated politics. Edwards argues that the Trump administration treated the presidency very much like a reality TV show upon taking office. He writes that "the simulacrum board room of *The Apprentice* anticipates the transformation of the White House Cabinet Room at the televised live sessions in the early months of 2018."[32] Reality television dwells in the gap between the real and the contrived, and subsequently subverts the distinction between them. In a 2016 piece for *Decider*, Hirschorn asserts that the genius behind reality television "is not that it's fake, but that it lives uniquely between truth and fabrication."[33]

Television scholar Justin Lewis argues that reality television does not represent a paradigmatic shift in the way that people understand reality, but rather throws into sharp relief the complicated relationship to reality that has always accompanied the experience of watching television. He writes that reality TV "has not precipitated any profound shifts in popular consciousness; rather it expresses the epistemological contradictions already involved in watching television."[34] Lewis highlights a gap between academic discourses in which the notion of objective reality has been thoroughly deconstructed and the fact that "evocations of 'reality' are still a constant presence in public discourse. Our everyday conversations are full of references to reality and real life, and these conversations are filled with distinctions between what is real and what is not."[35] In the case of scripted fictionalized television, the savvy viewer knows that the reality presented there is, in fact, a construction. Lewis goes on to argue that one televised domain in which discourses of reality still pervade is in the realm of the news. At least at the time of his essay in 2004, the ideological integrity of "news" was such that "their claim to signify real life" is not questioned by the general television audience.[36] In fact, Lewis asserts that "use of everyday words like 'real,' realistic,' or 'authentic' does not coalesce into a coherent system of references. In other words, it is neither clear what is meant by real life or how it is signified televisually.'[37] For Lewis, in the terrain of television, the scripted fiction, the reality program, and the nightly news offer different relationships to reality rather than one having more authority to claim reality than the others. Trump's coterminous position as a celebrity, as a reality television star, and as a political figure relies upon his ability to blur the lines between the coherent systems of reference that situate reality in each of those frameworks. Trump's concomitant ability to fabricate truths while never breaking character from the performance he honed as a celebrity and reality television star offers a confusing version of reality, one that is polysemic in that different audiences can understand him to be making competing reality claims. Liberals consistently work to show Trump for who he really is by pointing out the lies and inconsistencies, while Trump supporters show their admiration by signaling their devotion to any truth claims that he makes—regardless of how outlandish they may be.

His followers buy into Trump's notion of truth because he comes across as authentic, a trait highly valued in the logic of reality television. One way of thinking about how discourses of reality circulate within reality television is that the shows offer not necessarily an objective reality about what "really" happened but instead an ostensibly authentic insight into the "real" self of the contestants. As cultural studies scholars Anita Biressi and Heather Nunn contend, "the reality TV subject is enjoined to share their pain, their surprise or their joy in a realm of mediated sociality and most successful contestants of series such as *Big Brother* are often those who have allegedly remained 'true' to themselves and who have been frank with their audience."[38] In his campaign and his presidency, Donald Trump appeals to his audience not by presenting them with "real" facts but by tapping into "real" emotions pervasive among certain segments of the population. The supposedly objective truth that the economy improved dramatically in the eight years of the Obama administration did not "feel" true to many of the working class who had lost their jobs or experienced a decreased quality of living during those times. Even though Trump does not have humble origins or any visible ties with working-class struggles, he projects an ability to "get" his audience's experience by tapping into their very real anger and frustration.

Even though Trump often lies, dissembles, and distorts, he is still seen as authentic because he "tells it like it is." As cultural studies scholar Mark Andrejevic explains, reality television offers the promise that it "might cut through the vagaries of mediation to allow direct access to the character or 'soul' of its participants."[39] In fact, Trump seems his most Trumpian when he is riffing, rather than speaking from a script, and disregarding facts as traditionally understood. Further, his adoring supporters are much more inspired when he is riffing in his speeches and tweeting in ways that the Washington establishment labels as "undisciplined." That establishment seems to long for the days of Ronald Reagan, a president who had so honed his traditional skills as a celebrity that even when acting spontaneously, he seemed to be "on script." Reagan famously confused actual events from his past with roles from his Hollywood past, and he consistently played the part of a movie star, removed from the ordinariness of his supporters. In *Showbiz*

*Politics*, historian Kathryn Cramer Brownell notes that in Reagan's era, politics and Hollywood were so intertwined that "Ronald Reagan would wonder how anyone could be president without having a background as an actor."[40] If Reagan's presidency rested upon the logic of narrative Hollywood, then the Donald Trump presidency has foregrounded the logic of the reality show. Rather than existing as a coherent character within a scripted framework, Trump belies narrative structure in favor of short soundbites, multiple political positions, and a constant Manichean drive to separate the "winners" from the "losers."

A moment that defined the Trump campaign was his infamous "off the record" banter with Billy Bush, in which he bragged about sexually assaulting women, invoking his celebrity standing as currency. Trump crowed, "I just start kissing them. It's like a magnet. Just kiss. I don't even wait, and when you're a star they let you do it. You can do anything... Grab them by the pussy. You can do anything."[41] This conversation became arguably the most (in)famous moment of the 2016 campaign, and for many, these off-camera remarks seemed to mark the end of the road for Trump. Many were baffled when he won the presidency despite these revelations; however, the interaction did not reveal Trump as something he had not already purported to be. Trump's persona was already constructed as an alpha male with a history of womanizing and other appalling qualities vis-à-vis women; his boorishness was "baked in" to the structure of an established persona. Unlike candid celebrity pics that expose stars for who they "really" are, in a way that diverges from their public persona, Trump's misogyny played to type. When Toto pulled the curtains and exposed The Wizard, he was exactly who we thought he was. Trump never purported to be anything other than who he is.

Cultural studies scholar Liane Tanguay takes this a step further, arguing that the amenability to misogyny is baked not only into the Trump candidacy but also into the contemporary media landscape that has been saturated with a logic of reality TV. She writes:

> Although the racism and misogyny should have been a "deal breaker" for all but the most extreme of supporters, I believe that the grounds for such a "deal" were never really there, that they were eroded by a mediascape in which his racist and sexist proclamations, as well as other unsavory revelations about his character, were never simply objects about his character, but instead were always already subjected to the media logic in which they were swept up. That is, they were hollowed-out and reconfigured by a reality-TV, post-truth, neoliberalized mediascape in a way that made them less "real," and thus more palatable for Trump's more moderate supporters. (pp. 23–4)[42]

In Tanguay's logic, viewers found themselves observing the campaign as if it were a reality show, and Trump's despicable behavior was just him playing the part of a boorish candidate. When the Billy Bush tape surfaced, it felt like a "surprise twist," so common to the genre, and didn't necessarily register as "real," but rather just seemed like another wacky episode in the sordid tale of the rakish Trump and his over-the-top shenanigans. The Billy Bush tape was simply one "deal breaker" in a series of "deal breakers" that should have disqualified Trump on countless occasions, but any walls between the "real" reality of politics and the "fake" reality of reality TV had ceased to register with a segment of the voting public.

By the time Trump became a player in national presidential politics, the presidential politics had become so deeply inscribed by media events and rituals and saturated by established media outlets and new social media that any line between the reality of politics and the showbusiness of the entertainment industries that covered it had been completely erased. A reality show president became the logical extension of a media environment in which these boundaries had become dissolved; professional wrestling is an apt pastime to consider in relation to Trump and reality television. Professional wrestling challenges the notion of how sports are won or lost by prescribing the outcomes of matches in advance while the performers and the audience act as if the outcome is nevertheless in the balance. Similarly, the Trump supporter may know very well that the words Trump speaks are not true in any empirical sense of the word; nevertheless, they maintain a devotion to the version that he espouses in order to demonstrate their fidelity to his politics and all that entails.

## Pro Wrestling, Kayfabe, and Reality

Professional wrestling is a cultural phenomenon that foreshadows the rise of reality television, and scholars of reality television have linked the genre to professional wrestling. In *Reality TV*, Mark Andrejevic references an MTV show called *Tough Enough* (2001–15), a pro wrestling-themed reality show. He notes that "the marriage of these two formats seems particularly appropriate, since pro wrestling represents the culmination of the demise of symbolic efficacy: it thematizes cynical savviness by not even trying to make viewers believe the action is real."[43] The consumer of both reality television and pro wrestling knows very well that the events are staged, but nevertheless participates in the conditions that construct reality. Andrejevic goes on to say that "the impasse of the savvy subject position is that, even as it collapses the imaginary into the real, it remains locked into the desperate search for some reality that would sustain its dismissal."[44] In this schema, the consumer of reality television and professional wrestling continues to crave something authentic despite knowing very well that the authentic is exactly that which is being produced and manipulated in these genres. The Trump supporter lauds their candidate because he "tells it like it is," despite knowing full well that what Trump says does not have any basis in objective reality. The Trump opponent becomes frustrated because they can see through the ruse; however, they are playing the game on the wrong terrain.

Donald Trump was involved with professional wrestling for many years before he entered politics. He had a business relationship with Vince McMahon and McMahon's league, WWE (wrestling's flagship brand), in the 2000s. Highlights of his associations with professional wrestling include twice hosting Wrestlemania (1985–) at his hotels and participating in a "Battle of the Billionaires" in which surrogates for Trump and McMahon wrestled for billionaire supremacy.[45] He even was on the receiving end of a "Stone Cold Stunner," the signature move of wrestling star "Stone Cold" Steve Austin. On another occasion, he and Austin publicly shaved the head of Vince McMahon, and Trump was eventually inducted into the WWE Hall of Fame in 2013.[46] Trump's association with professional wrestling reveals itself as salient in Trump's devotion to spectacle, his Manichean nationalistic worldview, and his complicated relationship to truth and reality.

Scripted professional wrestling has its roots in the 1930s and has enjoyed periods of tremendous success in the 1930s, 1950s, and 1980s. The genre continues to maintain cultural resonance in the 2020s; while its primary audience is working-class white men, it has crossover appeal to a larger audience as evidenced by stars such as John Cena, Hulk Hogan, and Dwayne "The Rock" Johnson, who maintain popularity with a mass audience. As with reality television, to question the reality of professional wrestling is to engage on the wrong register—the reality of each is beside the point. Wrestling and reality TV may not be "real" in the sense that they are spontaneous and not staged or choreographed in advance; however, their fans maintain a strong affective relationship to the characters and the morality plays that structure their narratives. Cultural critic Henry Jenkins argues that wrestling "externalizes emotion, mapping it onto the combatant's bodies and transforming their physical competition into a search for moral order. Restraint or subtlety has little place in such a world. Everything that matters must be displayed, publicly, unambiguously, and unmercilessly."[47] Jenkins describes a Manichean world with clear dividing lines between good and evil, or in wrestling terms, the "babyface" or "face" and the "heel."

Popular culture scholar Jeffery Mondak links professional wrestling's success in different eras to moments of political ambiguity or national insecurity. He maintains that wrestling's morality plays frame political and international events within the contours of easily distinguishable heroes and villains, or in the parlance of Trump, winners and losers. He argues that "wrestling's periodic popularity should be viewed as a function of its ability to make complex events comprehensible."[48] Especially in the 1980s, wrestling looked to simplify international politics and relations by creating an ultranationalist jingoism wherein the United States perpetually represented the good guys, and an array of international challengers were the bad guys. For Mondak, this allowed for a new understanding of the "reality" of international politics, one that simplifies the subtleties that characterize international issues in a global environment. He maintains that "in staging presentations sympathetic to societally prevalent isolationist and nationalist sentiments, wrestling can act to extend and reinforce those views."[49] Donald Trump maintained a savvy relationship to professional wrestling, adopting its xenophobic nationalism, its Manichean morality play, and an accepted notion of a constructed reality. For both reality television and professional wrestling, truth and reality are of secondary importance to the drama and narratives that run through the genres.

Audiences familiar with reality television and professional wrestling are already primed to think about truth in ways that are seemingly incompatible with rational truth, and thus were able to see the appeal of Trump and take him seriously while pedantic fact-checkers were busy taking him literally. Rhetorical scholar Shannon Bow O'Brien explains the ways that Trump is able to use the logic of wrestling to gain the trust of his followers, even if the truths that he is asserting are only true in Trump's own logic. She maintains that "within the world of wrestling, trustworthiness is derived from the vigorousness of your assertions. Apologies, backtracking, or admitting faults are a sign of weakness and lack of truthfulness."[50] Trump steadfastly refuses to ever admit defeat or error, and his audience develops a faith that he will always maintain his word, even when he seems to be obviously in error. O'Brien argues that Trump has "utilized aspects of manufactured reality to create a stylized world where his beliefs are the guiding principles and the only point of trusted information."[51] For her, as long as he refuses to back down, his fans will follow him, even when confronted with the "big lie" of the 2020 presidential election in which Trump claims that the election was rigged and that he is the legitimate winner.

Journalists and scholars have suggested that understanding Trump through a lens of professional wrestling offers a way to see that Trump is playing a different political and epistemological game than his opponents. In a 2015 essay, Judd Legum offered this provocative clickbait: "This French Philosopher is the Only One who Can Explain the Donald Trump Phenomenon." Legum reads Trump through the semiotician Roland Barthes and the theorist's reading of professional wrestling. Very early in the presidential campaign, Legum notes that "in the current campaign, Trump is behaving like a professional wrestler while Trump's opponents are conducting the race like a boxing mach."[52] In his influential *Mythologies*, Barthes notes the distinction between a boxing match and a wrestling match—the former is focused on the outcome, while the latter is concerned with the spectacle of individual moments and is ultimately unconcerned with who wins. He writes that "wrestling is a sum of spectacles, of which no single one is a function: each moment imposes the total knowledge of a passion which rises erect and alone, without ever extending to the crowning moment of a result."[53] This logic applied to the debates, after which pundits declared that Trump had surely lost and would subsequently fall in the polls and lose the election. Trump, of course, maintained his lead and prevailed in the primaries and the general election. Just as the public for a pro wrestling match does not ultimately care who wins or loses, the logic of Trump holds that he wins by simply being the center of attention. He took advantage of this strategy during the Republican debates involving many candidates on stage. Trump was always situated in the center and received the most questions and the most media attention—that was what mattered to him. Journalist Chauncey Devega argues that traditional media institutions were not prepared for a candidate who defined winning and losing by the amount of press coverage that he received. He writes that "supposed journalistic standards of balance and neutrality were ill-equipped to deal with a presidential candidate who learned from reality TV and professional wrestling that the way to win is to always keep the camera focused on him."[54] Other critics have suggested that wrestling's peculiar relationship with reality—one that shares much in common with reality television—provides a framework for conceptualization of reality and truth in the Trump era.

Writing during the 2016 campaign, journalist Jeremy Gordon asks, "Is Everything Wrestling?" and argues that the performed reality of the wrestling ring now proliferates in many aspects of contemporary society. Gordon writes, "With each passing year, more and more facets of popular culture become something like wrestling: a stage-managed 'reality' in which scripted stories bleed freely into real events, with the blurry line between truth and untruth seeming to heighten, not lessen, the audience's addiction to the melodrama."[55] Donald Trump invites his supporters and the media to indulge in this world in which reality and "reality" commingle. He insisted that thousands of Muslims in New Jersey celebrated 9/11.[56] He asked the public to disbelieve visual evidence about the number of attendees at his inauguration, and his press secretary assured journalists that the unemployment numbers were bogus during the Obama administration, but suddenly were accurate once he took office. Sean Spicer quipped, "They may have been phony in the past, but it's very real now."[57] Spicer and the journalists at the press conference laughed at this moment with the press secretary, and the humor stemmed from the savvy acknowledgment that Spicer was involved in the construction of reality. They all recognized that the strange ritual of a press conference is no different from a pro wrestling match in the way in which its reality is constituted by a mutual understanding between the performers and the audience.

Trump's multiple encounters with professional wrestling and his long tenure on a reality show prepared him to strive for attention at all costs even if it meant sometimes playing the part of the "heel." In professional wrestling, the heel is the "bad guy" whom the audience revels in cheering against. They flaunt their dastardly ways, and the audience often cheers the most voraciously when the heel gets their comeuppance. Devega explains:

> in keeping with that role [the heel], Trump has shown a flagrant disregard for the truth, pretends to be a victim when in fact he is the aggressor, is a bully, lords his wealth over others, cheats and has little regard for the rules. Trump's version of the heel professional wrestler is also a bellicose, verbally dexterous womanizer and misogynist.[58]

While Trump is indeed a heel and does perform as a character who seems morally reprehensible, he continues to enjoy a great deal of political popularity. His base seems to support him in spite of any transgressions or even more bizarrely, because of his performance as a heel. As former professional wrestler Marissa Alexa McCool explains, "Sometimes the bad guy is just so awesome that you find yourself liking them, despite yourself." She goes on to write that "heels are allowed to have more fun, and can even seem more authentic, since they aren't perfect. The bad guys aren't constrained by fans' preconceptions of who they can reasonably attack, or what they can say."[59] Trump is often lauded for being more authentic, for "telling it like it is" even if what he has to say is not "politically correct."

As Trump plays the part of the heel, he and his supporters luxuriate in his disdain for the concept of "political correctness," a concept that for Trump and his supporters was constructed by the Left to limit free speech and to disadvantage those white men who have enjoyed political and cultural power for centuries. In an August 2015 debate, Trump opined, "I think the big problem this country has is being politically correct. I've been challenged by so many people, and I don't frankly have time for total political correctness. And to be honest with you, this country doesn't have time either."⁶⁰ This is one of the ways that Trump gains support despite his "heel" status or perhaps because of it; he declares himself a champion in the face of the evils of this country, and political correctness is one of the evils that the cultural left has supposedly imposed upon "average Americans" for several decades. Journalists Karen Tumulty and Jenna Johnson cite celebrity conservative pollster Frank Luntz, who argues that "'political correctness' are the two words that best respond to everything that a conservative feels put upon." For Luntz, the label is "a validation that what many on the right see as legitimate policy and cultural differences are not the same as racism, sexism or heartlessness."⁶¹ By choosing to engage in the war on political correctness, Trump defers some of the heel status that he attains by being brash and uncouth and resituates it onto liberals, who are more concerned with language and labels than they are with actually protecting the country.

The nebbish, effete liberal is a recognizable heel figure in the terrain of pro-wrestling, and Trump's supporters laud him for standing up to the proprietors of political correctness. During the Trump presidency, a wrestling heel emerged who went by the name of "The Progressive Liberal." He would go into towns in Appalachia, wearing a shirt emblazoned with pictures of Hillary Clinton, and threatened to take the crowd's guns and make them use renewable energy.⁶² At a festival dedicated to the 1980s television show *The Dukes of Hazzard* (1979–85), The Progressive Liberal pretended to wipe his rear end with the confederate flag, though he did have to wear a diaper and drink milk out of a bottle as his comeuppance.⁶³

While the character like The Progressive Liberal is the ultimate heel in Appalachian professional wrestling circles, Trump played a heel figure for the mainstream media and Hollywood establishment, who were not used to his boorish behavior. Trump highlights his heel persona through his antipathy toward immigrants and his brand of "America first" nationalism. Historically in pro wrestling, heels have often taken the form of caricaturized versions of racial and ethnic "Others" who threatened the unquestioned hegemony of the United States. Professional wrestling's jingoism is so intense that former wrestler Marissa McCool maintains that one of the easiest ways to get "cheap heat" as a heel is to "just to pretend to be from Canada. In most small towns, it's easy to get cheap heat [applause] by just being 'not American.'"⁶⁴ Trump's professional wrestling performance is thus especially savvy because he is able to mobilize the emotional vitriol that heels often use to generate "heat," but is able to redirect that heat toward politically correct liberals and foreign intruders as his supporters see him as standing up for the values of "real America," while his detractors continue to see him as just a common heel.

Ironically, though Trump offered a version of truth that did not always conform to the confines of objective reality, his authenticity was one of the qualities that supporters cited as a reason to vote for him. Silicon Valley tycoon Peter Thiel, one of Trump's more famous supporters, uses wrestling terminology to explain Trump's success. In an interview with the *New York Times* Maureen Dowd, he maintains that "many people assumed Mr. Trump was 'kayfabe'—a move that looks real but is fake. But then his campaign turned into a 'shoot'— the word for an unscripted move that suddenly becomes real."[65] He goes on to note that "maybe pro wrestling is one of the most real things we have in our society and what's really disturbing is that the other stuff is much more fake. And whatever the superficialities of Mr. Trump might be, he was more authentic than the other politicians."[66] French theorist Jean Baudrillard presaged this move in his famous essay "The Precession of Simulacra." He writes that "when the real is no longer what it was, nostalgia assumes its full meaning. There is a plethora of myths of origin and of signs of reality—a plethora of truth, of secondary objectivity, and authenticity."[67] Trump's "authenticity" exists in the same way Thiel suggests that pro wrestling is one of the most real things we have in society. Just as Baudrillard contends that Disneyland exists as imaginary to convince its consumers that the rest of Los Angeles is indeed real, pro wrestling exists as fake in order to convince its audience that the rest of the world is indeed real. Trump's authenticity is a secondary authenticity that is produced and constructed like wrestling's kayfabe.

Celebrity studies scholar Benjamin Litherland examines the notion of kayfabe, specifically its complicated role in the multimediated experience of contemporary professional wrestling. Litherland explains that the term comes from old carnival slang and "refers to the practice of sustaining the in-diegesis performance into everyday life."[68] While he does not write about Trump, he does talk about the ways in which Twitter, Trump's medium of choice, complicates the relationship between a celebrity's real self and their persona. In Litherland's schema, Twitter calls into question any distinction between a celebrity's true self and that which they present to the public. For him, "the borders of diegesis and 'in' and 'out' of character performance are stretched to breaking, especially in the wake of structured reality television genres. The complexities of kayfabe, therefore, may serve as a useful starting point for considering the layers of performance in modern celebrity, both on Twitter and beyond."[69] Trump uses the ambiguity of Twitter as a means of allowing himself to play multiple roles and to create a gap between the presidential Trump who appears in meetings in the Oval Office, and his Twitter handle, which is ostensibly the same as his presidential persona, but through which he can blur the lines between reality and celebrity in ways consistent with WWE performances and reality performances.

Blogger Gregory Quinn specifically links Donald Trump with the practice of kayfabe in a piece for *Bullshitist*. He asserts that "Donald Trump is our first kayfabe president" and goes on to note that while wrestling is fake "it's *complicated fake*. It's fakeness treated as real."[70] The complicated nature of the fake stems from the fact that the performers do not break character or break kayfabe. During his presidency, many in the media kept hoping or assuming that Trump would break character and "pivot" to being more presidential. They assumed that it was in the best interest of Trump to transition from his role as "heel," to one that assumed the more traditional "face" status of the president or one that more closely resembled who he was. They saw his undisciplined tweets, acknowledged that they were "part of the act," but assumed that at some point he would move beyond the character or caricature of himself who appeared undisciplined, buffoonish, and potentially unhinged. The astute wrestling fan understands that such a pivot would have been unlikely; Trump and his supporters created a bond with each other by maintaining kayfabe to the dismay of the liberals and mainstream media who insisted on trying to show that the whole act was simply a performance and had no basis in reality.

Anthropologist Adam Hodges shows that by maintaining kayfabe, Trump is able to construct the terms of his own epistemological bubble in which versions of truth circulate that are completely separate from those in mainstream media. He writes that

> kayfabe allows Trumpian discourse to create its own internal reality filled with "alternative facts" that are used to determine what is true. In other words, kayfabe ensures that questions of truth and accuracy are not judged according to standards established outside the fourth wall of the theater, but inside the storyworld constructed on the stage or in the wrestling ring—or on the reality-television set of the Trump White House.[71]

Diligent Trump supporters never break kayfabe; they never acknowledge that the truth that they recognize within their media environment is incompatible with the truth accepted in the mainstream media. As such, when Trump claims that the 2020 election was rigged and that Joe Biden is an illegitimate president, he has an entire history of an alternative epistemological performance to support his claim as he advocates for the "big lie." What persists is a bifurcated country whose sides exist in different epistemological bubbles; without a common reality from which to deduce the truth, democratic politics becomes unworkable. The example of an attempt at reality programming in Putin's Russia provides a contrast to the success of reality television in the United States.

## Russia and Reality

The popularity and pleasure that reality television provides rely upon a world in which some notion of an unmediated access to reality still holds purchase. Even if the savvy viewer of reality television knows very well that what they are watching in a reality television program is staged, the viewer still needs to uphold some kind of version of a real/fake dichotomy, even if the reality television program upends or challenges that dichotomy. Peter Pomerantsev is a British television and filmmaker who was living in Russia in the 2000s. There, he was tasked with creating a reality television show for a Russian audience. What he found was that reality television, which was extraordinarily popular in the United States and Western Europe at the time, did not resonate with a Russian audience. Reality television relies on a premise that on some basic level there is a distinction between reality and falsehood. Even if the savvy reality television viewer knows that what is presented to them may not, in fact, be "real," the viewer is never forced to question the very notion of reality as such. If reality television in the United States blurs distinctions between binaries such as real/fake, frontstage/backstage, authenticity/artifice, it nevertheless relies upon an assumption that such a reality exists, however malleable it might be.

However, in Russia, reality has been afforded no such luxury. In *Nothing Is True and Everything Is Possible*, Pomerantsev offers his thoughts about why reality television did not succeed in Russia. He argues that "part of the problem was that the audience wouldn't believe the stories in the show were real. After so many years of fake reality, it was hard to convince them this was genuine."[72] Seven decades of Soviet rule, followed by ten years of relatively loose government authority, followed by nearly two decades of Putinism have left the populace disoriented and disillusioned in their relationship to the media and the government. Pomerantsev details the ways in which the Putinist government works to amplify this disorientation and to mobilize it for political ends. Putin's government has become deft at using the media to enhance the feeling of disorientation and not only to spread falsehoods to the people but to dismiss the very notion of truth itself.

Writing in 2014, Pomerantsev suggests that Russia was ahead of the United States in using the media to dismantle the concept of truth; further, Russia has a much more complicated history in terms of politicians and truth-telling. For most of the twentieth century, most people in the United States assumed that their politicians would tell small lies to get elected, but that they mostly were acting in good faith. Conversely, under Soviet rule, most Russians assumed they were always being lied to by their leaders and largely ignored the government-controlled media. Pomerantsev argues that the canniness of the new Russian media regime is the way that it keeps television interesting and entertaining, while still maintaining complete control over content. He avers that "the new Kremlin won't make the same mistake the old Soviet Union did: it will never let TV become dull. The task is to synthesize Soviet control with Western entertainment."[73] In fact, part of the show that Russian television features is a show about democracy. Putin does not win elections like many two-bit dictators with 99 percent of the vote; he often wins by plausible numbers by seemingly plausible candidates, handpicked by the Kremlin, of course. Pomeransev writes that "it was television through which the Kremlin decided which politicians it would 'allow' as its puppet-opposition."[74] He refers to this phenomenon as a "sort of postmodern dictatorship that uses the language and institution of democratic capitalism for authoritarian ends."[75] However, just as the savvy viewer of reality television knows that reality television is not actually real, the Russian populace knows that the whole operation—the government, the media, the president riding shirtless on a horse—is all a simulation. They are in on the secret; as such, when Russian television and Pomerantsev tried to sell a reality television program to Russia, the Russian audience was confused for they already were existing on the register of simulation. Reality television only holds purchase if on some level the audience believes in a reality that undergirds the whole endeavor.

Writing during the 2016 campaign, Pomerantsev was one of the first to connect the political strategies of Donald Trump to those of Vladimir Putin. In "Why We're Post-Fact," he compares Trump's recollection of thousands of Muslims cheering in New Jersey when the World Trade Center Towers were attacked to Putin coyly denying the existence of Russian soldiers in Ukraine. Pomerantsev argues that "it's clear we are living in a 'post-fact' or post-truth' world. Not merely a world where politicians and media lie—they have always lied—but one where they don't care whether they tell the truth or not."[76] For him, this lack of a stable base of truth leads to a dark cynicism or nihilism. In his logic, "if everyone is lying then anything goes." He concludes the piece by suggesting that being freed from the confines of truth produces a dark joy. "All the madness you feel, you can now let it out and it's okay. The very point of Trump is to validate the pleasure of spouting shit, the joy of pure emotion, often anger, without any sense. And an audience which has already spent a decade living without facts can now indulge in a full, anarchic liberation from coherence."[77] In the wake of the insurrection brought about by Trump's "big lie" about the election results, Pomerantantsev's words seem particularly prescient and dourly pessimistic. In Chapter 6, I look more closely into the idea that contemporary society reflects a "post-truth" moment and look for ways that future scholars and activists might work on repairing a democratic politics in a country without a shared version of reality.

## Notes

1. Jeff Nesbit, "Donald Trump Is the First True Reality TV President," *Time*, December 9, 2017, https://time.com/4596770/donald-trump-reality-tv/
2. Ibid.
3. Laurie Ouellette and Susan Murray, "Introduction," in *Reality TV: Remaking Television Culture*, 2nd ed., eds. Susan Murray and Laurie Ouellette (New York: New York University Press, 2009), 3.
4. Jennifer C. Dunn, "Critical Rhetoric in the Age of the First Reality TV President: A Critique of Freedom and Domination," *International Journal of Communication* 14 (2020): 824–5.
5. Tyson Smith, "Wrestling with 'Kayfabe'," *Contexts* 5, no. 2 (2006): 54.
6. David S. Escoffery, "Introduction: The Role of Representation in Reality Television," in *How Real Is Reality TV?: Essays on Representation and Truth*, ed. David S. Escofferey (Jefferson, NC: McFarland & Company, 2006), 2.
7. Tom Syverson, *Reality Squared: On Reality TV and Left Politics* (Washington, DC: Zero Books, 2021), 19.
8. Ouellette and Murray, 9.
9. John Corner, "Performing the Real: Documentary Diversions," in *Reality TV: Remaking Television Culture*, 2nd ed., eds. Susan Murray and Laurie Ouellette (New York: New York University Press, 2009), 45.
10. Donald J. Trump and Tony Schwartz, *Trump: The Art of the Deal* (New York: Random House, 1987).
11. Jane Mayer, "Donald Trump's Ghost Writer Tells All," *The New Yorker*, July 25, 2016, https://www.newyorker.com/magazine/2016/07/25/donald-trumps-ghostwriter-tells-all
12. Erving Goffman, *The Presentation of Self in Everyday Life* (New York: Anchor Books, 1959).
13. Syverson, 11.
14. Patrick Radden Keefe, "How Mark Burnett Resurrected Trump as an Icon of American Success," *The New Yorker*, December 27, 2018, https://www.newyorker.com/magazine/2019/01/07/how-mark-burnett-resurrected-donald-trump-as-an-icon-of-american-success
15. Ibid.
16. Ibid.
17. Mayer.
18. Emily VanDerWerff, "Donald Trump's Secret Weapon Is His Mastery of Reality TV," *Vox*, August 14, 2015, https://www.vox.com/2015/8/14/9151251/donald-trump-apprentice-president
19. James Hamblin, "Donald Trump: Sociopath?" *The Atlantic*, July 20, 2016, https://www.theatlantic.com/health/archive/2016/07/trump-and-sociopathy/491966/

20. Mayer.
21. Sara Booker and Bradley M. Waite, "Humilitainment? Lessons from *The Apprentice*: A Reality Television Content Analysis," in *17th Annual Convention of the American Psychological Society*, Los Angeles, 2005.
22. John W. Whitehead, "Nothing Is Real: When Reality TV Program Masquerades as Politics," *Counterpunch*, January 19, 2017, https://www.counterpunch.org/2017/01/19/nothing-is-real-when-reality-tv-programming-masquerades-as-politics/
23. Joy Lazendorfer, "How Reality TV Made Donald Trump President," *Vice*, November 18, 2016, https://www.vice.com/en_nz/article/avak5a/how-reality-tv-made-donald-trump-president
24. Ibid.
25. Dan Spinelli, "Trump Revives Rumor Linking Cruz's Father to Kennedy Assassination," *Politico*, July 22, 2016, https://www.politico.com/story/2016/07/trump-ted-cruz-jfk-assassination-226020
26. Reena Flores, Republican Debate: Donald Trump Defends the Size of His Hands, and More, *CBS News*, March 3, 2016, https://www.cbsnews.com/news/republican-debate-donald-trump-defends-the-size-of-his-hands-and-other-body-parts/
27. Rachel E. Dubrofsky, "Monstrous Authenticity: Trump's Whiteness," in *Interrogating the Communicative Power of Whiteness*, eds. Dawn Marie D. McIntosh, Dreama G. Moon, and Thomas K. Nakayama (New York: Routledge, 2019), 166.
28. Dubrofsky, 167–8.
29. Dubrofsky, 171.
30. Ibid.
31. Michael Hirschorn, "The Case for Reality TV," *The Atlantic*, May 1, 2007, https://www.theatlantic.com/magazine/archive/2007/05/the-case-for-reality-tv/305791/
32. Brian T. Edwards, "Trump from Reality TV to Twitter, or the Selfie-Determination of Nations," *Arizona Quarterly: A Journal of American Literature, Culture, and Theory* 74, no. 3 (2018): 33.
33. Michael Hirschorn, "Celebreality Values Have Come Home to Roost in Donald Trump's Rise to Power," *Decider*, July 20, 2016, https://decider.com/2016/07/20/donald-trump-scott-baio-antonio-sabato-michael-hirschorn-celebreality/
34. Justin Lewis, "The Meaning of Real Life," in *Reality TV: Remaking Television Culture*, eds. Susan Murray and Laurie Ouellette (New York: New York University Press, 2004), 289.
35. Ibid.
36. Lewis, 290.
37. Ibid., 291.

38  Anita Biressi and Heather Nunn, *Reality TV: Realism and Revelation* (London: Wallflower Press, 2005), 5.
39  Mark Andrejevic, "The *Jouissance* of Trump," *New Media and Society* 17, no. 7, 652.
40  Kathryn Cramer Brownell, *Showbiz Politics: Hollywood in American Political Life* (Chapel Hill, NC: University of North Carolina Press, 2014), 8.
41  "Donald Trump's Taped Comments about Women," *The New York Times*, October 8, 2016, https://www.nytimes.com/2016/10/08/us/donald-trump-tape-transcript.html
42  Liane Tanguay, "Reality TV 'Gets Real': Hypercommercialism and Post-Truth in CNN's Election Coverage of the 2016 Election Campaign," in *Neoliberalism in the Media*, ed. Marian Meyers (New York: Routledge, 2019), 23–4.
43  Mark Andrejevic, *Reality TV: The Work of Being Watched* (Lanham, MD: Roman & Littlefield, 2004), 226.
44  Andrejevic, 212.
45  Dan Gartland and Extra Mustard, "It's Been 10 Years since the Leader of the Free World Shaved Vince McMahon's Head," *Sports Illustrated*, March 30, 2017, https://www.si.com/extra-mustard/2017/03/30/donald-trump-vince-mcmahon-wrestlemania-hair-match
46  Richard Langford, "Donald Trump to Be Inducted into WWE Hall of Fame," *Bleacher Report*, February 25, 2013, https://bleacherreport.com/articles/1544081-donald-trump-to-be-inducted-into-wwe-hall-of-fame
47  Henry Jenkins III, Henry, "'Never Trust a Snake': WWF Wrestling as Masculine Melodrama," in *Steel Chair to the Head: The Pleasure and Pain of Professional Wrestling*, ed. Nicholas Sammond (Durham, NC: Duke University Press, 2005), 34.
48  Jeffery J. Mondak, "The Politics of Professional Wrestling," *Journal of Popular Culture* 23, no. 2 (1989): 146.
49  Ibid.
50  Shannon Bow O'Brien, *Donald Trump and the Kayfabe Presidency: Professional Wrestling Rhetoric in the White House* (Cham, CH: Palgrave MacMillan, 2020), 6.
51  Ibid.
52  Judd Legum, "This French Philosopher Is the Only One Who Can Explain the Donald Trump Phenomenon," *Think Progress*, September 14, 2015, https://archive.thinkprogress.org/this-french-philosopher-is-the-only-one-who-can-explain-the-donald-trump-phenomenon-47afad40647c/
53  Roland Barthes, "The World of Wrestling," in *Mythologies* (New York: Hill & Wang, 1972), 16.
54  Chauncey Devega, "Peter Thiel Pulls Back the Curtain: Donald Trump Is a Pro-Wrestling Villain Turned President," *Salon*, January 17, 2017, https://www.salon.com/2017/01/15/peter-thiel-pulls-back-the-curtain-donald-trump-is-a-pro-wrestling-villain-turned-president/

55  Jeremy Gordon, "Is Everything Wrestling?," *The New York Times Magazine*, May 27, 2016, https://www.nytimes.com/2016/05/27/magazine/s-everything-wrestling.html

56  Tessa Berenson, "Video Debunks Trump's Claim That Thousands of American Muslims Celebrated 9/11," *Time*, December 1, 2015, https://time.com/4131439/donald-trump-muslims-9-11-video/

57  Madeline Conway, "Spicer Claims That Job Numbers 'May Have Been Phony' before, but Now They're 'Very Real'," *Politico*, March 10, 2017, https://www.politico.com/story/2017/03/trump-monthly-jobs-numbers-sean-spicer–235936

58  Devega.

59  Marissa Alexa McCool, "Heel in Chief: Donald Trump and the Psychology of Pro Wrestling," *The Huffington Post*, April 1, 2017, https://www.huffpost.com/entry/heel-in-chief-donald-trump-and-the-psychology-of-pro_b_58df1a80e4b0d804fbbb7317

60  Kat Chow, "'Politically Correct: The Phrase Has Gone from Wisdom to Weapon," *NPR*, December 14, 2016, https://www.npr.org/sections/codeswitch/2016/12/14/505324427/politically-correct-the-phrase-has-gone-from-wisdom-to-weapon

61  Karen Tumulty and Jenna Johnson, "Why Trump May Be Winning the War on 'Political Correctness'," *The Washington Post*, January 4, 2016, https://www.washingtonpost.com/politics/why-trump-may-be-winning-the-war-on-political-correctness/2016/01/04/098cf832-afda-11e5-b711-1998289ffcea_story.html

62  Jacob Pinter, "Appalachian Wrestling's Greatest Villain: 'The Progressive Liberal'," *NPR*, June 30, 2017, https://www.npr.org/2017/06/30/534969928/appalachian-wrestlings-greatest-villain-the-progressive-liberal

63  Samer Kalaf, "The 'Progressive Liberal' Wipes His Butt with the American Flag," *Deadspin*, August 15, 2017, https://deadspin.com/the-progressive-liberal-wipes-his-butt-with-the-confe–1797864121

64  McCool.

65  Maureen Dowd, "Peter Thiel, Trump's Tech Pal, Explains Himself," *The New York Times*, January 11, 2017, https://www.nytimes.com/2017/01/11/fashion/peter-thiel-donald-trump-silicon-valley-technology-gawker.html

66  Ibid.

67  Jean Baudrillard, "The Precession of Simulacra," in *Simulation and Simulacra* (Ann Arbor, MI: University of Michigan Press, 1994), 6–7.

68  Benjamin Litherland, "Breaking Kayfabe Is Easy, Cheap, and Never Entertaining: Twitter Rivalries in Professional Wrestling," *Celebrity Studies* 5, no. 4 (2014): 531.

69  Litherland, 533.

70  Gregory Quinn, "There's a Perfect Word to Describe Donald Trump's Unreality. It's Kayfabe," *Bullshitist*, December 22, 2016, https://bullshit.ist/theres-a-perfect-word-to-describe-donald-trump-s-unreality-it-s-kayfabe-ab9351d90b27

71 Adam Hodges, "Wrestling with 'The Donald'," *Anthropology News*, September 5, 2017, https://anthrosource.onlinelibrary.wiley.com/doi/abs/10.1111/AN.593

72 Pomerantsev Peter, *Nothing Is True and Everything Is Possible: The Surreal Heart of the New Russia* (New York: Public Affairs Books, 2014), 64.

73 Pomerantsev, 6.

74 Ibid.

75 Pomerantsev, 42.

76 Peter Pomerantsev, "Why We're Post-Fact," *Granta*, July 20, 2016, https://granta.com/why-were-post-fact/

77 Ibid.

# 4

# The President Is Tweeting

In May 2020, Donald Trump published two tweets about mail-in ballots and the possibility for voter fraud that were severe exaggerations if not complete lies. The executives at Twitter deemed the falsifications to be so egregious as to supplement Trump's tweets with disclaimers, offering a link for users to become better informed about mail-in ballots and the actual rates of fraud that accompany them.[1] Trump responded that Twitter was "interfering in the 2020 Presidential Election" and "completely stifling FREE SPEECH."[2] Within two days, Trump had crafted an executive order to "prevent online censorship," which was targeted at social media platforms such as Twitter.[3] He even threatened to "'strongly regulate' or shut down social media platforms, which he accused of silencing conservative viewpoints."[4] The idea of Trump shutting down Twitter seemed preposterous as during his presidency Trump had utilized the medium more than any other politician or candidate to circumvent the mainstream news outlets and to drive the content of those outlets. An early adopter of the microblogging service, Trump made Twitter an integral part of his candidacy and his presidency; he has relied on Twitter so heavily that authors have written numerous articles and books dubbing Trump "The Twitter President" or the "Twitter Candidate." Just as Trump was able to absorb the media norms that made a figure like Rush Limbaugh successful on conservative talk radio, and to take advantage of the logic of reality television and its relationship to contemporary politics, he was able to fully intuit the advantages that Twitter allowed.

In *The Twitter Presidency*, Brian Ott and Greg Dickenson argue that "as a mode of communication, Twitter is defined by three key features: simplicity, impulsivity, and incivility" and suggest that "Trump's manner of speaking and Twitter's underlying logic, as a modality or medium of communication, are virtually homologous."[5] Ott and Dickenson take a media ecological approach and suggest that the messages of certain media are contained by the structure. They use the famous example that Neil Postman provides in

*Amusing Ourselves to Death* in which he explains that smoke signals provide a terrible medium for delivering a philosophical treatise.[6] Twitter similarly offers certain limitations due to its character limit; from its inception it limited its users to 140 characters per tweet, and since 2017 it has limited its users to 280 characters. Like smoke signals, Twitter is a suboptimal medium for constructing a philosophical treatise. In explaining why Donald Trump is so effective at the medium, cultural critic Virginia Heffernan notes that he makes "himself heard in fragments, monosyllables and exclamation points, a proud male hysteric with the deafening staccato and hair-trigger immune system that Twitter exists to host. He embraces odd abbreviations, erratic capitalization and typos in his invariably reactive rants."[7] Ott and Dickenson are right that the character limit on Twitter makes the medium more amenable to certain kinds of discourse—the fragments and monosyllables that Heffernan observes. However, I am not certain that they are correct that the medium necessarily leads to incivility; Twitter as a medium is a great way to cultivate community. Donald Trump has found it a useful medium for incivility, but he has also found press conferences to be useful for incivility, as well as talk radio, Fox News, and just about any medium that he has used as part of his campaign or his presidency.

Rather than viewing the medium as having inherent properties that are more amenable to a certain type of discourse or politics, I suggest that Twitter is ambivalent to these types of distinctions. While it is, of course, better suited to discourse that can be expressed in short, pithy bursts, those bursts need not take a particular affective form. I would also argue that Twitter is ambivalent about the type of candidate that uses the medium for their political success. Ott and Dickinson maintain that the medium is the perfect conduit for Trump's demagogic instincts. For them, "Twitter breeds dark, degrading, and dehumanizing discourse; it breeds vitriol and violence; in short, it breeds Donald Trump."[8] They go on to connect this to his style of politics. They contend that "Donald Trump is the walking, talking embodiment of white rage, which he enacts through his authoritarian management style, bullying manner, and hyperbolic, narcissistic, and demagogic discourse."[9] While they are correct that Trump uses all of the tools available to promote his demagogic discourse, I suggest that there is nothing inherent in the medium of Twitter that makes it an especially appealing medium for demagogues, just as I balk at their assumption that Twitter necessarily breeds dark and dehumanizing discourses, though it certainly has the potential to do so. Linguists Galen Stolee and Steve Caton explain that Twitter provides the conditions for a politician like Trump to promote his demagogic agenda, but also insist that a skilled politician with democratic instincts could have the same success with the medium. They argue that "a medium like Twitter is a Janus-faced figure or a double-edged sword, at once promoting the likes of a demagogue as easily as it might a democrat."[10] Twitter contains multitudes, and Trump used the medium in myriad ways.

## Constructing a Big Tent Community—Maybe Too Big

One of the ways that Twitter has proven to be an effective tool is to create community among its users. Writing during the primaries, Antoaneta Roussi, who describes Trump as "The Twitter Candidate," argues that Trump is so effective at using Twitter because he is able to capitalize on its ability to use Twitter for these purposes. For her, "Trump's Twitter feed has a strong sense of community and most of his followers are ardent supporters of his policies, again reflecting on the social media to ground support conversion. His social followers often create memes and witty hashtags for their chosen candidate, perhaps more so than any other presidential aspirant, in part because Trump so frequently retweets their support."[11] Twitter facilitates a seemingly close relationship between fans and celebrities, and Trump cultivated that during his candidacy by retweeting his supporters in order to show that his campaign was not far removed from his fans.

Trump continued this practice throughout his presidency, even getting into trouble on several occasions by retweeting posts from people representing extremist organizations. For example, during the primaries, he retweeted a supporter who was taking a shot at his opponent, Jeb Bush. The tweet itself is innocuous: "Poor Jeb, I could've sworn I saw him outside Trump Tower the other Day!" While the tweet was benign, the account that tweeted it belonged to @WhiteGenocideTM, an account maintained by an avowed white supremacist.[12] Trump has on more than one occasion "accidently" retweeted accounts from the fringes of the far right, giving him plausible deniability to excuse them as accidents, but simultaneously amplifying voices that are on the very fringes of the conservative movement. One of the ways in which the fringe of the conservative movement has been able to get their ideas out from the dark corners of the web to the mainstream is through memes, and these memes often found their way from imageboards like 4chan to Twitter. Journalist Ben Schreckinger examines the role that meme warfare played in the 2016 election and argues that the Trump campaign "paid rapt attention to meme culture from the start. It took it seriously, even pushing some memes out to the candidate's millions of

Twitter followers."[13] In the next chapter, I specifically examine the role that 4chan and Reddit, and memes played in the election of Donald Trump and the rise of the alt-right in mainstream US politics.

One instance in which the Trump campaign took material from the dark corners of the web and brought them into the campaign was when Trump retweeted an attack against Democratic rival Hillary Clinton featuring a picture of the former secretary of state with a headline reading "Most Corrupt Candidate Ever!" The headline was framed within a six-pointed star, and critics quickly pointed out that the star resembled the Star of David, and that the attack carried anti-Semitic implications. In fact, the attack was from a meme that originated on a neo-Nazi website, though the Trump campaign did not give credit to the original source. As journalist Ben Mathis-Lilley writes, "we have Trump's campaign acknowledging that it took the image from a Twitter user and reposted it without attribution.... We also have evidence of a neo-Nazi Twitter user posting the image under his/her own account name."[14] After the retweet caused a controversy, Trump claimed ignorance of any anti-Semitic connotations in the attack, though the campaign did remove the tweet. However, at a subsequent speech, Trump laments taking the post down, and used it as an opportunity to criticize the news media. He proclaimed, "CNN started this dialogue going: It's the Star of David and because it's the Star of David, Donald Trump has racist tendencies. These people are sick folks, I'm telling you, they're sick.... How sick are they? Actually, they're the ones with the bad tendencies when they can think that way."[15] So, Trump is able to use the retweet and the subsequent conversations about the retweet for three purposes: to align himself with a white supremacist website and to make an anti-Semitic attack against his (Methodist) opponent, to disavow any racist connotation by saying that he regretted removing the tweet, and to impugn those who might read the tweet's anti-Semitic content as the actual racists who are "sick" and have "bad tendencies." The logic of retweeting allows for Trump to create an ambiguous relationship with his constituencies, and to utilize the polysemic characteristics of social media. In this logic, he is obviously not the racist; rather, the corrupt media and his opponents must be racist for making such assumptions. Meanwhile, those right-wing white nationalists can rest easy knowing that Trump has not disavowed a tweet that came from their ranks and was clearly intended as an anti-Semitic gesture.

The Star of David tweet was consistent with a pattern in which Trump retweeted objectionable content while remaining unclear as to whether he endorsed the source of the content. At another point during the 2016 campaign, journalist John Nichols connected the Star of David scandal to an earlier moment in which Trump retweeted a quote that has been largely attributed (perhaps apocryphally) to Benito Mussolini. The quote, "It is better to live one day as a lion than 100 years as a sheep," came to Trump's attention by a parody account with an intent to embarrass the presidential candidate for accidentally associating himself with the infamous dictator. Nichols writes that "the realization that he was retweeting what was once understood as a fascist call to arms should have embarrassed, or at least unsettled, the frontrunner for the Republican presidential nomination.... But Trump did not appear to be embarrassed or particularly unsettled."[16] Instead, when asked about the quote, Trump maintained that "it was a good quote, it's a very interesting quote" and that he wanted to be associated with interesting quotes regardless of their source. Nichols ends his piece by chastising Trump, noting that "his is a candidate who seems to think that trafficking in crude stereotypes, making incendiary comparisons and comments, and retweeting lines from dark chapters in history will somehow 'make America great again.'"[17] Nichols brings to the fore the logic of retweeting as a political tactic; the medium allows Trump to dabble in fascist rhetoric without disqualifying himself for the presidency of a country that ostensibly prides itself on its anti-fascistic values. Trump can evoke those strains of what Richard Hofstadter famously called the "the paranoid style in American politics" without unequivocally endorsing them.[18]

The question of whether retweets constitute endorsement is a subject that circulates in journalistic circles. In 2014, journalism blogger Sam Kirkland noticed that different journalistic institutions had different assumptions about retweeting in their style guides; *The New York Times* did not think that readers would automatically assume that retweeting constituted endorsement, while National Public Radio and the *Associated Press* did.[19] Donald Trump is, of course, not a journalist, so he does not need to adhere to any particular style; however, he uses the ambiguity of retweeting to ally himself with marginal white supremacist discourses while not specifically endorsing the groups that unabashedly support white supremacy. Trump does suggest how he uses retweets to make the claim that "some people are saying" something without having to say it himself. Rhetorical scholar Jennifer Mercieca employs the Greek term *paralipsis* as the process, whereby a speaker says, "I'm not saying. I'm just saying." For her, *paralipsis* allowed Trump "to simultaneously embrace and disavow the white nationalists who supported him. *Paralipsis* allowed Trump to recirculate white nationalist sentiment without having to take responsibility for being a racist."[20] She uses retweeting as an example of how Trump is able to say and not say at the same time and thus be able to align himself with white nationalists and distance himself from them simultaneously.

Trump often mobilizes ambiguous terms in his speeches and tweets. In her blog for *Jezebel*, Ellie Shechet notices that Trump "likes to ominously cite 'somebody' or 'something' when referring to particularly imaginative scenarios, such as Mexicans being rapists or the President of the United States colluding with terrorists."[21] Another way in which Trump employs this ambiguity is by distancing himself by a statement by qualifying the statement with the preface, "some say" or "people think." Journalist Jenna Johnson notes Trump's propensity to preface his statements with these qualifiers and argues that this technique "allows him to share a controversial idea, piece of tabloid gossip or conspiracy theory without fully embracing it." She goes further and notes that Trump claims he uses the "people are saying" technique in the same way a Twitter user might "retweet" a claim. Trump used this argument after he had repeated a vulgar slur that a crowd member had used to describe one of his political foes, Ted Cruz. At a 2016 campaign event, an audience member called Ted Cruz a "pussy" and Trump repeated the line for the crowd. Afterward, in order to defend himself, Trump claimed that "it was like a retweet; I would never say a word like that."[22] Trump did, however, note that the crowd reacted favorably to the slur. Repeating what others have said allows Trump to simultaneously embrace an idea while distancing himself from it.

Journalists Ben Kharakh and Dan Primack analyze the instance in which Trump retweeted the white supremacist Twitter account with the handle @WhiteGenocideTM. They argue that

> it is possible that Trump… is unfamiliar with the term "white genocide" and doesn't do even basic vetting of those whose tweets he amplifies to his seven million followers. But the reality is that there are dozens of Tweets mentioning @realDonaldTrump each minute and he has an uncanny ability to surface ones that come from accounts that proudly proclaim their white supremacist leanings.[23]

I suggest that the question of Trump's intent is moot; he may, in fact, be oblivious to the sources that he retweets. However, by employing the logic of the retweet, he is able to simultaneously engage with and disavow a set of discourses about white supremacy. He uses the retweet to provoke the darker elements that lurk on social media while simultaneously providing distance. Karakh and Primack quote Hope Hicks, a Trump spokeswoman at the time, who rejects the ideas that a retweet is tantamount to endorsement. Hicks claims that "the retweets are based solely on the content, not the personal views of those individuals as they are not vetted, known or of interest to the candidate or the campaign."[24] Her logic is slippery; she suggests that the candidate endorses the content of the tweet but cannot be responsible for his origins. The logic becomes further muddled in the case of the Star of

David when Trump took down the potentially offending Tweet, and then openly lamented that decision. The indeterminate nature of retweeting allows Trump to linger in the ambiguous areas between the conventional terrain of politics and the more ominous strains of white supremacism that rarely see overt representation in the field of the political.

## Twitter and the Construction of Authenticity

Trump also creates an image that he is "of the people" by posting in the vernacular of Twitter. In her article dubbing Trump "The Twitter Candidate," Virginia Heffernan suggests that presidential candidates have a habit of remaining aloof from their constituencies and that even their Twitter accounts seem to be handled by staffers concerned with how each word will play with different markets. By contrast, "@realDonaldTrump is the opposite of aloof, the opposite of polished... Trump's errors pass for style. They add to the impression that he is unscripted, which is precisely what the Internet, and the American public, seems to be craving in this current media moment."[25] Twitter allows a New York millionaire/billionaire who has never struggled financially in his entire life to seem like a man of the people by allowing him to appeal directly to the people and speak without a filter. As rhetorical scholar Dawn Colley explains, Trump is credible "because his words are, ostensibly, not clothed in the colors of rhetoric. As such, his target audience is invited to accept what he says at face value his words are believable for the very fact they are not well considered. The plain style also suggest that he is of the people and for the people."[26] Trump is able to construct an authentic image of himself for his supporters; any misspellings, falsehoods, or exaggerations only work to enhance this perception to his supporters and reinforce the notion that his opponents who decry him for such things are aloof and elite.

One other way that Trump is able to construct this authentic image is that he is actually the person who is behind the Twitter account. Communication scholar Gunn Enli notes that during the 2016 campaign, nearly all of Trump's opponent Hillary Clinton's tweets were handled by staffers, and she noted the rare times when she was the author by attaching an "- H" after the tweet to proclaim its legitimacy.[27] Trump, conversely, either tweeted his himself or dictated them to a staffer, including punctuation. Clinton's tweets always took on an air of professionalism that eluded Trump's, which was exactly the point. Trump came across as an outsider, who did not need handlers to take care of his communication; he communicated directly to the people in an unpolished way. As Enli argues, "the fact that Trump delegated much less social media work to professionals than either of the Obama campaigns and the 2016 Clinton campaign meant that his candidate image on social media was much closer to his self-presentation. To a degree, Trump therefore came across as more consistent and authentic compared to Clinton."[28] The "behind the scenes" Trump seemed to be a real person, unlike the Clinton campaign, which seemed to be a political machine to the core.

Twitter actually opens a possibility to offer some transparency in politics between the polished frontstage of US politics and the backstage, which is less polished. Erving Goffman famously outlined the ways in which individuals behaved differently when they were performing in public (their frontstage persona) and when they were behind the scenes (their backstage persona).[29] In the media era, politics has increasingly constructed a polished frontstage persona for politicians that has seemed distant from the actual backstage machinations of politics. Writing in anticipation of "America's First Twitter President," Navneet Alang laments the possibilities that Twitter might have in the hands of a more adept personality for bridging the gap between the polished politician and the gritty backrooms of Washington politics. He notes that "the modern relationship between politics and mass media has produced a strange situation in which we all acknowledge there is a difference between the public discourse of politics and how it is practised behind closed doors We *know* that lofty campaign speeches bear no resemblance to the profanity-laden arguments in backrooms where power is truly exercised."[30] For him, a more capable president might have used the medium to bridge that gap and to employ the medium's power to actually show the public politics' backstage while maintaining the decorum of the office. However, "Donald Trump will likely reign as the Twitter President, and he will do so like the worst of Twitter itself—primed for outrage, and quick to react with only the barest amount of thought." Like Ott and Dickenson, he argues that the possibility of using Twitter without thoughtful engagement allows for the medium potentially to bring out the worst of people. However, Alang does not maintain the same kind of technological determinism because he can also see the possibility of the medium allowing for social good. In his term in office, Trump used the medium to construct community, but only for his followers. In constructing that community, he has alienated a community that is just as large if not larger. However, neither side of the Manichean split has been able to ignore him, which has been his strategy all along. The goal of Trump is to rule all media, and he is able to use Twitter as a springboard to gain attention on other mainstream media platforms.

Media scholar Richard Grusin argues that Trump saw all of the various media—Twitter, television, print media, etc.—as real estate properties to be monopolized. Thinking like a real estate mogul, Trump saw that his best interests involved dominating all of the different media. He writes that "in treating print, televisual, and networked media during the primaries and the presidential election as if they were real estate properties to be developed, Trump was able to garner free media coverage estimated by media economists to be worth roughly five billion dollars, far more than all his opponents combined."[31] When Trump tweeted something controversial or outlandish, it was picked up by the other media, discussed by pundits, and effectively blocked out the messaging of other campaigns. Moreover, he did not have to spend any money to attain this level of coverage; the other candidates spent more money and received less coverage because whatever they said was less newsworthy simply by dint of it being more banal. Even if the news he was receiving across the media landscape was not positive, he was dominating the airwaves, making it seem as if he were more important than the other candidates. Grusin suggests that "our formal and informal socially networked media helped bring President Trump into existence, in large part by making it seem as if he was already president on TV."[32] For him, "the fact that throughout the fall election campaign he occupied national print, televisual, and networked news media far more than either President Obama or Hillary Clinton made it feel almost inevitable that he would become the next president."[33] That Trump was able to create this feeling of inevitability without spending a great deal of money and using Twitter as the predominant means of addressing his fans speaks to an upended relationship between Trump and the media gatekeepers that he established through his Twitter usage.

Until the rise of twenty-four-hour news channels and talk radio in the 1980s, national news was distributed through three national news channels—ABC, NBC, and CBS—and a handful of national newspapers such as *The New York Times*, *The Washington Post*, *The Los Angeles Times* and *The Wall Street Journal*. These sources created an oligopolistic system of gatekeeping, and for the most part these sources decided which news would become part of the mainstream national discourse and which would remain in relative obscurity. Historian Devan Bisonnette describes the traditional process of gatekeeping wherein "journalists (and editors) vetted news, picking and choosing what made it to the public, and in what form. Such a method helped the public from information overload and gave news context, including fact-checking, but it also gave media a huge gatekeeping power over public knowledge and a key role in setting the public agenda."[34] Because all of the journalists adhered to similar guidelines of objectivity and newsworthiness, and many were trained at the same journalistic schools, what they decided was news at the major gatekeeping outlets was remarkably similar. Thus, the Overton window of stories that were fit to print was relativity small, and the types of candidates who could succeed within this process were limited. A candidate that was too outlandish would never be able to communicate their message because they would immediately be dismissed by the gatekeepers and the message would never make it to a large audience.

Until the Trump campaign, the power of the gatekeeping process in the televised era proved to be extraordinarily powerful and enduring. Even with the rise of talk radio and CNN in the 1980s and 1990s, the established news organizations still maintained most of their gatekeeping status. Fox News began to shift the Overton window as it gained popularity in the 2000s, but the real key to the challenge to the traditional gatekeepers was the rise of social media in the mid-2000s. Media scholars Silvio Walsbord, Tina Tucker, and Zoey Lichtenheld go so far as to claim that "the digital revolution has shaken up the quasi-monopolistic position the press held in large-scale production and dissemination of news, information, and opinion for the past two centuries."[35] All political campaigns since the mid-2000s have relied upon using social media to some extent; however, Trump was able to use it to evade and to feed into the established media. He understands that social media are most powerful when they connect to the existing social media, even if at times that connection is abrasive; establishment media are often the object of Trump's scorn on social media.

Trump is able to both insult the "dishonest media" as "fake news" and continue to feed that media content that they cover; even if that content is not necessarily true, the established news media cover the controversy. Trump does not care how he is covered, as long as he remains the center of attention; he can speak directly to his supporters through Twitter and his surrogates on Fox News, while the traditional mainstream gatekeepers are discussing stories that would have traditionally been kept outside of their gates because they are so outlandish. Moreover, his followers can retweet and share in blogs and memes Trump's message outside of the influence of the mainstream gatekeepers. Media scholar Michael X. Delli Carpini explains, "His use of Twitter to bypass and/or influence traditional gatekeepers and speak directly to, motivate, and mobilize his followers epitomizes the blurring of interpersonal and mass communication. And the amplification and diffusion of his message through online social networks made his followers both consumers and producers of information and discourse."[36] By being able to bypass and feed into the traditional gatekeepers, Trump is able to take on the role of the agenda setter and expand the realm of acceptable truths within the political discourse. Further, he is able to expand the potential Overton window of political ideologies by engaging both mainstream politics and the further outreaches of the internet where members far to the right of the mainstream provide a level of support for Trump that far exceeds that of traditional Republican candidates and politicians.

Twitter is one way that Trump is able to offer alternative truths to those offered by the mainstream media and traditional gatekeepers. In *How Trump Thinks*, journalist Peter Oborne and media historian Tom Roberts suggest that he uses Twitter as a means of constructing this alternative way of constructing truth. They contend that "he exploited Twitter's ability to express raw sentiment instantly, without nuance or subtext, and its ability to blur, even extinguish the boundary between sentiment and fact."[37] For them, Twitter offers the possibility to conflate personal communication with public communication; it conflates the backstage persona with the frontstage persona and renders the potential contradictions between the truths inconsequential. If the public had previously understood that politicians were generally lying, they did so by maintaining a separate truth between the frontstage and backstage. Trump used Twitter to dissolve that line; as such, even though his statements did not comport with the consensual truth of public discourse, it did align with his personal truth and allowed him to remain authentic to his supporters, while still lying. As Oborne and Roberts explain, 'Trump told lies, smeared and fabricated in order to destroy opponents. If the facts proved what he was saying to be untrue, Trump didn't care. He constructed a personal epistemology. His truth claims were purely instrumental. He made assertions about his own honesty—and the lies of his enemies—in order to gain power and win arguments."[38] The notion of a personal epistemology conflicts with a traditional notion of how truth circulates in politics, but Trump is able to use it to his advantage through the use of Twitter.

For many, Twitter is a difficult medium on which to maintain authenticity because it relies upon the notion of context collapse; a variety of different audiences all read the same feed.[39] Media scholars Marwick and boyd explain that most people construct their authenticity in different contexts by selecting different aspects of themselves to reveal in different frontstage and backstage contexts. For example, a server at a restaurant acts differently when presenting the specials to the table than they do in the kitchen with their coworkers; if they did not, they would be considered rude or inauthentic because the expectations are vastly different. Marwick and boyd argue that "since authenticity is constituted by the audience, context collapse problematizes the individual's ability to shift between these selves and come off as authentic or fake." Because Twitter collapses the context, Twitter users use "two techniques to navigate these tensions: self-censorship and balance."⁴⁰ Trump seems to employ neither self-censorship nor balance in his tweets; or rather, Trump has created a persona for nearly forty years in popular media that is so consistent that if there is a "real" Donald Trump backstage doing the tweeting, then it is so far removed from any iteration of Trump the public has ever seen as to be unrecognizable. For example, conservative journalist Heather Higgins writes that

> by multiple accounts, the private Donald Trump is not what one would expect from the tabloid reporting. He's often described as charming—even by those who didn't want to like him or expect to be impressed—an attentive listener, a loyal friend, deeply interested in his lowest-level employees' lives and opinions, a great father, and someone generous to and concerned about others.⁴¹

This account just seems off—as if it were written by a public relations manager to describe some version of Donald Trump who has never appeared in public. If he were these things, one might assume that he would do them just for his own personal advancement as the will to power has been the only motivating factor that Trump has ever presented himself as having or wanting. This insatiable drive is alluring to many people, and despicable to many others, but it keeps Trump from having to censor or balance himself or Twitter; Trump comes across as being who he always is and who he always has been, and this authenticity is one of the great allures of the man.

Part of Trump's ability to maintain the same outward presentation of himself is through his unwavering optimism about himself and his ability, which presents to some as egoism or narcissism. Trump needs his buildings not just to be good but to be the best and tallest. He needs not just to be smart but to be the smartest. He needs his economy not just to be good but to be the greatest of all time. He needs all of these things to be true, and he does not need for empirical facts to align with his conception of them. His personal epistemology will work fine. Rhetorical scholar Lance Cummings traces this back to Trump's upbringing in Norman Vincent Peale's Marble Collegiate Church. Peale is famous for penning *The Power of Positive Thinking* (1952), and at his church, he "focused his preaching on developing self-confidence through Christian principles derived from specific verses that could be used as a kind of hypnotic suggestion."⁴² Cummings uses the metaphor of alchemy to describe the ways in which Trump wills things into being true through his unwavering optimism. For him, Twitter is the perfect medium for such transformation because it uses so few characters that the audience participates in creating the meaning of the text. While the openness of the text assures that not everyone will have the same type of affective relationship to the tweets, some will feel a strong investment in them and will come to share Trump's personal epistemology. Cummings explains that "because Twitter tends to collapse context and flatten audiences, followers respond to these algorithms in different ways, explaining why many feel a strong identification with Trump, while others feel a strong aversion." Because some are able to connect through this strong identification, Trump is able "not only to promote ways of thinking through repetitive algorithms but also as a way to extend the self into the public sphere."[43] In this logic, Trump is able to bring something into being as truth through his own hyper-inflated sense of self and the power of positive thinking and is able to transfer this personal truth to others through the medium of Twitter.

For Cummings, the alchemy lies in Trump's ability to alter reality through this process. A good example of this process is the "birther" controversy that elevated Trump to the national political conversation. The idea that Barack Obama was not born in the United States, his birth certificates were forged, and that his entire life story was a large conspiracy hiding the fact that he was a secret Muslim had germinated in the darker, more conspiratorial outskirts of internet culture. In 2012, Trump started to ask questions about Obama's country of origin and to demand to see his birth certificate; he, of course, used Twitter to link to less-than credible sources confirming the conspiracy. By dint of his persistent tweeting, the birther controversy became a mainstream issue, and Obama had to formally deny claims on several occasions and had to produce a long-form birth certificate, which still did not satisfy many hardcore birthers.[44] While there were no facts to support his conspiracy theory, by 2016 Trump had sown enough doubt that nearly three-quarters of Republicans either doubted or were not sure whether President Obama was indeed born in the United States.[45] For that group of people, no matter what evidence Obama provided would not have satisfied their insistence that he was not born here, because they had aligned with a different epistemological model. If Donald Trump was confident that he was born overseas, and he tweeted about it consistently, then that was evidence enough for them. In Cummings's schema, through the dark alchemy of Twitter, reality has shifted. He argues that "Twitter becomes a mechanism for deliberately altering reality through discourse. If I can change my personal reality through the power of positive thinking, then I can also change the public reality with the appropriate conduit, in this case, Twitter."[46] On Trump's Twitter feed, everything is always positive for Trump and his allies, and everything is always negative for his enemies. Trump never admits defeat, changes his mind, or acknowledges bad news;

rather, he alters the reality of his Twitter feed in such a way as to consistently portray himself in the best possible light; the power of positive thinking is alive and well on that feed.

## Twitter and Censorship

When Trump presented his 2020 executive order accusing online social media companies of censorship, he was following in a line of conservative media voices who believe in free speech absolutism and who feel that social media are intent on stifling conservative voices. The executive order asserts that "Twitter, Facebook, Instagram, and YouTube wield immense, if not unprecedented, power to shape the interpretation of public events; to censor, delete, or disappear information; and to control what people see or do not see" and that "online platforms are engaging in selective censorship that is harming our national discourse."[47] The Trump administration specifically highlighted Twitter, which they claims "selectively decides to place a warning label on certain tweets in a manner that clearly reflects political bias" and compares Trump's tweets which were given a warning label as having factual errors with that of a Democratic opponent Adam Schiff, whose Tweets never received such a warning.[48] The executive order suggests that Democrats and Republicans should be treated equally on Twitter, regardless of the underlying truth or facts. For free speech absolutists, any speech should be afforded the same liberties on a platform such as Twitter; the content does not matter, only freedom in its purist form.

For the company's part, Twitter has been very lenient in terms of the content that it allows on its site; at the time of Trump's executive order, which claimed to be concerned about leftist bias on the site, Richard Spencer, a prominent leader of the alt-right who has demonstrated many affinities with Nazism, still had many followers on the platform. Getting banished or censored from Twitter is very difficult because the company believes itself to be a form of a public sphere. For them to go to such lengths as to put a warning on Trump's tweets and eventually to ban him altogether shows the extent to which he was abusing the site, as the company knew full well what the backlash would be.

One of the first prominent public figures to be banned from Twitter was the alt-right personality Milo Yiannopoulos, whom the site ousted for cyberbullying in 2016. Yiannopoulos and his hundreds of thousands of Twitter fans started an assault on the all-woman remake of *Ghostbusters* (2016), and specifically targeted one of its stars, Leslie Jones, the only one of the titular ghostbusters who was a woman of color. They employed a tactic called "brigading," which involves "the act of a group targeting specific subjects and strategizing ways to collectively harass or threaten them,"[49] and Jones was subjected to an onslaught of racist, misogynist, and transphobic comments from Yiannopoulos and his followers. Because this was not the first time Yiannopoulos had used the power of his Twitter following to harass people ruthlessly, Twitter pulled his account.[50]

In their analysis of the incident, media scholars Milosavljević and Micova argue that Twitter has taken on the role of gatekeeper and as such has certain responsibilities in terms of maintaining free speech in the digital era. They maintain, "The Yiannopoulos case appears to be an example of an arbitrary decision-making process" and that Twitter's Terms of Service "indicate a lack of transparency and public accountability in the system and suggest a lack of consistency in the application."[51] For them, because Twitter has taken over the role of gatekeeper from the broadcast networks and print journalism, they have an enhanced role of responsibility to the public and should have been more transparent before taking action against Yiannopoulos. However, when establishment media maintained their power, the kind of direct harassment of a celebrity like Leslie Jones would not have been possible. I suggest that calling Twitter a gatekeeper is disingenuous because Twitter allows the floodgates to open between celebrities and their fans, and well-organized trolls such as Milos Yiannopoulos were able to use those floodgates to verbally assault a woman of color.

In some ways, however, this logical argument about liberal democracy, the public sphere, and the terms of engagement is exactly the wrong register for the freedom of speech argument that Yiannopoulos is making or that Trump is exploring in his executive order. Political scientist Joseph Mello maintains that the argumentative tactic that Yiannopoulos employs is to make an absurdist argument to anger his opponent, and then when the opponent tries to either silence him or resort to shouting or violence, Yiannopoulos can claim victory because the opponent is not following the rules of "freedom of speech." Mello provides the example of Yiannopoulos arguing that women should not take birth control because it makes women "'ugly,' 'crazy,' or 'slutty.'"[52] This is, of course, not an argument of any kind, but rather a series of misogynist attacks. In internet parlance, Yiannopoulos is trolling, trying to evoke a response that will attempt to silence him and demonstrate that he was the one playing by the rules of free speech. Mello explains, "Yiannopoulos' goal is not to win an argument based on substance, but to make his audience so angry that they will attempt to silence him, thus giving him the moral high ground and elevating his cause."[53] Yiannopoulos only maintains the high ground if one insists that free speech trumps all other morals; in the traditional media landscape, gatekeepers have limited speech tremendously by only allowing certain points of view to appear on television or to be printed in newspapers. Twitter is unquestionably more democratic in that it allows many more voices to be heard without having the same gatekeeping rules. As such, when a troll like Yiannopoulos is banished from a platform that still gives a voice to Nazis such as Richard Spencer, I might argue that the platform has not relinquished its free speech ideals. However, even though its free speech possibilities are nearly unlimited, when the site banishes Yiannopoulos or fact-checks Trump, some are wont to insist that their personal liberties have been challenged.

Yiannopoulos used his fame from getting booted from Twitter to procure speaking engagements on college campuses where he could present himself as a free speech warrior, valiantly battling the politically correct social justice warriors who thrive on college campuses. In 2017, Yiannopoulos was slated to speak at the University of California-Berkeley, but the event was canceled at the last minute when over 1,000 protesters showed up, and the protesters did damage to campus property. University security did not believe that they could safely hold the event. Fox News picked up the story, and, of course, Donald Trump felt the need to opine on the situation, tweeting "If U.C. Berkeley does not allow free speech and practices violence on innocent people with a different point of view—NO FEDERAL FUNDS?"[54] Here, Trump shows his affinity with a troll like Yiannopoulos because they both rely upon the notion of free speech at any costs to spew their rhetoric and they position it against the notion of political correctness as a strawperson against whom they can stake their claim to free speech absolutism. Yiannopoulos is also more outrageous than Trump in his racism and misogyny, which offers Trump a rare opportunity to seem like a moderate discursively, while still defending the right to free speech and challenging political correctness at all costs.

Donald Trump specifically dismissed the idea of political correctness in his campaign, saying that it "hinders progress and wastes valuable time."[55] Trump then is able to express racist, sexist, and misogynist things and claim that only those who are politically correct worry about such things. In fact, according to anthropologists Kira Hall, Donna Goldstein, and Matthew Ingram, when Trump tells the truth (or at least his truth), he does so by eschewing the norms of political correctness. They write that "when Trump promises to tell the truth (Muslims are terrorists; some women are uglier than others; Mexicans are rapists), he aligns himself with opposition to political correctness, with a stance that rejects rhetorical caution regarding minority religions, genders, and ethnicities."[56] For Trump, avoiding being politically correct is simply "telling it like it is," which for him is as close to truth as he is going to get; it aligns with his personal epistemology and Twitter is the perfect conduit for that.

Media studies scholar Jessica Shafer uses Goffman's notion of frontstage and backstage to describe the ways in which Trump uses his aversion to political correctness to foreground his racist points of view. She contends that many of Trump's supporters held racist views, but always felt the need to maintain them in their backstage personae because social norms, or political correctness, necessitated that they not overtly express those racist views. For her, "bringing white racism to the forefront in this manner dismisses continued structural inequality and normalizes racist thinking as logical. This bringing back of backstage racist feelings to the frontstage is justified under the guise of being honest and simply 'telling it like it is,' which creates an illusion of subtlety in expressing racist interpretations of issues."[57] As Twitter serves as both the frontstage and backstage platforms for Trump (insofar as those distinctions make sense in Trump's persona), Trump gives permission for his followers to embrace their inner racist and see the value in that truth.

In July of 2020, Trump took to Twitter to blast Twitter for hosting trending topics that did not portray Trump in a positive light. Trump tweeted, "So disgusting to watch Twitter's so-called 'Trending', where sooo many trends are about me, and never a good one. They look for anything they can find, make it as bad as possible, and blow it up, trying to make it trend. Really ridiculous, illegal, and, of course, very unfair!"[58] Trump did not mention which trending topics angered him, but in response to Trump's tweet, the hashtags #ThePresidentIsACrybaby and #TrumpleThinSkin both trended on the social media site.[59] The obvious irony is that Trump's annoyance with Twitter would not have received media attention had he not had Twitter as a platform to air his grievances; he needed Twitter to complain about Twitter. He was dissatisfied that the platform did not hew to his every demand, and calling the trending topics "illegal" exposed Trump's totalitarian instincts and his desire to be in control of media. However, the very fact that Twitter is not easily controllable is exactly what allowed Trump to use the medium to his advantage through the course of his campaign and his presidency.

If politicians traditionally had to play by the rules of traditional print media and network and cable television news to get their message across to an audience, then Twitter allowed Trump to go over the heads of those traditional news sources. Moreover, because Trump's tweets came to be of such import, those traditional news sources had to cover them as if they were traditional news stories. Even Trump's tweet about trending Twitter topics being unfair and illegal was not just a Twitter story; it was picked up by myriad news sources, because when the president of the United States claims that a media source is potentially doing something illegal by criticizing him, that becomes news. The only downside to the Twitter system that Trump consistently took advantage of was that not everyone on Twitter loved him. The same tool can also be used by those who resist Trump, and they can mobilize with anti-Trump tweets and hashtags and can voice their opinion against the president. A less thin-skinned president might perceive that anti-Trump trending hashtags would not make news beyond the Twittersphere if the president himself did not make a big deal about it; only when Trump called those tweets illegal and unfair did the story get picked up by the larger media universe and make bigger news. Whether Trump did this strategically is an arguable point, but the mainstream media amplified Trump's tweets in ways that were unique to him. As political scientists Matthew Miles and Donald Haider-Markel explain, "Even if few people actually follow Trump directly through a Twitter account, news media coverage of nearly everything that he posts on Twitter makes it likely that many people without Twitter accounts become aware of the tweet."[60] They go on to explain that because of the "amplification effect," once one mainstream news media outlet starts to cover a story, it will be covered by multiple outlets.[61] Trump's tweets were a goldmine for print and television news sources looking for content—especially when he said something outrageous.

## The End of Trump's Twitter

Twitter came under quite a bit of fire for blindly allowing Donald Trump to post any content he wanted without repercussion. The company has a policy about "newsworthiness" that ensures that elected officials with a certain number of followers will not have their tweets removed or their accounts suspended for tweeting content that falls outside of the standard rules of content that Twitter employs.[62] However, Donald Trump abused the privilege to such an extent that Twitter started putting warning labels on many of Trump's tweets, especially in the lead-up to and aftermath of the 2020 election, during which Trump made many false claims about the election process. Beginning in August 2020, many of Trump's tweets were appended by Twitter with the note that the content "violated the Twitter Rules about civic and election integrity."[63] The misleading tweets escalated after the election, when Trump disputed the results and Twitter felt the need to include a warning label on an increasing number of Trump's tweets.[64] Whether the warning labels on Trump's tweets constituted a form of censorship is a point of debate; however, the practice shows the tension that Trump puts on the medium in terms of its relationship to the notion of truth. For Trump, he wants to be the official arbiter of truth, and he sees Twitter as a medium that should allow him to present an unvarnished version of that truth to the public with no resistance from the platform. Despite the exception in their terms of use for elected officials, Twitter feels pressure to serve the interests of a larger public forum and understands that this means having an obligation to a version of truth that is shared by more than an audience of one. Thus, the warning labels ostensibly work to suggest that Trump's version of truth deviates from that of the larger Twitter community and the larger public sphere. Twitter understands the danger of a singular powerful figure controlling messaging and producing a truth that is more powerful than that collectivity produced by the public sphere that is the whole of the platform.

Donald Trump was able to intuit the logic of Twitter as a medium like no other politician, and his campaign and presidency were characterized by a constant stream of tweets that provided a glimpse into the mind and strategy of the president. Mainstream media covered Trump's tweets as if they were official presidential decrees, though the tweets often maintained a stream-of-consciousness shape that typifies the medium. Trump's administration made it clear that tweets were official White House policy, though the Twitter feed from @theRealDonaldTrump often contradicted the messaging that came from the communications team or other surrogates. For Trump, the beauty of the medium is that he could communicate directly to his supporters (and haters) without going through the intermediaries of his communications team or the mainstream media and could broadcast his ideas at any time of the day or night. Only at the very end of his presidency did Twitter begin to curtail his every indulgence by putting warnings on the tweets that they might not be factual or might not comport with the facts of the 2020 election. Trump ultimately collided with the outer edge of Twitter's free speech limits, where it chose to warn the public about the speech of even a public elected official.

Trump's entire media presence changed dramatically when Twitter banned him from the platform in January 2021. The relative silence that ensued after Trump was no longer consistently tweeting was deeply felt across media environments. Writing for *The Washington Post*, Craig Timberg compares Trump's first impeachment, during which he tweeted an average of fifty-eight times a day, and his second impeachment, which occurred after the Twitter ban, and notes the surreal quiet that transpired during the second impeachment. For Timberg, "the silence was momentous… This emerging new world—free from Trump's tweets and the kaleidoscope of reactions to Trump's tweets—has dawned suddenly, costing the president his ability to speak directly with 88 million followers, unfiltered by journalists or other traditional gatekeepers."[65] During his first impeachment, Trump was able to offer a meta-commentary over the events and to criticize consistently the Democrats for their unfair treatment of him, and to decry the mainstream media for their unfair coverage of the process. He was able to frame himself as the victim in the process. However, during the second impeachment, in the wake of the insurrection, he was forced to remain muzzled.

Writing several months after Trump's Twitter ban and several months into Biden's presidency, journalist Sarah Lyall writes that Twitter is a much calmer place in the wake of a campaign and presidency characterized by the persistent, escalated tweeting style of Donald Trump. She notes that "a strange quiet has descended after a four-year bombardment of presidential verbiage."[66] The relative calm that Lyall explains seems to have spread across all media as political news lost some of its urgency without the consistently energetic drive of Trump's Twitter account. In fact, the entire news industry saw a dramatic decline in viewership/readership in the first quarter of 2021 after Trump left office and was no longer able to tweet. Media expert Scott Robson attributes this to the fact that "people are relieved they don't have to check the news every night to see what the latest crisis is."[67] Trump's tweets, along with their relationship to other media, created a media environment characterized by consistent crisis in which people felt obliged to be constantly connected so as not to miss whatever might be coming next. When the flow of tweets was turned off at the source, many in the public felt a sense of quiet or relief because they no longer felt the need to be constantly tuned in to national politics. When Trump's Twitter account was finally turned off, Trump no longer was able to maintain control of the media environment as he had done for the five years prior, and the public was able to feel a certain amount of relief by not having to engage in the chaotic mediascape that Trump produced.

# Notes

1. Kate Conger and Davey Alba, "Twitter Refutes Inaccuracies in Trump's Tweets About Mail-In Voting," *The New York Times*, May 26, 2020, https://www.nytimes.com/2020/05/26/technology/twitter-trump-mail-in-ballots.html
2. Ibid.
3. Margaret Harding McGill, "What Trump's 'Executive Order on Preventing Online Censorship' Orders," *Axios*, May 28, 2020, https://www.axios.com/what-trumps-executive-order-on-preventing-online-censorship-orders-3f5fcd6d-a160-49b7-9add-26551bd0ba61.html
4. Shannon Bond and Avie Schneider, "Trump Threatens to Shut Down Social Media after Twitter Adds Warning to His Tweets," *NPR*, May 27, 2020, https://www.npr.org/2020/05/27/863011399/trump-threatens-to-shut-down-social-media-after-twitter-adds-warning-on-his-twee
5. Brian Ott and Greg Dickenson, *The Twitter Presidency: Donald J. Trump and the Politics of White Rage* (New York: Routledge, 2019), 61, 59.

6   Neil Postman, *Amusing Ourselves to Death: Public Discourse in the Age of Show Business* (New York: Penguin Books, 1985), 7.
7   Virginia Heffernan, "How the Twitter Candidate Trumped the Teleprompter Candidate," *Politico*, May/June 2016, https://www.politico.com/magazine/story/2016/04/2016-heffernan-twitter-media-donald-trump-barack-obama-teleprompter-president-213825
8   Ott and Dickenson, 64.
9   Ibid., 94.
10  Galen Stolee and Steve Caton, "Twitter, Trump, and the Base: A Shift to a New Form of Presidential Talk?" *Signs & Society* 6, no. 1 (2018): 157.
11  Antoaneta Roussi, "The Twitter Candidate: Donald Trump's Mastery of Social Media Is His Real Ground Game," *Salon*, February 18, 2016, https://www.salon.com/2016/02/18/the_twitter_candidate_donald_trumps_mastery_of_social_media_is_his_real_ground_game/
12  Peter Oborne and Tom Roberts, *How Trump Thinks: His Tweets and the Birth of a New Political Language* (London: Head of Zeus Books, 2017), 176.
13  Ben Schreckinger, "World War Meme," *Politico*, March/April 2017, https://www.politico.com/magazine/story/2017/03/memes-4chan-trump-supporters-trolls-internet-214856
14  Ben Mathis-Lilley, "Trump Apparently Took Star of David Image from Neo-Nazi's Twitter Account," *Slate*, July 5, 2016, https://slate.com/news-and-politics/2016/07/neo-nazi-twitter-account-created-trump-star-of-david-image-watermark-indicates.html
15  Jenna Johnson, "Trump Says Campaign Shouldn't Have Deleted Image Circulated by White Supremacists," *The Washington Post*, July 6, 2016, https://www.washingtonpost.com/news/post-politics/wp/2016/07/06/trump-says-campaign-shouldnt-have-deleted-image-circulated-by-white-supremacists/
16  John Nichols, "As Long as We're Taking Note of Trump's Anti-Semitic Tweeting, Shall We Address His Mussolini Messaging?" *The Nation*, July 6, 2016, https://www.thenation.com/article/archive/as-long-as-were-taking-note-of-trumps-anti-semitic-tweeting-shall-we-address-his-mussolini-messaging/
17  Ibid.
18  Richard Hofstadter, *The Paranoid Style in American Politics and Other Essays* (New York: Vintage Books, 2008).
19  Sam Kirkland, "Retweets Are Endorsements at NPR and AP, but Not at NYT," *Poynter*, July 10, 2014, https://www.poynter.org/reporting-editing/2014/retweets-are-endorsements-at-npr-and-ap-but-not-at-nyt/
20  Jennifer Mercieca, *Demagogue for President: The Rhetorical Genius of Donald Trump* (College Station, TX: Texas A&M University Press, 2020), 90.
21  Ellie Shechet, "8 Things Trump Keeps Saying We 'Have' to Do That We Absolutely Do Not Have to Do," *Jezebel*, July 6, 2016, https://theslot.jezebel.com/8-things-trump-keeps-saying-we-have-to-do-that-we-absol-1783131244

22  Jenna Johnson, "'A Lot of People are Saying...': How Trump Spreads Conspiracies and Innuendos," *The Washington Post*, June 13, 2016, https://www.washingtonpost.com/politics/a-lot-of-people-are-saying-how-trump-spreads-conspiracies-and-innuendo/2016/06/13/b21e59de-317e-11e6-8ff7-7b6c1998b7a0_story.html
23  Ben Kharakh and Dan Primack. "Donald Trump's Social Media Ties to White Supremacists," *Fortune*, March 15, 2016, https://fortune.com/longform/donald-trump-white-supremacist-genocide/
24  Ibid.
25  Heffernan.
26  Dawn F. Colley, "Of Twit-Storms and Demagogues: Trump, Illusory Truths of Patriotism, and the Language of the Twittersphere," in *President Donald Trump and His Political Discourse: Ramifications of Rhetoric Via Twitter*, ed. Michelle Lockhart (New York: Routledge, 2019), 38.
27  Gunn Enli, "Twitter as an Arena for the Authentic Outsider: Exploring the Social Media Campaigns of Trump and Clinton in the 2016 Presidential Election," *The European Journal of Communication* 32, no. 1 (2017): 57.
28  Ibid.
29  Erving Goffman, *The Presentation of Self in Everyday Life* (New York: Anchor Books, 1959).
30  Navneet Along, "Trump Is America's First Twitter President. Be Very Afraid," *The New Republic*, November 15, 2016, https://newrepublic.com/article/138753/trump-americas-first-twitter-president-afraid
31  Richard A. Grusin, "Donald Trump's Evil Mediation," *Theory and Event* 20, no. 1 (2017): S–92.
32  Grusin, S-88.
33  Ibid., 93.
34  Devon Bissonette, "'Modern Day Presidential': Donald Trump and American Politics in the Age of Twitter," *The Journal of Social Media in Society* 9, no. 1 (2020): 192.
35  Silvio Waisbord, Tina Tucker, and Zoey Lickenheld, "Trump and the Great Disruption in Public Communication," in *Trump and the Media*, eds. Pablo J. Boczkowski and Zizi Papcharissi (Cambridge, MA: The MIT Press, 2018), 26.
36  Michael X. Delli Carpini, "Alternative Facts: Donald Trump and the Emergence of a New U.S. Media Regime," in *Trump and the Media*, eds. Pablo J. Boczkowski and Zizi Papcharissi (Cambridge, MA: The MIT Press, 2018), 20.
37  Oborne and Roberts, ix–x.
38  Ibid., xi.
39  Alice E. Marwick and danah Boyd, "I Tweet Honestly, I Tweet Passionately: Twitter Users, Context Collapse, and the Imagined Audience," *Media & Society* 13, no. 1 (2011): 122.
40  Marwick and boyd, 124.

41  Heather R. Higgins, "Trump as Communicator," *The National Review*, March 6, 2017, https://www.nationalreview.com/magazine/2017/03/06/donald-trump-persona-president/
42  Lance Cummings, "The Dark Alchemy of Donald Trump: Re-inventing Presidential Rhetorics through Christian and 'New Age' Discourses," in *President Donald Trump and His Political Discourse: Ramifications of Rhetoric via Twitter*, ed. Michelle Lockhart (New York: Routledge, 2019), 53.
43  Cummings, 54.
44  Michael D. Shear, "With Document, Obama Seeks to End 'Birther' Issue," *The New York Times*, April 27, 2011, https://www.nytimes.com/2011/04/28/us/politics/28obama.html
45  Josh Clinton and Carrie Roush, "Poll: Persistent Partisan Divide over 'Birther' Question," *NBC News*, August 10, 2016, https://www.nbcnews.com/politics/2016-election/poll-persistent-partisan-divide-over-birther-question-n627446
46  Cummings, 54.
47  "Executive Order on Preventing Online Censorship," *Whitehouse.Gov*, May 28, 2020, https://www.whitehouse.gov/presidential-actions/executive-order-preventing-online-censorship/
48  Ibid.
49  Aja Romano, "Milo Yiannopoulos's Twitter Ban, Explained," *Vox*, July 20, 2016, https://www.vox.com/2016/7/20/12226070/milo-yiannopoulus-twitter-ban-explained
50  Ibid.
51  Marko Milosavljević and Sally Broughton Micova, "Banning, Blocking and Boosting: Twitter's Solo-Regulation of Expression," *Media Studies* 7, no. 13 (2016): 52.
52  Joseph Mello, "Free Speech from Left to Right: Exploring How Liberals and Conservatives Conceptualize Speech Rights through the Works of Lenny Bruce and Milo Yiannopoulos," *Law, Culture, & the Humanities* 17, no. 2 (2021): 348.
53  Mello, 348–9.
54  Alana Horowitz Satlin, "Donald Trump Defends Far-Right Troll Milo Yiannopoulos," *Huffington Post*, February 2, 2017, https://www.huffpost.com/entry/donald-trump-defends-troll-milo-yiannopoulos_n_589315e9e4b0af07cb6b992f
55  Jessica Gantt Shafer, "Donald Trump's 'Political Incorrectness': Neoliberalism as Frontstage Racism on Social Media," *Social Media & Society* 3, no. 3 (2017): 1.
56  Kira Hall, Donna M. Goldstein, and Matthew Bruce Ingram, "The Hands of Donald Trump: Entertainment, Gesture, Spectacle," *Hau: Journal of Ethnographic Theory* 6, no. 2 (2016): 74.
57  Shafer, 3.

58  Justine Coleman, "Trump Blasts 'Trending' Section on Twitter: 'Really Ridiculous, Illegal, And, Of Course, Very Unfair!'," *The Hill*, July 27, 2020, https://thehill.com/homenews/administration/509286-trump-blasts-trending-section-on-twitter-really-ridiculous-illegal

59  Mia Jankowitz, "#ThePresidentIsACrybaby and #TrumpleThinSkin Became Twitter Trends after Trump Complained about Mean Twitter Trends," *Business Insider*, July 28, 2020, https://www.businessinsider.com/anti-trump-trends-surge-on-twitter-after-he-complains–2020–7

60  Matthew R. Miles and Donald P. Haider-Markel, "Polls and Elections. Trump, Twitter, and Public Dissuasion: A Natural Experiment in Presidential Rhetoric," *Presidential Studies Quarterly* 50, no. 2 (2020): 440.

61  Miles and Haider-Markel, 440–1.

62  Alex Hern and Kari Paul, "Trump Will No Longer Receive Special Twitter Treatment if He Loses Election," *The Guardian*, November 6, 2020, https://www.theguardian.com/us-news/2020/nov/06/donald-trump-twitter-rules-newsworthy-election

63  Kate Conger, "Twitter Flags Trump Tweet for Dissuading Voters," *The New York Times*, August 23, 2020, https://www.nytimes.com/2020/08/23/technology/twitter-trump-tweet-warning.html

64  Meg Wagner et al., "Joe Biden Elected President," *CNN.com*, November 8, 2020, https://www.cnn.com/politics/live-news/trump-biden-election-results-11-07-20/h_4b7431d7ff5ea6dc0fb40e8247492de8

65  Craig Timberg, "Twitter Ban Reveals That Tech Companies Held Keys to Trump's Power All Along," *The Washington Post*, January 14, 2021, https://www.washingtonpost.com/technology/2021/01/14/trump-twitter-megaphone/

66  Sarah Lyall, "100 Days without Trump on Twitter: A Nation Scrolls More Calmly," *The New York Times*, April 17, 2021, https://www.nytimes.com/2021/04/17/us/politics/trump-twitter.html

67  Thomas Moore, "TV News Readership, Online Readership Plunge during Biden's First 100 Days," *The Hill*, April 30, 2021, https://thehill.com/homenews/media/551210-tv-news-ratings-online-readership-plunge-during-bidens-first-100-days

# 5

# 4chan, Reddit, Far-Right Politics, and Insurrection

On June 29, 2020, Reddit banned one of its subreddits, "r/the_donald" from the site, marking and end of an era for one of the most controversial internet forums.¹ While ostensibly a site dedicated to the election and eventually the presidency of Donald Trump, r/the_donald was a hotbed of racist, misogynist, Islamophobic, and homophobic content. During the 2016 presidential campaign, some of the darkest content from r/the_donald was able to move into the mainstream by the ability of its members to loosely veil its most abhorrent content through the playfulness and polysemic nature of memes and to game the Reddit algorithm to bring its content to the frontpage of Reddit.² Another space that produced similar discourse to Reddit was the imageboard 4chan; many of the memes that circulate in mainstream sites like Facebook and Twitter have their origins in 4chan, as well as its successors 8chan and 8kun, all of which are known for embracing very broad free speech protocols. Extreme racist, sexist, or homophobic content that might get one banned from Facebook or Twitter can find a perfectly acceptable home on 4chan. In the days following the election, members of 4chan felt that they had an outsized role in swinging the election to Trump, and their favorite cartoon mascot, Pepe the Frog, had gained some national notoriety during the campaign, causing one member to quip that "we actually elected a meme as president."³ While this sentiment suggests that members of Reddit and 4chan may have found humor in the process of electing Donald Trump to the White House, the ramifications that the two sites had in terms of bringing hateful content into the mainstream are, in fact, totally serious. In other words, these sites not only played a part in bringing Donald Trump the presidency but they increasingly shuttled the ideas of the nascent alt-right into dominant discourse.

In this chapter, I look at the ways in which far-right content emerges on anonymous websites such as Reddit and 4chan and how the content from these sites comes to circulate across more mainstream media outlets. Media scholar Julia DeCook notes that "the specific brand of extremist ideology that has taken rise is prominent in web forums like 4chan, reddit, and many others that provided anonymity for its users and allowed for content creation and proliferation across platforms in multiple modalities (text, video, audio, etc.) to cater to people's information needs."[4] The ascendency of Donald Trump occurred concomitantly with the rise in national prominence of the alt-right, and many of the ideas that fueled groups on the alt-right initially percolated on sites such as 4chan and reddit before being distributed across more mainstream media outlets. Moreover, many of the racist and misogynist messages that characterize contemporary alt-right ideologies were initially presented in the form of humor and irony packed into and dispersed through memes, wrapping the hateful ideology into a cloak of plausible deniability, allowing the content to gain access to audiences that might not otherwise have an appetite for far-right material. By the end of the Trump presidency, several far-right groups had used the internet to boost their membership, resulting in real-world violent skirmishes and culminating in the insurrection at the Capitol, where a number of different alt-right groups came together in a show of violent support for Donald Trump. Here, I consider the Boogaloo Bois, the Proud Boys, and QAnon in particular, and show how they used the internet to organize and emerge as some of the most visible far-right groups that participated in the insurrection on January 6, 2021.

## The Alt-Right

The alt-right came to mainstream prominence in the middle of the 2016 presidential campaign as a relatively recent phenomenon in far-right politics that challenged establishment conservatism and swung the pendulum of the conservative movement to the right. They came to be ardent supporters of Donald Trump and used social media as their dominant way of communicating with each other and of bringing their ideas from the depths of the internet to the fore of mainstream political discourse. Journalist Mike Wendling offers a generous definition of the movement, claiming that "the alt-right is an incredibly loose set of ideologies held together by what they oppose: feminism, Islam, the Black Lives Mater movement, political correctness, a fuzzy idea they call 'globalism,' and establishment politics of both the left and the right."[5] A more critical reading of the alt-right would call it a euphemistic term that avoids labeling the movement "white nationalist" or "Nazi," even though it definitely has elements that might point to those labels. As the term was gaining national attention during the 2016 election, Andrew Anglin wrote "The Normie's Guide to the Alt-Right" for *The Daily Stormer*, an internet publication with no compunction about its ties to white nationalism and neo-Nazism. Anglin argues that the main components of alt-right ideology are anti-Semitism, the establishment of an exclusive state for "white" people, a commitment to scientific racism (i.e., opposition to the claim of equality for all races), as well as an opposition to feminism, and an "endorsement of white history."[6] This ambiguity between the definition that Wendling gives, which still promotes a far-right ideology but seems more palatable to a mainstream audience, and the definition that Anglin gives, which seems most decidedly white nationalist, is purposeful. Most often the alt-right shows this ambiguity by presenting their ideologies in terms of irony, jokes, and memes. This ultimately created a rift between those who were decidedly committed to the racial politics of a white ethno-state, who continue to be known as the alt-right, and those who revel in the potential confusion of a more ambiguous politics. The less radical side of this rift has been dubbed the "alt-lite" and is able to reach a larger audience and serve as a stepping-stone between mainstream conservative politics and the far reaches of the alt-right, where comparisons to Nazis are lauded rather than abhorred.[7]

While giving a talk at a conference to like-minded individuals in November 2016, Richard Spencer, perhaps the most well-known member of the alt-right, hit upon many of the key white nationalist notes that define the movement, purposefully echoing the style and tone of Adolf Hitler in his remarks. He ended his speech by praising a new era that was dawning with the election of Donald Trump and shouted, "Hail Trump! Hail Our People! Hail Victory!" The room responded by returning a Nazi salute and shouting, "Sieg Heil!" (Heil Victory!) in the original German.[8] While this seems to remove any doubt about Spencer and his followers' adherence to Nazism, when questioned, Spencer shook off the critique by saying it was merely a joke. For him, the homage to Nazism was just "in fun" and "clearly done in a spirit of irony and exuberance."[9] Another person who was at the conference and in the room for the Nazi salute noted that it was not a performance for those in the room but rather for those in the media and the "normies" who would take the gesture seriously. He stated that "the whole thing is we have jokes that offend the outside and we laugh. It's hilarious."[10] By framing Nazi references as a joke, they displace some of the potential outrage away from the group, suggesting that those who are offended might just be too politically correct. This potential gap between what the members of the alt-right "really" mean and what they say allows space for them to be taken up by those who do not necessarily fully endorse their white nationalist agenda or who do not necessarily want to bear the political consequences of that association.

The process of expressing something terrible and then claiming that it is simply a joke that people need to get over is one tactic of trolling, a phenomenon that has been part of internet culture since its beginning and gained more mainstream notoriety as it percolated in sites like 4chan and reddit and moved outward to the more mainstream sectors of the internet. In "A Normie's Guide to the Alt-Right," Andrew Anglin argues that "the core identity of the current Alt-Right originates from the highly intellectual meme and trolling culture which was birthed on 4chan in the 00's."[11] For an alt-right insider, trolling is not just one aspect of the alt-right but it is indeed its "core identity." If we can take Anglin at his word (and definitionally that might be difficult), the goal of the alt-right is less to actually implement every aspect of its white nationalist agenda than it is to create chaos by trolling and irritating others by making others think that they are serious. Anglin is slippery, though, as he then says that the opposite is true; nihilism is a cover for an actual sincere agenda. He contends that "the true nature of the movement, however, is serious and idealistic. We have in this new millennium an extremely nihilistic culture. From the point when I first became active in what has become the Alt-Right movement, it was my contention that in an age of nihilism, absolute idealism must be couched in irony in order to be taken seriously."[12] Thus, while trolling and internet culture are part of the core identity of the alt-right, and nihilism is the primary goal of the trolling, the ultimate goal is the white nationalist agenda that they are advocating at face value. Their worldview depends on chaos and nihilism, but they want to harness that chaos and nihilism toward a white nationalist agenda.

Rhetorical scholars Heather Woods and Leslie Hahner argue that to dismiss the irony and nihilism that characterizes memes on the alt-right is to underestimate their power. In *Make American Meme Again*, they take up the notion of "lulz" as a way of understanding that the ostensible nihilism of the alt-right is actually performing a kind of ideological work. Lulz, which is a take on the internet jargon LOL (laughing out loud), implies that when a person is engaging in memes, they are doing it "for the lulz," or because it is funny, not because the person actually believes or adheres to a particular ideology. They maintain that "for the Alt-right, the deployment of ironic images through lulz supplies rhetorical cover for hate-filled messages... Such disavowal recognizes the racism contained in far-right memes but refuses to accept responsibility for conveying racism. This mode of engagement has long been central to trolling and lulz."[13] In fact, in the way of thinking on these imageboards, to convey any feelings or ideological leanings with sincerity is a sign of weakness. Instead, one must be able to present as having a complete irreverence for everything and should be able to never take offense. As such, when a person on the alt-right plays the part of a Nazi, they can claim plausible deniability because they have a history of doing outrageous things, just for the lulz. Woods and Hahner are quick to challenge the assumption that one can avoid charges of racism by circulating racist images ironically. For them, even if one takes them at their word that they are only engaging in white nationalist discourses for the lulz, once those images start to circulate through message boards and across the internet at large,

> these vicious messages and images can never be ironic. White nationalist, misogynist, and other hateful memes circulate these ideas and certainly attract an audience who finds affinity with these claims, even in jest. In this way, despite the pretensions of the original user claiming ironic distanciation, that irony is itself a form of racism given that the user seems to presume that they can singularly determine the meaning of memes regardless of context.[14]

Their implication of the ironic racist would also apply to those giving an ostensibly ironic Nazi salute to Richard Spencer at the conference; those engaging in those racist signifiers do not necessarily know how they might be taken up when circulated through a larger audience, who might see more into it than them just doing it for the lulz.

Evidence suggests that some of the support that Trump originally got for president was simply because some of the people on 4chan and Reddit thought that it would be funny if a buffoon like Trump were to become a candidate and create chaos in the political system. Media scholar William Merrin notes that "there's evidence that 4chan's support for Trump was at first ironic, with the trolls enjoying the idea of trying to get a joke candidate elected president."[15] An anonymous member of the 4chan community argues that when Trump first announced his candidacy, it inspired many people on the site to launch a joke campaign. He explains that "for a lot of people, on the first day it was like, 'This would be fucking hilarious,' and then when he started coming up with policy stuff—the border wall, the Muslim ban—people on the boards were like, 'This can't be real. This is the greatest troll of all time.'"[16] Despite the fact that many in the online community were not taking the candidacy seriously, their involvement may indeed have helped to propel Trump to the presidency. Merrin maintains that 4chan and Reddit culture "played a central role on the attack on mainstream media, mainstream politics, the culture of 'political correctness' and Left-wing identity politics, and… coopted, diverted and weaponized troll culture for neo-Fascist purposes, supporting and aiding the election of Donald Trump."[17] The question of whether the members of the 4chan community actually thought Trump would be the best candidate for president becomes moot when Trump found himself sitting in the Oval Office implementing many of the alt-right ideas that percolated on sites like 4chan and Reddit.

Unlike other media, such as Twitter and cable television, which Donald Trump himself specifically engaged, 4chan and Reddit message boards operated independently from Trump and his campaign. Trump himself is known to be barely computer literate, not using email, preferring to have the stories of the day printed out, and only relying on his phone for his favorite app, Twitter, until that was taken away from him.[18] At times, the reality of the 4chan universe endorsed wildly speculative conspiracy theories that were far afield from the mainstream news outlets, but which ended up attracting mainstream attention when they brought real-life danger into the speculative world of the message board communities. The so-called PizzaGate controversy is one example when a conspiracy theory that was concocted by 4chan, perhaps entirely for the lulz, put actual people in danger. The PizzaGate theory asserted that Hillary Clinton and John Podesta, who was chief of staff during the Bill Clinton administration and a close ally of Hillary Clinton, were running a pedophile ring out of a pizza shop in Washington, DC. The absurdity of the situation became amplified when someone who was following the set of memes that developed around this theory—again, probably just for the purpose of joking—drove from his home in North Carolina and brought a gun into a pizza shop in DC. The man was apparently quite shocked when upon entering the pizzeria with an assault rifle found only pizza and handed himself over to the authorities.[19] In their analysis of the PizzaGate incident, media scholars Marc Tuters, Emilija Jokubauskaité, and Daniel Bach argue that because 4chan does not archive its content and its content is subsequently ephemeral, it is prone to spreading what they call "bullshit," which appeals to people's preconceived notions of the existing order. They argue that 4chan's "ephemerality affordance contributed to an environment that is remarkably productive of bullshit. As a type of knowledge-accumulation, bullshit confirms preconceived biases through appealing to emotion—this at the expense of the broader shared epistemic principles, an objective notion of 'truth' that arguably forms the foundation for public reason in large and complex liberal societies."[20] Thus, for them, 4chan operated as a space in which ideas could circulate that had no relation to the version of truth that was operating in mainstream media. At times, however, meme culture and mainstream culture intersected, which Shreckinger defines as "the ability of their trolling to create real-world effects."[21] Thus the truths that operated in the deeper spaces of the internet were able to percolate up to the mainstream. Memes were, in fact, a means through which many ideas that developed in spaces like 4chan and Reddit were able to gain purchase in more mainstream channels. The humorous structure of memes provides a way for the alt-right to employ their joking tactics in ways that are much more palatable to a mainstream audience than a conference with members giving Nazi salutes.

Media scholars Tuters and Hagen specifically analyze memes and their capacity to circulate between the deeper realms of the internet to more mainstream areas. They coin the term "memetic antagonism" to describe the process exemplified on 4chan/pol/ in which "political memes can be extremely effective in the formulation of an organic and classless 'us' bound together by existential antagonisms against a nebulous 'them.'"[22] Tuters and Hagen show that while the meanings of memes might seem extraordinarily fixed and linked to the far-right ideologies from which they emerged, once they become unhinged from their original mediated environment, their meanings become unfixed. They go on to argue that "as a meme develops and finds new audiences, initially overt antagonism can become nebulous, in the process becoming a floating signifier—the semiotic term for a sign whose ultimate meaning is changing and open-ended."[23] For them, this is what makes the process so dangerous, because it allows for discourses that might otherwise fall outside of the Overton window of acceptability to emerge in the mainstream because of their ambiguity. In their analysis, "It is this very blurriness that makes the subcultural milieu of political discussion on 4chan/pol/ a kind of petri dish for concocting extreme and extremely virulent forms of right-wing populist antagonism."[24] The figure of "Pepe the Frog" is an example of a meme with deep ties to far-right internet culture that found its way into mainstream politics and served as a sign that Donald Trump held allegiance to the darker corners of right-wing internet culture while allowing enough possible semiotic blurriness to avoid a direct connection.

In September 2016, with the election season in full swing, Donald Trump Jr. retweeted a meme called "The Deplorables" that was a take on the movie *The Expendables* (2010), and the Hillary Clinton gaffe in which she referred to a segment of Trump's base as "deplorable." The meme featured prominent members of Trump's team and of the alt-right in battle-ready clothing, and included Trump, his adult sons, Alex Jones, and Milos Yiannopoulos, among others. What brought media attention to the meme was the inclusion of 4chan's own "Pepe the Frog," a cartoon that has come to stand in for an affiliation with white supremacy. While racism on the part of Trump and his family has always been present, albeit often with plausible deniability, the inclusion of the cartoon frog was seen by the media as a bridge too far. However, the cartoon offers just the kind of ambiguity that allows for plausible deniability. Donald Trump Jr. appeared on *Good Morning America* (1975–) and stated, "I've never even heard of Pepe the Frog. I mean, bet you 90 percent of your viewers have never heard of Pepe the Frog."[25] He is thus able to have it both ways; he is able to wink at those in the know who circulate in the 4chan community and white supremacist circles and simultaneously to disavow any association with that community because the meaning of the cartoon frog is not widely known enough.

In her investigation of the roots and history of Pepe's circulation, Olivia Nuzzi outlines the cartoon frog's origins on the defunct social media site MySpace to its oversaturation as a meme by the general internet population, to his transformation to a symbol of white supremacy.[26] She argues that the appeal of most memes is their openness, their ability to have their meaning transformed into different contexts. Apparently, a handful of white supremacists have been working to associate the meaning of the frog so heavily with the white power movement that it can no longer be co-opted by "normies," or those who are not heavily invested in the dark corners of internet culture and patois. She quotes one of these white supremacists who maintains that Pepe is "a reflection of our souls, to most of us. It's disgusting to see people ('normies,' if you will) use him so trivially. He belongs to us. And we'll make him toxic if we have to." The same message-board white supremacist goes on to claim that "In a sense, we've managed to push white nationalism into a very mainstream position. Trump's online support has been crucial to his success, I believe, and the fact is that his biggest and most devoted online supporters are white nationalists. Now, we've pushed the Overton window. People have adopted our rhetoric, sometimes without even realizing it." The anonymous white supremacist knows that they have worked to fix the meaning of Pepe the Frog; they also know that by couching white nationalism in the character of a seemingly harmless cartoon figure, they make Pepe a more palatable symbol to a mainstream audience than either white sheets or burning crosses would. So, when Donald Trump Jr. retweets a seemingly innocuous tweet that just happens to have Pepe the Frog alongside presidential candidate Donald J. Trump, it leaves some room for plausible deniability, but it also brings a discussion of Pepe the Frog and white nationalism into the current of mainstream discourse. ABC News anchor George Stephanopoulos did an entire piece about Pepe and white nationalism on broadcast television, so regardless of Donald Trump Jr.'s intent, he was able to get the idea of Pepe and white nationalism into mainstream circulation, even as he maintained a thin veil of plausible deniability for himself and his father.

Pepe the Frog was just one example of a meme that percolated up from the depths of the internet and found resonance with a mainstream audience. The internet has a long history of housing hate groups and providing a sanctuary for extreme free speech. As social media came to dominate mainstream media, it became an avenue from which content from sites like 4chan and Reddit could find broader exposure. The humorous modality of memes provided an alibi for despicable content to move into the mainstream in palatable ways, because, after all, the people creating that content were just doing it for the lulz. Offensive memes may not have singlehandedly brought about the mainstreaming of the alt-right and the election of a cartoonish far-right president, but they did work to move the Overton window of acceptability, so that when Richard Spencer or Donald Trump dismisses a racist act as "just a joke," the template for that has been pressed.

## The Internet and Hate

Since the internet's inception, those who have constructed and maintained the internet have adhered to a notion of cyber-libertarianism in which free speech absolutism and freedom from government censorship prevailed as anchoring forces in internet discourses. Barbrook and Cameron famously coined the term "Californian ideology" to describe the seemingly bizarre hybrid of free-market capitalism and hippie creative individualism that pervaded in the construction of the internet culture in the 1980s and 1990s. For them, "Californian Ideology simultaneously reflects the disciplines of market economics and the freedoms of hippie artisanship," and central to the hippie dream and the capitalist dream was freedom from government interference.[27] This guiding principle of the internet was ingrained in the medium from its inception and has continued to circulate among those who are deeply invested in computers, programming, and gaming as subcultures. Many patrons of 4chan and the subreddits that created and fostered the alt-right would identify with some of these subcultures.

In the twenty years between Barbrook and Cameron's article in the early days of the World Wide Web and the Trump campaign in 2015, the internet increasingly became a place for a wide range of global identities, cultures, and ideologies, not just a place dominated by libertarian-leaning white men with absolutist understandings of freedom of speech. However, the white, male, cyber-libertarian strand still holds considerable purchase in some corners of the internet, and clashes with what they see as intrusions on an outside world that wants to impose its politically correct concepts of race, gender, and sexuality onto an internet culture that has thrived on relative anonymity and comparatively few rules and regulations. One particularly salient moment when the traditional forces of an "anything goes" internet pushed against what they saw as an intrusion into their territory was the "#GamerGate" controversy, which started as a disagreement in the gamer community about a positive review of a game developed by a woman. While the details of the review are inconsequential, what followed in the gaming community was a torrent of misogyny and sexism that included rape threats, death threats, doxing, and general abuse of many of the women in the community.[28] While the threats and harassment on the part of many in the community were horrible, it brought to the foreground the resistance to change by many members of the gaming community and brought the culture's misogyny to the fore. For many members of the computing world and gaming world, the #GamerGate controversy demonstrated that the "SJWs" (social justice warriors) had it out for their way of life and were trying to impart norms of political correctness on their internet culture. Journalist Simon Parkin writes:

> Gamergate is an expression of a narrative that certain video-game fans have chosen to believe: that the types of games they enjoy may change or disappear in the face of progressive criticism and commentary, and that the writers and journalists who cover the industry coordinate their message and skew it to push an agenda. It is a movement rooted in distrust and fear.[29]

#GamerGate was just one battle in a larger internet culture war and a precursor to what was to come in the 2016 election.

Many of the wounds from #GamerGate were still fresh when Donald Trump began running for the presidency in 2016, and one of the things he promised was freedom from political correctness. As journalist Angela Nagle writes in *Kill All Normies*, "one of the things that linked the often nihilistic and ironic chan culture to a wider culture of the alt-right orbit was their opposition to political correctness, feminism, multiculturalism, etc., and the encroachment in to their freewheeling world of anonymity and tech."[30] Many who were involved in the #GamerGate controversy were baffled when they made death threats or rape threats and found harsh opposition; in their eyes, they were simply expressing their freedom of speech in an argumentative form and doing it for the lulz. For hardcore members of the community, internet arguments always digress to their lowest common denominator. From their point of view, that does not necessarily translate into actually meaning that the person behind the discourse is misogynist; in their schema, people need to learn how to take a joke, even if that joke is about death or rape. When women insisted that these types of jokes were not, in fact, funny and did, in fact, cross lines of decency, the women were dismissed as SJWs and accused of ruining the utopian free speech community for everyone involved.

The alt-right offered a welcome space where such alienated folks could find a compassionate ear; similarly, sites like 4chan and Reddit offered spaces where those who felt injured by the political correctness espoused by #GamerGate could find safe refuge. Writing for *Politico*, Ben Shreckinger notes that "The 'Gamergate' harassment campaigns against women in the video-game industry were often organized on 4chan" and goes on to note that "Gamergate also hardened anti-political correctness sentiment on 4chan."[31] #GamerGate was a moment in time directly preceding the 2016 presidential campaign when far-right ideologies were solidifying in the deeper corners of the web, and they were using social media to gain a larger audience. Further, trolls from #GamerGate learned how to organize in ways that would transfer their anger from adolescent pranks online into tactics with terrifying real-world consequences. The trolls bombarded their opponents with death threats, rape threats, threats against their family, and doxing—sharing personal information such as address and phone number. Antia Sarkeesian, who critiques video games for their problematic representations of gender, was a common target of death threats and rape threats; she was ultimately forced to cancel a public-speaking appearance at Utah State University when trolls called in a credible threat that a mass shooting would happen at her event if she went through with the talk.[32]

Another phenomenon that emerged out of the #GamerGate mobilization was the increased popularity of several far-right activists who came to be associated with the so-called "alt-lite," such as Milo Yiannopoulos and Mike Cernovich. These personalities distanced themselves enough from the likes of Richard Spencer that they could attract a larger audience or sites such as YouTube and deliver far-right politics without the harsher edges. Both of them made a name for themselves during #GamerGate, and both were able to feed upon the politics of white male resentment that fueled the alt-right and the presidential campaign of Donald Trump. As journalist Matt Lees argues, "by leveraging distrust and resentment towards women, minorities and progressives, many of Gamergate's most prominent voices—characters like Mike Cernovich... and Milo Yiannopoulos—drew power and influence from its chaos."[33] The differences between the alt-right and the alt-lite are perhaps minimal, or perhaps about branding, but the alt-lite is definitely able to reach a larger audience as many of its ideas are circulated on the popular Breitbart News, which is very much in its corner. Journalist Andrew Marantz explains that both groups are adherents of "anti-feminism, opposition to political correctness, online abuse, belligerent nihilism, conspiracy theories, inflammatory Internet memes." What divides them is that the alt-right is explicitly white nationalist and in favor of the tactics of Richard Spencer, while the alt-lite prefers softer terms such as "American nationalist" or "civic nationalist" and is not avowedly in favor of a white ethno-state.[34]

The alt-lite offers a space where people with an interest in anti-feminist, pro-Western politics can enjoy the nihilistic memes and the 'politically incorrect" humor without having to feel like they are supporting actual Nazis.

As Bob Moser argues, "far more effectively than a straight-up white nationalist like Spencer could ever manage, the alt-lite peddles big lies that regularly work their way into 'normie' right-wing discourse."[35] The alt-lite provides a middle ground between the most hardcore militant activists and mainstream discourse and proved to be incredibly popular. Through sites such as Breitbart News, it was able to become a powerful political force in the 2016 campaign, and Breitbart's executive chairman, Steve Bannon, was a head strategist in the early days of the Trump administration. The alt-lite provided a stepping-stone between mainstream conservative politics and ultra-far-right ideologies. In meme culture, differences between those who were proponents of white nationalism and those who were proponents of American nationalism might be subtle or nonexistent, especially because both groups relied on humor to avoid critique. As actual real-world groups formed with far-right ideologies and political agendas, they would embrace the power of memes, humor, and the ambiguity of internet culture to cultivate followings.

## Boogaloo Bois, Proud Boys, and QAnon

The insurrection at the Capitol on January 6, 2021, was led in part by three groups of far-right Trump supporters, all with ties to the darker corners of the internet, and all with different objectives. The Boogaloo Bois are a loose configuration of armed insurrectionists, intent on bringing about a second civil war in the United States. Their name, attire, and digital presence make them seem like a meme joke gone awry, but their heavy armament suggests that they should be taken seriously. Like the Boogaloo Bois, the Proud Boys are a hyper-masculine group with violent tendencies. Their ideology is better defined, as they characterize themselves as "Western chauvinist," and are concerned about the potential for a "white genocide," a racist conspiracy theory about the elimination of the white race.[36] They share in common with the Boogaloo Bois a penchant for violence and guns. QAnon is a conspiracist organization whose ideas are often far-fetched—one of the tenets associated with the group is that beloved actor Tom Hanks drinks the blood of children—but whose devotion to Trump has migrated from its origins on 8chan (an offshoot of 4chan) to the real world of politics.[37] QAnon does not have a coherent ideology beyond an amalgamation of conspiracy theories, but its members are convinced that Donald Trump is the savior that will save them from the cannibals and the pedophiles who are currently in the highest positions of power in Washington and Hollywood. All three of these groups received some mainstream media attention before the Capitol insurrection, but the events of

January 6 brought them together and to the fore of media attention, revealing the danger that they presented to the established order.

## Boogaloo Bois

Dismissing the Boogaloo Bois (or Boogaloo Boys) as simply a joke would be easy; their sartorial choice for the great second civil war is to don Hawaiian shirts. This future war is referred to as a Luau (a derivation of Boogaloo), which makes the Hawaiian shirts appropriate, and their name comes from a 1980s breakdancing movie, *Breakin' 2: Electric Boogaloo* (1984). However, the goal of the Boogaloo Bois is to show up at protests on any side of the political spectrum and escalate conflict. Journalist Bulent Kenes describes the group as "a decentralized movement that organizes largely online but whose presence has increasingly been felt in the real world, the Boogaloo Boys is a group favoured by the militia, gun rights, and anarcho-capitalist movements."[38] While it has its origins on 4chan, the group organized and grew its membership primarily through Facebook (though in 2020, Facebook banned over 200 accounts associated with the group because of its violent tendencies).[39] Ever the tricksters, many Boogaloo Bois strategically changed their Facebook titles to names that could not be as easily detected by the Facebook scanners. (For example, they started referring to themselves as "CNN Bois," under the assumption that Facebook would never be ever to search and delete everything with CNN in the title.[40])

Media scholar Bradley Wiggins examines the ways in which the Boogaloo Bois used memes as a way to solidify group identity, positioning themselves as an in-group who were better able to understand the realities of the contemporary world than the enemies they were fighting. Specifically, they used their ability to be able to abide horrific content as a way to differentiate themselves from those outside of the group. Wiggins argues that "in-group messages as memes carry with them deeply contextualized and situated logics that may seem humorous and critically viable to the in-group but offensive to an out-group. The use of strong emotions embedded in memes-as-messages reinforces identity to encourage users to spread and communicate message conformity among disparate members of boogaloo discourse."[41] While he pays lip service to their notion of memetic antagonism, Wiggins seems to diverge from Tuters and Hagen's notion that the process of constructing memes creates ambiguous messages that allow them to become more palatable for the mainstream. Instead, for Wiggins, the unseemly content of many of the memes enjoyed in Boogaloo Bois spaces is precisely what separates them from the normies who would not be able to handle that level of content.

I suggest that the seemingly playful nature of the Boogaloo Bois allows them to seem less frightening to a mainstream audience, and that playfulness stems from their engagement with memetic content. By naming their group after a 1980s movie, donning Hawaiian shirts, and engaging in the process of shitposting, they separate themselves from other right-wing groups who take themselves much more seriously.

Despite the seemingly playful nature of the group, the Boogaloo Bois are indeed a dangerous group who are interested in instigating and escalating violence. Writing a few months before the insurrection at the Capitol, journalist Salvador Hernandez explains that "the so-called boogaloo boys may not be just disconnected extremists who share a penchant for Hawaiian shirts and chaos. They may have built nationwide systems to coordinate acts of violence and terror."[42] While the group has an ideology built around extreme libertarianism and gun rights, its main goal is the violent overthrow of the US government, which it feels will come about by accelerating any chaos or protests, regardless of their place on the political spectrum. Bulent Kenes explains that they get their tactics from William Luther Pierce's white supremacist fantasy novel *The Turner Diaries* (1978), popularized by Timothy McVeigh, who used the book as a template for carrying out the terrorist attack on the federal building in Oklahoma City in 1995.[43] Specifically, the Boogaloo Bois take from *The Turner Diaries* an accelerationist mindset in which they "promote violence to speed up the collapse of society, and often seek to exploit moments of political or civil unrest, including widespread protests."[44]

Seemingly counterintuitively, one of the first times that the Boogaloo Bois received national attention was during the protests in Minneapolis in the summer of 2020 following the killing of George Floyd by a police officer. While the majority of the people protesting in Minneapolis were challenging the role of policing from the political Left, members of the Boogaloo Bois showed up to encourage and escalate an already tense situation. In fact, members of the Boogaloo Bois have been known to wear BLM (Black Lives Matter) or LGBTQ+ iconography in order to confuse authorities, blame chaos on the Left, or perhaps just to do it for the lulz.[45] One member of the organization was arrested for his participation in the protests; Hernandez notes that the young man traveled all the way from Texas to Minneapolis "wearing a tactical vest on his chest and a skull mask over his face. In grainy video footage captured outside of Minneapolis's 3rd Police Precinct on the night of May 28, the man can be seen pulling out an AK-47 style rifle and blasting 13 shots into the police building. The shooting happened shortly before the structure was set ablaze."[46] The fact that a member of the organization would make the trip all the way from Texas to Minnesota to take part in protests that he did not even agree with shows the fervor of the group's members as they became increasingly radicalized through online sites. Throughout 2020 and early days of 2021, members of the Boogaloo Bois would find ways to insert themselves into the political and social tumult that transpired during the end of Trump's term.

Because their main goal is chaos, and the group is willing to glam onto political protests on any side of the political spectrum, the Boogaloo Bois' relationship to Donald Trump is complicated. The Boogaloo Bois specifically call for the violent overthrow of the established government; thus, when Donald Trump was president, this included him. As journalist Michael Mooney writes,

> the boogaloos don't appear interested in fighting for Donald Trump—they tend to despise him, mostly because they think he panders to the police. But for the past year, boogaloo bois all over the United States have been cheering on the country's breakdown, waiting for the moment when their nihilistic memes would come to life and the country would devolve into bloody chaos.[47]

Yet, when Trump led his followers to the insurrection at the Capitol, Boogaloo Bois were among the members of the crowd, seeking to participate in the melee. In fact, in an interview, one of the members of the Boogaloo Bois (part of a faction called The Last Sons of Liberty) claims that the Boogaloo Bois were responsible for helping to fire "up the crowd and 'may' have penetrated the [Capitol] building."[48] While the Boogaloo Bois may not have had any particular affinity for the forty-fifth president, they were more than happy to join in a crowd that was breaking into the Capitol and chanting "hang Mike Pence" as they searched the building for any official members of the government. The Boogaloo Bois make use of the systems that allow for joking memes to circulate and use humor in their attire and discourse to show reverence toward that meme culture. However, their commitment to heavy artillery and investment in a second civil war shows the possible terrifying ramifications of violent internet culture materializing in the real world.

## *The Proud Boys*

The Proud Boys have a more coherent ideology than the Boogaloo Bois; they are committed to the ideas of "Western chauvinism" and patriarchal norms. Their membership rituals read like a fraternal organization. To become a member, one has to go through a series of initiations that include getting "the crap beaten out of you by at least five guys until you can name five breakfast cereals," foregoing masturbation (or at least reducing it to at least once a month), and ultimately being tattooed to signify membership in the group.[49] The goal of these rites is to make a "real man" out of the members, as the Proud Boys believe that the United States has become overly feminized and they want to revive a version of masculinity based upon a severe gender divide that necessitates masculine violence. While reciting breakfast cereals may seem like a juvenile endeavor, the Proud Boys became one of the most widely known white nationalist groups when they were brought up in a 2020 debate and Donald Trump refused to disavow the group, instead suggesting that they "stand back and stand by."[50]

Like the Boogaloo Bois, the Proud Boys are a loosely connected network that uses the power and flexibility of the internet for their organization. Bulent Kenes writes that

> the group is distinct from other neo-conservative movements because of their heavy and strategic use of social media, and although other factions of the alt-right are known for their digital media savvy, the Proud Boys have specifically harnessed the power of digital technologies and have used Instagram, Facebook, and other platforms for recruitment, identity reinforcement, and to highlight the visibility of members in the world.[51]

Groups like the Boogaloo Bois and the Proud Boys are enabled by and take advantage of the toxic environments found on sites like 4chan and Reddit. They are then able to use more mainstream digital technologies to take their message to a larger audience. The internet allows for the Overton window to shift to allow groups that might otherwise remain confined to a remote corner of online space to organize into groups with large memberships and strong visibility and notoriety. Julia DeCook states that the Proud Boys post their memes on Instagram, rather than on 4chan or Reddit, in order to reach a broader audience and bring their alt-right message out from the deeper recesses of the internet. She argues that "perhaps the move to Instagram is an intentional one to gain a wider audience who may not participate in web forums like 4chan, 8chan, and Reddit due to Instagram's popularity and reach among youth."[52] The Proud Boys consistently take steps to distance themselves, however slightly, from the most radical elements of the alt-right, while adhering to an ideology that is decidedly racist and misogynist.

One way that the Proud Boys were able to increase their national visibility was by showing up at protests on both ends of the political spectrum. If the Boogaloo Bois preferred to show their violence by proudly displaying high-caliber rifles, the Proud Boys were more interested in brawling. They were particularly interested in beating up members of the Left; in fact, one can "level up" in the Proud Boy hierarchy by beating up a member of Antifa.[53] (How one definitively identifies a member of Antifa is unclear.) The group received national attention when members of the group did, in fact, beat up protesters associated with the Antifa movement; they were ultimately arrested, convicted, and sentenced to prison time.[54] The altercation happened outside of the Republican Club, as members of the Proud Boys, including their founder Gavin McInnes, were mingling with establishment Republicans. While fascinated with violence and extremist politics, the Proud Boys also aspire to influence politics on the national level.

One effort to make themselves more palatable to a mainstream audience came after the "Unite the Right" rally in Charlottesville, Virginia, in which an array of different far-right groups came together to protest the removal of a Confederate statue. The event ultimately ended in violence, leaving three people dead and at least thirty-three injured.[55] One of the organizers of the event was a member of the Proud Boys, Jason Keller, but founder Gavin McInnes condemned the event and kicked Keller out of the group, trying to distance himself from the overt racism on display. McInnes, somewhat disingenuously, insists that the Proud Boys "is simply a right-wing men's drinking club in the vein of the Elks Lodge," and he "hides under a guise of irony, freely using racial slurs and making incendiary comments about women, Muslims and African Americans in the name of mocking political correctness."[56] The *Southern Poverty Law Center* argues that because McInnes nominally disavows the alt-right and because he uses irony and humor to cushion the blow of his misogyny and racism, he is a good stepping-stone to more hardcore far-right politics. McInnes is often lumped in as a member of the alt-lite, though his politics are quite extreme. In their entry about the Proud Boys, which they characterize as a hate group, the *Southern Poverty Law Center* maintains that "white nationalists and neo-Nazis themselves have cited McInnes as a gateway to the alt-right... one former Proud Boy who went on to embrace white nationalism said he was originally drawn to the group because of its 'pro-white sentiment.'"[57] Because McInnes is able to be coy about his extremism, he was, at least for a time, able to find a platform on mainstream media. In 2018, ABC News' *Nightline* (1980–) had him on for an interview, an opportunity that would not have been afforded to more hardcore members of the alt-right.[58] Perhaps that was an anomaly, however, because Facebook and Twitter banned the Proud Boys and McInnes from their platforms that same year.[59] The ambiguity of the Proud Boys is exactly what enables them to serve as a "gateway" to the more hardcore segments of the alt-right.

The biggest boost in national attention that the Proud Boys received was during a 2020 presidential debate when Fox News' Chris Wallace asked Donald Trump if he would disavow white supremacists who were provoking violence at the anti-police brutality demonstrations that prevailed across the country in 2020 and asked if he would tell those groups to "stand down." Trump responded, "Sure, I'm willing to do that but I would say almost everything I see is from the left wing, not from the right wing." From his podium, Joe Biden asked him to "do it, say it," urging him to specifically condemn the white supremacists at these rallies. Donald Trump asked him to "give me a name," and Biden shot back: "Proud Boys." Trump took the bait, retorting, "Proud Boys—stand back and stand by. But I'll tell you what. I'll tell you what. Somebody's got to do something about Antifa and the left because this is not a right-wing problem."[60] At no point did Trump disavow the white nationalist group, and by telling them to "stand back and stand by," the media and members of the Proud Boys felt that this was an explicit endorsement of their organization. One member of the Proud Boys reacted to the Trump quote by posting, "Stand back and stand by for when the commies start a full escalation of war and he can call on us to essentially 'let loose the dogs of war.'"[61] Another exclaimed, "Trump basically said to go fuck them up. This makes me so happy."[62] Almost immediately after the debate, an online site was selling T-shirts emblazoned with the Proud Boys insignia and the slogan "Proud Boys: Standing By."[63] For his part, Trump walked back his comments the day after the debate, stating that "I don't know who the Proud Boys are. I mean, you'll you have to give me a definition because I really don't know who they are."[64] That Trump was unaware of the Proud Boys seems unlikely, but his knowledge of the group is unimportant. Through his comments at the debate, he had energized the alt-right and provided a call to arms, whether explicitly or tacitly. When the time came in January 2021 to storm the Capitol, the Proud Boys would indeed be ready, armed with the knowledge that Donald Trump was on their side, despite his tepid protestations that he had no idea who they were.

On January 6, 2021, The Proud Boys were one of the largest groups on the ground, with around 200 assembling before the Trump rally that kicked off the events.[65] One of the leaders of the group had posted on Parler, a microblogging service favored by extremist right-wing groups, in advance of the demonstration that "every law makers [sic] who breaks their own stupid Fucking laws should be dragged out of office and hung."[66] True to the spirit of the post, the crowd constructed a gallows outside of the Capitol, and the "Hang Mike Pence" chant was a frequent refrain among the group. The Proud Boys were on the front line of the insurrection; one of the broken windows that allowed for the crowd to enter the Capitol building was smashed by a shield wielded by a member of the organization.[67] While many who stormed the Capitol may have been doing so as a form of demonstration or to show their support for Donald Trump, members of the Proud Boys specifically wanted to assassinate Vice President Mike Pence and Speaker of the House Nancy Pelosi.[68] At the debate, Trump had encouraged the Proud Boys to "stand back and stand by," and they had stood by in anticipation of action. When the rally on January 6 turned into an assault on the Capitol, the hate group was more than ready for their assignment and dutifully participated in an effort to keep Trump in power.

## *QAnon*

While the Boogaloo Bois were interested in overthrowing the government as an end in and of itself, and the Proud Boys were interested in maintaining Trump as leader in an effort to forward their white supremacist agenda, the members of Qanon saw Trump as a kind of messiah who was chosen to cleanse the country of an elite cabal who thrived on cannibalism and pedophilia. Qanon is much larger than either the Proud Boys or the Boogaloo Bois; it boasts a membership in the millions with at least a loose affiliation to the group.[69] Journalist Jason McGahan characterizes the conspiratorial group as "the big-budget sequel to Pizzagate," and many of the themes of the PizzaGate narrative—pedophilia, nefarious cabals, Hillary Clinton—are present in QAnon lore. Q, the movement's leader, is an anonymous poster which began on 8chan, a descendent of 4chan, which has now been rebranded as 8kun. The name of the imageboard is unimportant; however, the anonymity of Q is important as the poster maintains an air of mystery as they post clues about the supposed cabal of Washington and Hollywood elites, such as Tom Hanks and Lady Gaga, who are involved in a giant pedophilia ring. Journalist Clive Thompson explains that Q, "this supposedly high-ranking insider claims that the deep state—an alleged cabal led by Barack Obama, Hillary Clinton, and George Soros and abetted by decadent celebrities—is running a global child-sex-trafficking ring and plotting a left-wing coup. Only Donald Trump heroically stands in the way."[70] While the group started in the deeper corners of the internet, it has grown to become a worldwide phenomenon, and has even produced two members of Congress—Lauren Boebert and Marjorie Taylor Greene, elected in 2020—who are avowed QAnon believers.[71] The group formed a particular affinity with Donald Trump; they showed up in numbers at many of his rallies, and before his account was blocked, Trump retweeted content that originated from members of QAnon over 145 times.[72] Of course, by retweeting QAnon content, the sitting president provided "proof" for QAnon believers that Trump was indeed the messianic figure that was diligently fighting to rid the world of the cannibals and pedophiles that were rampant in Hollywood and Washington.

Like many conspiracy groups, the process of searching for clues that confirm what they already believe is a key part of the process. Writing for *Wired* magazine, Clive Thompson argues that participation in the world of QAnon is like participating in a game; members are crowdsourcing, looking for clues that provide proof of the outlandish theories that form the bedrock of their conspiratorial universe. Thompson writes that perhaps QAnon is the "quintessence of internet culture. The web has always been about making willy-nilly connections: This links to that which links to this. And cyberspace facilitates the obsessive joint scrutiny of everything, from TV shows to knitting patterns to the belief that reptilians walk among us."[73] This game-like enjoyment is possibly one of the reasons that QAnon's membership numbers in the millions; the act of researching and finding clues that affirm one's beliefs is pleasurable, especially when the president of the United States, who is the group's messiah figure, drops hints that he too might be playing the game. Like the Boogaloo Bois riffing on a b-grade 1980s movie or the Proud Boys incorporating a breakfast cereal bit into their initiation rites, QAnon brings pleasure to what might otherwise be a horribly depressing tale of pedophilia, blood libel, and dreams of overthrowing the government.

While members of QAnon wanted to replace most of the members of the existing members of government, they, of course, wanted to keep Donald Trump, the central figure who would ultimately lead the true believers to the promised land. According to the lore, the last days of the Trump presidency were the "calm before the storm," and the events of January 6, 2021, were the supposed "storm" when Trump would reveal the massive conspiracy of cannibals and pedophiles, have them all arrested, and assume his rightful place as a savior figure. As journalist Amanda Marcotte explains, "the belief was January 6 was the prophesied day when Trump would supposedly ascend to his true power and have all their political enemies, who QAnon adherents believe are blood-drinking pedophiles, arrested."[74] While the prophesy did not come true and Trump did not even accompany his supporters to the Capitol, January 6, 2021, was the day that QAnon became a more of a household name as one of its supporters, dubbed the QAnon shaman, became a visual icon representing the attack on the Capitol. The shaman, Jacob Chansley, "was photographed inside the U.S. Senate chamber. He wore attention-grabbing red, white and blue face paint and an animal fur headdress, and carried a flagpole with a speared top."[75] His unique attire combined with his leadership role within the QAnon movement made him one of the faces of the insurrection, and highlighted the surreal feeling that characterized the events of the day. He seemed to be the personification of an internet meme, and he was holding court in the house chambers for several hours with no authority figure arresting him, Donald Trump observing with glee from afar. As outlandish as the ideas that QAnon websites circulate, one of their leaders was actually in the Capitol, and many of its followers were rooting for the insurrection that was actually transpiring. In their deep dive into the conspiracy group, Mia Bloom and Sophia Moskalenko maintain that members of QAnon were not only eagerly awaiting January 6 as a moment when Trump would jail the evildoers who resided in Washington and show his true faith as a defender of the country against pedophiles and blood drinkers but they were also actively involved in instigating the events. They argue that "QAnon propelled the events on January 6 just as much as the impeachment managers claimed that President Trump had done and as much as social media enabled the insurrection."[76] Though they did not necessarily share ideologies, members of QAnon, along with the Proud Boys and the Boogaloo Bois, were on the front lines of the assault on the Captiol on January 6.

Although Donald Trump ultimately did not fulfill the prophesy and arrest thousands of members of a nefarious cabal on-the-spot on January 6, 2021, followers of the QAnon conspiracy did not give up hope. Like any end-of-days cult, the lack of revelation on their assumed date of reckoning could only mean that they had misread the signs, not that their outlandish theories were mistaken. First, they believed that Joe Biden would not actually take office on Inauguration Day, January 20, and that Donald Trump would retain his rightful position as president that day. When that failed to materialize, they focused on March 4, which was the Inauguration Day prior to 1933, based on a fringe theory based that on an obscure law passed in 1871 every subsequent law has been illegitimate and that March 4 is therefore the rightful day that a president should take the oath of office.[77] When nothing happened on March 4, QAnon members claimed that word of that being the fateful date was a "trap" and a "false flag," and many members still hold out hope that in the not-too-distant future, Donald Trump will indeed save the world from the insidious pedophiles and cannibals who run rampant in Washington, Hollywood, and across the globe.[78]

## Conservative Media Ecosystem

In an analysis of the media habits of voters during the 2016 election cycle, a Harvard study showed that the leading source of information for conservative voters was Breitbart News, far surpassing Fox News.[79] Led at the time by Steve Bannon, Breitbart News was a decidedly alt-lite publication that used Twitter, Facebook, YouTube, and other social media sources to bring their news to millions of conservatives. Bannon himself has described Breitbart

News as a "platform for the alt-right."[80] According to the Harvard study, "a right-wing media network anchored around Breitbart developed as a distinct and insulated media system, using social media as a backbone to transmit a hyper-partisan perspective to the world."[81]

The study suggests two seemingly contradictory conclusions. First, the dominance of Breitbart as the go-to news source for the majority of conservatives created an isolated news ecosystem in which people were only exposed to views from a particular part of view. Second, the sheer dominance of the conservative ecosystem brought its discourse into national discussions and more mainstream news outlets. Thus, while those who got their news from Breitbart may have found it their only source for truth, those truths concocted within that bubble found their way into more mainstream discourses. So, Breitbart both "turned the right-wing media system into an internally coherent, relatively insulated knowledge community, reinforcing the shared worldview of readers and shielding them from journalism that challenged it" and "strongly influenced the broader media agenda, in particular coverage of Hillary Clinton."[82] As such, the right-wing media complex could construct their own reality through their own discursive pathways while also influencing the broader national conversation by inserting its version of truth into the mainstream political discourse. For example, if a wild conspiracy theory like PizzaGate was concocted on an imageboard like 4chan, percolated up through the alt-lite channels like Mike Cernovich's YouTube channel, and covered by Breitbart News, the underlying claim that Hillary Clinton was running a sex-trafficking ring is never disputed. That news story eventually gets covered by *The New York Times*, and even though those claims do not go undisputed in that venue, the story, linking Clinton with pedophilia, has entered mainstream political discourse.

The political Right has become so immersed in its own political reality that it rarely believes anything that circulates in mainstream news sources. One of the audience's favorite set pieces featured at Trump rallies is when Trump faces the members of the press and criticizes them for providing fake news and for being dishonest reporters while the audience hurls insults and off-color epithets in their direction. The terrain is consequently fertile for myriad conspiracy theories and alternative truths to circulate within the right-wing ecosystems. When a conspiracy theory as seemingly outlandish as QAnon can emerge from the deepest corners of the internet and grow to have over a million adherents and be a force in a violent insurrection at the US Capitol, the media environment can accommodate a variety of truths that push the Overton window of traditionally acceptable political discourse. Thus, when Trump started to lay the foundation for the possibility of a rigged election, which he actually began doing during the 2016 campaign, he found an audience willing to receive his message. A Reuters/Ipsos poll taken in May 2021, six months after the election, found that 25 percent of Americans felt that Donald Trump was, in fact, the true president of the United States and they did not accept the legitimacy of the election.[83] The Right is able to construct their own version of the truth and to dismiss the legitimacy of any competing narratives. They do this by constructing their own media ecosystem, which includes far-right extremists on less mainstream websites like 4chan and Reddit, seemingly innocuous memes with cute cartoon characters, and their own news systems that deny association with the most extreme characters in the movement while shifting the Overton window increasingly rightward. The audience in this media environment is so used to accepting the truths on offer in this media environment that when Trump presented them with the "big lie" that the election was rigged and that he is indeed the rightful leader of the free world, not only did they accept it without question but they were also willing to answer his call to action. In Chapter 7, I specifically look at the notion of truth and the "post-truth" environment that brought Trump into power and in which Trump flourishes.

## Notes

1. Jason Koebler, "The Great Ban: Reddit Bans 2,000 Communities Including the_donald, ChapoTrapHouse," *Vice*, June 29, 2020, https://www.vice.com/en_us/article/bv8v3v/the-great-ban-reddit-bans-2000-communities-including-the_donald-chapotraphouse?utm_content=1593452701&utm_medium=social&utm_source=VICE_facebook
2. Jason Koebler, "How r/the_donald Became a Melting Pot of Frustration and Hate," *Vice*, July 12, 2016, https://www.vice.com/en_us/article/53d5xb/what-is-rthedonald-donald-trump-subreddit
3. Abby Ohlheiser, "'We Actually Elected a Meme as President': How 4chan Celebrated Trump's Victory," *The Washington Post*, November 9, 2016, https://www.washingtonpost.com/news/the-intersect/wp/2016/11/09/we-actually-elected-a-meme-as-president-how-4chan-celebrated-trumps-victory/
4. Julia R. DeCook, "Memes and Symbolic Violence: #proudboys and the Use of Memes for Propaganda and Construction of Collective Identity," *Learning, Media, & Technology* 43, no. 4 (2018): 487.
5. Mike Wendling, *Alt Right: From 4chan to the White House* (London: Pluto Press, 2018), 3.
6. Andrew Anglin, "A Normie's Guide to the Alt-Right," *Daily Stormer*, August 31, 2016, https://dailystormer.name/a-normies-guide-to-the-alt-right/
7. "From Alt Right to Alt Lite: Naming the Hate," *Anti-Defamation League*, https://www.adl.org/resources/backgrounders/from-alt-right-to-alt-lite-naming-the-hate

8   Joseph Goldstein, "Alt-Right Gathering Exults in Trump Election with Nazi-Era Salute," *The New York Times*, November 20, 2016, https://www.nytimes.com/2016/11/21/us/alt-right-salutes-donald-trump.html
9   Jeet Heer, "Ironic Nazis Are Still Nazis," *The New Republic*, November 25, 2016, https://newrepublic.com/article/139004/ironic-nazis-still-nazis
10  Adam Gabbatt, "Hitler Salutes and White Supremacism: A Weekend with the 'Alt-Right,'" *The Guardian*, November 21, 2016, https://www.theguardian.com/world/2016/nov/21/alt-right-conference-richard-spencer-white-nationalists
11  Anglin.
12  Ibid.
13  Heather Suzanne Woods and Leslie A. Hahner, *Make America Meme Again: The Rhetoric of the Alt-Right* (New York: Peter Lang Publishing, 2019), 105.
14  Woods and Hahner, 130.
15  William Merrin, "President Troll: Trump, 4chan and Memetic Warfare," in *Trump's Media War*, eds. Catherine Happer, Andrew Hoskins, and William Merrin (Cham, CH: Palgrave & Macmillan, 2019), 207.
16  Ben Shreckinger, "World War Meme," *Politico*, March/April 2017, https://www.politico.com/magazine/story/2017/03/memes-4chan-trump-supporters-trolls-internet-214856
17  Merrin, 207.
18  Jeremy Diamond, "Trump, the Computer and Email Skeptic-In-Chief," *CNN*, December 30, 2016, https://www.cnn.com/2016/12/29/politics/donald-trump-computers-internet-email/index.html
19  Matthew Haag and Maya Salam, "Gunman in 'Pizzagate' Shooting Is Sentenced to 4 Years in Prison," *The New York Times*, June 22, 2017, https://www.nytimes.com/2017/06/22/us/pizzagate-attack-sentence.html
20  Marc Tuters, Emilija Jokubauskaité, and Daniel Bach, "Post-Truth Protest: How 4chan Cooked Up the Pizzagate Bullshit," *M/C Journal: A Journal of Media and Culture* 21, no. 3 (2018).
21  Shreckinger.
22  Marc Tuters and Sal Hagen, "(((They))) Rule: Memetic Antagonism and Nebulous Othering on 4chan," *New Media & Society* 22, no. 12 (2020): 2223.
23  Ibid.
24  Ibid.
25  Nick Gass, "Trump Jr.: 'I've Never Even Heard of Pepe the Frog,'" *Politico*, September 16, 2016, https://www.politico.com/story/2016/09/donald-trump-jr-pepe-the-frog-228268
26  Olivia Nuzzi, "How Pepe the Frog Became a Nazi Trump Supporter and Alt-Right Symbol," *The Daily Beast*, April 13, 2017, https://www.thedailybeast.com/how-pepe-the-frog-became-a-nazi-trump-supporter-and-alt-right-symbol?ref=scroll

27  Richard Barbrook and Andy Cameron, "The Californian Ideology," *Mute*, September 1, 1995, https://www.metamute.org/editorial/articles/californian-ideology

28  Caitlin Dewey, "The Only Guide to Gamergate You Will Ever Need to Read," *The Washington Post*, October 14, 2014, https://www.washingtonpost.com/news/the-intersect/wp/2014/10/14/the-only-guide-to-gamergate-you-will-ever-need-to-read/

29  Simon Parkin, "Gamergate: A Scandal Erupts in the Video-Game Community," *The New Yorker*, October 17, 2014, https://www.newyorker.com/tech/annals-of-technology/gamergate-scandal-erupts-video-game-community

30  Angela Nagle, *Kill All Normies: The Online Culture Wars from Tumblr and 4chan to the Alt-Right and Trump* (Washington, DC: Zero Books, 2017), 16.

31  Shreckinger.

32  Nick Wingfield, "Feminist Critics of Video Games Facing Threats in 'GamerGate' Campaign," *The New York Times*, October 15, 2014, https://www.nytimes.com/2014/10/16/technology/gamergate-women-video-game-threats-anita-sarkeesian.html

33  Matt Lees, "What Gamergate Should Have Taught Us about the Alt-Right," *The Guardian*, December 1, 2016, https://www.theguardian.com/technology/2016/dec/01/gamergate-alt-right-hate-trump

34  Andrew Marantz, "The Alt-Right Branding War Has Torn the Movement in Two," *The New Yorker*, https://www.newyorker.com/news/news-desk/the-alt-right-branding-war-has-torn-the-movement-in-two

35  Bob Moser, "Why the Alt-Lite Celebrated the Las Vegas Massacre," *The New Republic*, October 6, 2017, https://newrepublic.com/article/145192/alt-lite-celebrated-las-vegas-massacre

36  Martin Belam and Adam Gabbatt, "Proud Boys: Who Are the Far Right Group That Backs Donald Trump?" *The Guardian*, September 30, 2020, https://www.theguardian.com/world/2020/sep/30/proud-boys-who-are-far-right-group-that-backs-donald-trump

37  Virginia Heffernan, "QAnon's Monstrous Conspiracy Theories Fit the Trumpian Moment," *The Los Angeles Times*, September 18, 2020, https://www.latimes.com/opinion/story/2020-09-18/qanon-tom-hanks-blood-libel-protocols-of-the-elders

38  Bulent Kenes, "Boogaloo Bois: Violent Anti-Establishment Extremists in Festive Hawaiian Shirts." *European Center for Populism Studies*, February 2021, https://www.populismstudies.org/wp-content/uploads/2021/03/ECPS-Organisation-Profile-Series-2.pdf

39  Shirin Ghaffery, "Facebook Nears a Tipping Point When It Comes to Moderating Hate Speech," *Vox*, June 30, 2020, https://www.vox.com/recode/2020/6/30/21307529/facebook-hate-speech-boogaloo-ban-moderation-boycott

40  Kenes.

41. Bradley E. Wiggins, "Boogaloo and Civil War 2: Memetic Antagonism in Expressions of Covert Activism," *New Media & Society* (2020): 17.
42. Salvador Hernandez, "This Is How the FBI Says a Network of 'Boogaloo Boys' Sparked Violence and Death," *Buzzfeed News*, October 24, 2020, https://www.buzzfeednews.com/article/salvadorhernandez/boogaloo-bois-network-fbi-violence-extremism
43. Kenes.
44. Ibid.
45. Hatewatch Staff, "Who Are Boogaloos, Who Were Visible at the Capitol and Later Rallies?," *Southern Poverty Law Center*, January 27, 2021, https://www.splcenter.org/hatewatch/2021/01/27/who-are-boogaloos-who-were-visible-capitol-and-later-rallies
46. Hernandez.
47. Michael J. Mooney, "The Boogaloo Bois Prepare for Civil War," *The Atlantic*, January 15, 2021, https://www.theatlantic.com/politics/archive/2021/01/boogaloo-prepare-civil-war/617683/
48. A. C. Thompson, Lila Hassan, and Karim Hajj, "The Boogaloo Bois Have Guns, Criminal Records and Military Training. Now They Want to Overthrow the Government," *ProPublica*, February 1, 2021, https://www.propublica.org/article/boogaloo-bois-military-training
49. Alexandra Minna Stern, *Proud Boys and the White Ethnostate: How the Alt-Right Is Warping the American Imagination* (Boston: Beacon Press, 2019), 71–2.
50. Kathleen Ronayne and Michael Kunzelman, "Trump to Far-Right Extremists: 'Stand Back and Stand By,'" *Associated Press*, September 30, 2020, https://apnews.com/article/election-2020-joe-biden-race-and-ethnicity-donald-trump-chris-wallace-0b32339da25fbc9e8b7c7c7066a1db0f
51. Bulent Kenes, "The Proud Boys: Chauvinist Poster Child of Far-Right Extremism," *European Center for Populism Studies*, February 2021, https://www.populismstudies.org/wp-content/uploads/2021/03/ECPS-Organisation-Profile-Series-1.pdf
52. DeCook, 501.
53. Ibid.
54. Colin Moynihan, "Two Members of Proud Boys Convicted in Brawl Near Republican Club," *The New York Times*, August 19, 2019, https://www.nytimes.com/2019/08/19/nyregion/proud-boys-verdict-trial.html
55. Benjamin Hart and Chaz Danner, "3 Dead and Dozens Injured after Violent White-Nationalist Rally in Virginia," *New York Magazine*, August 13, 2017, https://nymag.com/intelligencer/2017/08/state-of-emergency-in-va-after-white-nationalist-rally.html
56. Cassie Miller, "McInnes, Molyneux, and 4chan: Investigating Pathways to the Alt-Right," *Southern Poverty Law Center*, April 19, 2019, https://www.splcenter.org/20180419/mcinnes-molyneux-and-4chan-investigating-pathways-alt-right

57  "Proud Boys," *Southern Poverty Law Center*, https://www.splcenter.org/fighting-hate/extremist-files/group/proud-boys

58  "Proud Boys Founder Denies Inciting Violence, Responds to whether He Feels Responsible for Groups Behavior," *ABC News*, December 12, 2018, https://abcnews.go.com/US/proud-boys-founder-denies-inciting-violence-responds-feels/story?id=59758209

59  David Ingram, "Facebook Removes Pages Belonging to Far-Right Group 'Proud Boys,'" *NBC News*, October 30, 2018.

60  "President Donald Trump White Sup remecist Group Proud Boys Should "Stand Back and Stand By," *YouTube*, September 30, 2020, https://www.youtube.com/watch?v=JZk6VzSLe4Y

61  David Gilbert, "'Trump Basically Said to Go Fuck Them Up': Here's How the Proud Boys Reacted to Trump's Comments," *Vice*, September 30, 2020, https://www.vice.com/en/article/n7wxxk/trump-basically-said-to-go-fuck-them-up-heres-how-the-proud-boys-reacted-to-trumps-comments

62  Ibid.

63  Ibid.

64  Libby Cathey, Allison Pecorin, Trish Turner, and Katherine Faulders, "Trump Denies Knowing Who 'Proud Boys' Are, Again Declines to Condemn White Supremacy By Name," *ABC News*, September 30, 2020, https://abcnews.go.com/Politics/trump-denies-knowing-proud-boys-declines-condemn-white/story?id=73342275

65  Ben Leonard, "Capitol Police Turned Attention from '200' Proud Boys Gathered on Jan. 6, Lawmaker Said," *Politico*, May 10, 2021, https://www.politico.com/news/2021/05/10/zoe-lofgren-capitol-police-proud-boys-486681

66  Luke Mogelson, "Among the Insurrectionists," *The New Yorker*, January 15, 2021, https://www.newyorker.com/magazine/2021/01/25/among-the-insurrectionists

67  Ibid.

68  Aila Slisco, "Proud Boys Intended to Kill Mike Pence and Nancy Pelosi, FBI Witness Says," *Newsweek*, January 15, 2021, https://www.newsweek.com/proud-boys-intended-kill-mike-pence-nancy-pelosi-fbi-witness-says-1562062

69  Sophia Moskalenko and Clark McCauley, "QAnon: Racical Opinion versus Radical Action," *Perspectives on Terrorism* 15, no. 2 (2021): 142.

70  Clive Thompson, "QAnon Is Like a Game—A Most Dangerous Game," *Wired*, September 22, 2020, https://www.wired.com/story/qanon-most-dangerous-multiplatform-game/

71  Jack Brewster, "Congress Will Get Its Second QAnon Supporter, as Boebert Wins Colorado Seat," *Forbes*, November 4, 2020, https://www.forbes.com/sites/jackbrewster/2020/11/04/congress-will-get-its-second-qanon-supporter-as-boebert-wins-colorado-house-seat/?sh=1664d4ec568f

72  Jason McGahan, "Inside QAnon, the Conspiracy Cult that's Devouring America," *Los Angeles Magazine*, August 17, 2020, https://www.lamag.com/citythinkblog/qanon-gop/

73  Thompson.
74  Amanda Marcotte, "March 4 Was a Dud—but QAnon Will Persist because It Is Fueled by White Entitlement," *Salon*, March 5, 2021, https://www.salon.com/2021/03/05/march-4-was-a-dud–but-qanon-will-persist-because-it-is-fueled-by-white-entitlement/
75  Jaclyn Diaz, "Jacob Chansley, Self-Styled 'QAnon Shaman,' to Stay in Jail Pending Trial," *NPR*, March 9, 2021, https://www.npr.org/2021/03/09/975097124/judge-rejects-qanon-shamans-bid-for-early-release-from-jail
76  Mia Bloom and Sophia Moskaleno, *Pastels and Pedophiles: Inside the Mind of QAnon* (Sanford, CA: Redwood Press, 2021), 41.
77  Shayan Sardarizadeh, "Why Are QAnon Believers Obsessed with March 4?" *BBC News*, March 4, 2021, https://www.bbc.com/news/blogs-trending-56260345
78  Tina Nguyen, "'It Is a Trap': Inside the QAnon Attack That Never Happened," *Politico*, March 7, 2021, https://www.politico.com/news/2021/03/07/qanon-trap-violence-474034
79  Yochai Benkler, Robert Faris, Hal Roberts, and Ethan Zuckerman, "Breitbart-Led Right-Wing Media Ecosystem Altered Broader Media Agenda," *Columbia Journalism Review*, March 3, 2017, https://www.cjr.org/analysis/breitbart-media-trump-harvard-study.php
80  Jessica Roy, "What Is the Alt-Right?: A Refresher Course on Steve Bannon's Fringe Brand of Conservatism," *The Los Angeles Times*, November 14, 2016, https://www.latimes.com/nation/politics/trailguide/la-na-trailguide-updates-201611-htmlstory.html#what-is-the-alt-right-a-refresher-course-on-steve-bannons-fringe-brand-of-conservatism
81  Benkler et al.
82  Ibid.
83  Matthew Brown, "Poll: A Quarter of Americans Say Donald Trump Is "True President" of the US, *USA Today*, May 25, 2021, https://www.usatoday.com/story/news/politics/2021/05/25/poll-quarter-americans-surveyed-say-trump-true-president/7426714002/

# 6

# The Press as "Enemy of the People": A Crisis of Epistemic Authority

In a 2018 tweet, Donald Trump attacked the mainstream media by labeling them "fake news" and an "enemy of the people." He opined: "There is great anger in our Country caused in part by inaccurate, and even fraudulent, reporting of the news. The Fake News Media, the true Enemy of the People, must stop the open & obvious hostility & report the news accurately & fairly. That will do much to put out the flame..."[1] While attacking mainstream journalism has been part of Trump's political strategy since he began running for president, characterizing the press as an "enemy of the people" was chilling for journalists, pundits, and scholars invested in the ideal of normative media practices being a necessary condition for a liberal democracy. According to dominant discourses in journalism and journalism studies, a well-functioning media are necessarily on the side of the public and critical of those in positions of power. In the media's role as the "fourth estate," journalists are charged with serving as "watchdogs" for the people against those working for institutions of power who were wont to abuse their position.

As many populist leaders do, Trump positions himself as the true champion of the people as he rails against journalists and any other forces that challenge his authority. By pitting the media against "the people," Trump constructs a populist dichotomy that positions him on the side of authentic public support and the media as an elitist enemy. Trump's strategy of attacking the mainstream media is particularly effective because it resonates with decades of right-wing talking points about liberal bias in mainstream media. Moreover, journalists have struggled with how to counteract Trump's attacks because the profession of journalism is experiencing a crisis of confidence in the changing landscape of journalism and the epistemological foundations that undergird the profession.

In this chapter, I explain the traditional normative function of the press that journalists and scholars of journalism have endorsed and often taken for granted. From there, I explore the crisis of confidence that the discipline of journalism has undergone as the dominance of print journalism has dwindled and an array of new modes of media production and consumption have emerged. This crisis of confidence among journalists has transpired concomitantly with an increasing distrust in experts throughout the general public—a public trust necessary for journalism to perform its traditional functions. Trump has masterfully exploited the challenge to journalistic epistemological assumptions and the public's loss of faith in institutions for his own gain. For Trump and his supporters, only Trump can serve as an arbiter of truth against those "enemies of truth" that comprise the mainstream media. I conclude by examining potential strategies for countering Trump's hostility toward journalism. Some scholars maintain that returning to the roots of journalistic professionalism is the best strategy, while others worry that doubling down on existing practices is insufficient to counteract a singular threat to the role of media. The fear of those working in journalism and those studying the discipline is that Trump's consistent attacks on an institution that many believe is a keystone of a functioning democracy will ultimately be the downfall of liberal democracy in the United States.

## Journalistic Norms, Epistemic Authority, and Liberal Democracy

While the practice of journalism in some form has existed at least since the development of the printing press, the version of journalism that came to be synonymous with the mainstream press in the United States has its roots in the twentieth century. Specifically, a set of practices and institutions brought about a "professionalization" of journalism, which had previously been predominantly a working-class occupation. Sociologist and historian of journalism Michael Schudson explains that "only in the twentieth century did journalism's growing occupational self-consciousness acquire elements of a professional pride and a set of moral rules or patterns about what a reporter should do—in relation to accuracy, fairness, neutrality or what would be called by the 1920s 'objectivity.'"[2] The set of rules governing what a reporter "should" do solidified through a set of norms, which were developed and inculcated through journalism schools that began to emerge at the beginning of the twentieth century.

In their *Normative Theories of the Media*, Clifford Christians et al. outline a distinction between a set of media practices that have become the norm and a set of cultural ideals to which journalists should aspire. They assert that

> the role of media, or of journalists working within the media, has a component that describes journalistic tasks or practices and another dimension that refers to their larger purposes and obligations. Because a free press in a democratic society cannot be compelled to follow any particular purpose, the normative element in media roles is often a matter of choice, often reinforced by custom and the force of social ties.[3]

For Christians et al., by adhering to a set of established rules and practices, journalists can avoid having to consistently reflect upon the ways in which those customs contribute to a democratic society. By dint of journalists following the rules, the norms established by a set of practices should result in journalism that promotes democratic practices.

Media scholar Mats Extröm shows the ways in which those particular customs and practices that structure normative journalism work to produce "knowledge claims," which for him constitute the epistemology of journalism and work to validate its existence and promote its importance. He holds that epistemology "refers to the rules, routines and institutionalized procedures that operate within a social setting and decide the form of the knowledge produced and the knowledge claims expressed (or implied)."[4] Further, "the legitimacy of journalism is intimately bound up with claims to knowledge and truth."[5] These norms situate journalists as authorities in the production of truth. Journalism scholars Matt Carlson, Sue Robinson, and Seth Lewis argue that this epistemic authority 'is not guaranteed. It is the product of ongoing legitimation strategies meant to establish, maintain, or repair the status of journalism in the face of contestation... epistemic contests are conflicts over what truthful accounts ought to look like and who ought to create them."[6] For many years in the middle of the twentieth century, most of the public trusted mainstream journalistic media and acknowledged the epistemic authority that normative journalistic practices espouse.

Perhaps the apotheosis of the general public's acceptance of journalists' epistemic authority occurred in the wake of the Watergate scandal and the diligent reporting that led to the resignation of a president. Journalist Margaret Sullivan cites the *Washington Post's* coverage of Watergate as well as *The New York Times* publishing of the Pentagon papers in the early 1970s as the halcyon days of trust in journalism—a period when "the public clearly believed that the press represented their interests and worked on citizens' behalf to get the truth out."[7] Myriad factors during the last forty years—the rise of cable news, the decline of print journalism, the proliferation of social media, and a broad distrust in institutions—have led to low levels of trust in journalistic media and an erosion of epistemic authority.

While not the sole cause of this decline in the epistemic authority of journalistic media, Donald Trump has certainly exacerbated the problem. By insisting on identifying himself as a fount of knowledge and truth, Trump widened the chasm between the knowledge claims of the media and their authority as authenticators of truth. Carlson, Robinson, and Lewis contend that Trump's demagogic characteristics work to explain the ways in which he challenges journalistic practices by refusing to acknowledge their epistemic authority. For them, demagogues "base their authority on a unique ability to lead.... Traditional journalistic modes—the neutral, objective style of the standard model of news that dominates the journalistic imaginary—are not well equipped to confront the excesses of demagoguery."[8] The epistemic authority of journalists relies upon their commitment to procedures and practices that comprise journalistic norms. Donald Trump refuses to acknowledge or abide journalistic norms and consequently works to further erode the trust in the institution of journalism upon which its epistemic authority rests.

*New York Times* journalist Emily Bazelon worries that Donald Trump accelerated the ongoing deterioration of norms, both presidential and journalistic, which has consequently had deleterious effects on democracy in the United States. She holds that "norms are entirely up to us—they exist only as long as there's a consensus, even unspoken, to preserve them. Such consensus is probably as important as law to the functioning of a democracy."[9] By refusing to acknowledge these norms, Trump showcases a design flaw in liberal democracy; because they are not laws, Trump can ignore norms and face no legal repercussions. Journalism scholar Robert Gutsche troubles the assumption that journalistic norms work in the service of the public; rather, for him those norms work to reinforce existing structures of power. He holds that

> news media maintain a list of approved behaviors for society and present those lists through coverage that is designed to maintain order. News that dictates compliance to dominant ideology polices society and its members as a means to record patterns of misbehavior and ideological mismanagement for the sole purpose of instituting discipline that will bring society back in-line with the status quo.[10]

Gutsche's schema creates a quandary for journalists. On the one hand, dominant discourses about the role of Anglo-American journalistic norms assert that those norms work to strengthen the discipline of journalism and subsequently contribute to a robust democracy. On the other hand, rigid adherence to norms works to reinforce dominant ideologies about power that are potentially antithetical to democracy. By disregarding journalistic and presidential norms, Trump shows that those ideological norms are reinforced hegemonically through consensus. However, he does not have democracy in mind when he refuses to abide those norms; rather, he defies journalistic norms in order to promote populist demagoguery. Trump uses the dissolution of journalistic authority to position himself as an enemy of journalism and consequently as the one true source of epistemic authority.

## The Conservative Assault on the "Liberal Media"

According to a familiar narrative about the importance of journalism in US democracy, the zenith of journalistic authority occurred in the wake of the Watergate scandal and Nixon's subsequent resignation. Perhaps unsurprisingly, Nixon pioneered a political strategy that involved denigrating the media, particularly its "left-wing" leanings. Nixon took a decidedly combative relationship with the media—in fact, he was the first president to refer to reporters as "the media" rather than "the press," because he thought that the former sounded "more ominous."[11] Journalist Jon Marshall maintains that "Nixon's way of handling the press has prevailed in American politics. Intimidating journalists, avoiding White House reporters, staging events for television—now common presidential practices—were all originally Nixonian tactics."[12] Nixon often used Vice President Spiro Agnew as a surrogate in attacking the news media.

After the Nixon administration disagreed with the media's reaction to his famous 1969 "silent majority" speech, Agnew went on the offensive. He complained that after the speech, Nixon's "words and policies were subjected to instant analysis and querulous criticism. The audience of 70 million Americans gathered to hear the President of the United States was inherited by a small band of network commentators and self-appointed analysts, the majority of whom expressed in one way or another their hostility to what he had to say."[13] Here, Agnew pits an elitist media against a populist mass that has inherently different interests than the president. Through this dichotomy, Agnew positions the "70 million Americans" as agentic listeners who should "make up their own minds and form their own opinions about a Presidential address without having the President's words and thoughts characterized through the prejudices of hostile critics before they can even be digested."[14] In their deployment of a schism between everyday voters and "hostile critics" of the president, Nixon and Agnew are forging the foundation upon which fifty years of conservative attacks on the media have thrived.

The rise of talk radio in the 1990s and of Fox News in the 2000s provided mainstream media outlets that could position "everyday Americans" against the mainstream media. Fox News advertised itself as "fair and balanced" news and implemented the tagline: "We Report. You Decide." Both of these slogans imply that other networks' journalism is neither fair nor balanced; subsequently, mainstream news viewers are unable to make the crucial decisions about politics that Fox News empowers them to make. Communication scholar Prashanth Bhat contends that "this right-leaning channel cemented the notion of liberal bias among Republican voters leading to a steady decline of their trust in news media."[15] By the time Trump emerged onto the political scene, the idea that mainstream media had a liberal bias and that its reporters were part of a liberal elite was deeply engrained in dominant political discourse.

Vice-presidential candidate of 2008 Sarah Palin popularized a memorable, albeit ableist, riff on the notion of the mainstream media by referring to them as the "lamestream media."[16] Palin also trumpeted the notion of a "real America"— an idealistic, rural, white version of the United States. She embraced "real America's" authenticity in relation to liberal coastal elites, which, of course, included members of the "lamestream media." During the 2008 campaign, Palin claimed that "the best of America is in these small towns that we get to visit, and in these wonderful little pockets of what I call the real America, being here with all of you hardworking, very patriotic, um, very, um, pro-America areas of this great nation."[17] By characterizing certain swaths of the country as "real," Palin creates a Manichean divide between an authentic populace and those who are not "real" Americans. In her vision, members of the media are not real Americans; consequently, her dismissal of journalists and their profession is not only acceptable but also, in fact, laudable.

The term "lamestream media" has become a common epithet in right-wing discourses, and Donald Trump unsurprisingly embraced the term. In the midst of the spate of protests that erupted in 2020 in reaction to George Floyd being murdered by a Minneapolis police officer, Donald Trump deployed the term "lamestream media" and referred to journalists in a tweet as "truly bad people with a sick agenda" in response to police officers targeting members of the media with violence.[18] When mainstream news media—as well as Fox News—called the 2020 election in favor of Joe Biden, Trump tweeted: "Since when does the Lamestream Media call who our next president will be? We have all learned a lot in the last two weeks!"[19] While their reporting does not affect election results, journalists "calling" results is nothing new. Moreover, newsrooms began to employ greater methodological rigor in deciding when an election has been "called" after every major television station called the

2000 presidential election too early and/or incorrectly. Nevertheless, Trump implicates the media as co-conspirators in the delusional conspiracy about a stolen election that he concocted after the 2020 election. The process of division in which Trump characterizes media that do not promote his agenda as "fake" situates members of those fake media institutions as fake Americans who are his enemies rather than his opponents. By imagining himself as a synecdoche of the authentic public, Trump positions those fake Americans and fake media not just as enemies to him but as "enemies of the people."

## The Deterioration of Trust in Institutions of Power

In his 2012 book *Twilight of the Elites*, MSNBC journalist and media pundit Chris Hayes outlines a series of failures by dominant institutions that eroded the public trust in those institutions and indeed in powerful institutions more broadly. He points to the failure to elect a clear leader in the 2000 election, the collapse of Enron followed by the 2008 financial crisis, the sexual assault scandals that marred the Catholic Church and Penn State football, and the utter failure of the Iraq War as examples of previously revered institutions whose downfall has led to a loss of public trust. For Hayes, 'the cumulative effect of these scandals and failures is an inescapable national mood of exhaustion, frustration, and betrayal."[20] Further, for a complex society such as the United States in the twentieth century to properly function, its members must have some degree of faith that the folks in charge, that is, experts, know what they are doing. People must trust that the engineers who construct a bridge do so correctly, that the scientists who make vaccines are working in their best interest, and that the bureaucrats and volunteers who oversee democratic elections from the local level to the federal level are acting in good faith. Hayes explains:

> we do not trust our institutions because they have shown themselves to be untrustworthy. The drumbeat of institutional failure echoes among the populace as skepticism. And given both the scope and the depth of this distrust, it's clear that we're in the midst of something far grander and more perilous than just a crisis of government or a crisis in capitalism. We are in the midst of a broad and devastating crisis of authority.[21]

This crisis of authority that Hayes identifies includes a crisis of epistemic authority; it raises the question of how people come to know things if they no longer trust the institutions that have traditionally provided authoritative knowledge.

Writing in the same year as Hayes, communication scholar Zvi Reich concurs, identifying "the general decline in trust in expertise—and in journalism expertise in particular."[22] Trump takes advantage of this distrust by dismissing mainstream media—who according to professional journalistic norms should be a source of authority—and using the lack of trust in media to stand in for a distrust in authority more broadly. Trumpism suggests that if people do not trust the media, then they should similarly be wary of other institutions promising to serve as figures of authority and truth. To paraphrase Groucho Marx, Trump's supporters only need to believe him, not their lying eyes, which were already skeptical of receiving authoritative information from mainstream media. Though Hayes was writing three years before Trump declared his candidacy, the national mood of exhaustion and frustration remains in the wake of the Trump presidency; if anything, those feelings have been exacerbated. Trump was deftly able to exploit the distrust of authority and institutions that Hayes outlines.

One place in which Trump was able to exploit the public's distrust of authority is by questioning the validity of professional journalism. Communication scholars Zvi Reich and Hagar Lahav contend that journalistic expertise is complicated because journalists are "knowledge brokers."[23] In other words, they must learn the expertise of other professionals and serve as mediators between those with specialized expertise and a broader public who might not be familiar with a particular subject on which a journalist is reporting. For Reich and Lahav, "to carry out their roles, these brokers must develop proficiency not only in mediating knowledge (e.g., reporting, teaching, stock market analysis) but also in the mediated subject matter as well (e.g., physics, medicine, or finance)."[24] Because journalists are not necessarily experts themselves but rather are second-hand facilitators of information, their epistemic authority is inherently tenuous. A good journalist might understand that climate change is an important vital issue, but they most likely do not have the familiarity with physics, chemistry, or climatological methodologies that climate change scholars possess. In order to mask their inevitable lack of expertise in the areas they are reporting, reporters rely upon employing multiple sources that offer layers of support, complexity, and nuance. However, because the reporters are not experts in the area they are reporting, they often refrain from inserting themselves into the story and are reluctant to take a stance that might position them on one side of a controversy.

The journalist norm in which reporters refuse to take a position becomes problematic when those taking a controversial position do not act in good faith or employ a different epistemological framework than traditional journalists.

The ostensible controversies surrounding global climate change and vaccine science are two instances in which traditional journalistic norms have been unsuccessful in tackling serious problems. The aforementioned notion that mainstream media have a liberal bias is deeply pervasive in dominant discourses about media and politics. In "What Liberal Media?," journalist Eric Alterman states that "the myth of the 'liberal media' empowers conservatives to control debate in the United States to the point where liberals cannot even hope for a fair shake anymore." Because the quest for unbiased reporting—however Quixotic that quest may be—is indeed an entrenched norm of journalistic practice, reporters are keenly aware of the perception of its liberal bias and actively struggle to avoid those accusations.

Chuck Todd, the host of *Meet the Press* (1947–), a bedrock institution of mainstream television journalism, admits that journalists have internalized the notion that media are liberal and have consciously moved journalism rightward to avoid that claim. He laments that "we should have fought back better in the mainstream media. We shouldn't [have] accepted the premise that there was liberal bias. We should have defended.... We ended up in this both-sides trope."[25] He goes on to assert that "mainstream media overcorrected. And we bought into the Fox motto of 'balance.'"[26] By internalizing discourses that insist the mainstream media have liberal biases, journalists moved the Overton window rightward.

The journalistic strategy of providing balance to controversial issues provides cover against accusations of bias. Philosophers Natasha Rietdijk and Alfred Archer outline the concept of "false balance" as an institutional norm employed by journalists that works to undermine the notion of expertise. They examine the practice wherein journalists present the views of an expert and "balance" those views with those of a layperson, subsequently suggesting that both views are equally worthy of consideration. They provide the example of the anti-vaccine movement in which journalists often "balance" expert opinions about the importance of vaccines against celebrities who believe that vaccines lead to autism—a view thoroughly refuted by the scientific community. Rietdijic and Archer maintain that "reporting on the views of non-experts in this way runs the risk of sending the message that the views of non-experts should be paid the same amount of attention as those of experts."[27] For them, the consequences of this are that "it obscures the notion of epistemic authority itself. It muddies the epistemic model, misrepresenting who is an expert and for what reasons."[28] Rietdijic and Archer also show that journalists sometimes "balance" expert opinion with the aggregate beliefs of the general public—a public without the resources to have a credible opinion about an issue. They point to an instance in which journalists have often balanced the claims of experts on global warming with a prevalent belief by a sizable portion of the populace that global warming is a hoax.[29] The practice of juxtaposing the ideas of scientific experts against widely held beliefs legitimizes populist sentiment as an appropriate source of expertise. By refusing to explain which side is correct, journalists cede epistemic authority to "the people," and demagogues such as Donald Trump can seize upon the populist authority and use it to their political advantage.

Another way that journalists attempt to maintain neutrality through professional norms is by purporting to give "both sides" of an issue equal weight. The "both-sides trope," which Chuck Todd refers to in the above quote, allows for journalists to see both sides of any controversy as equal, even when evidence does not support that equivalence. The scientists and the doctors who warn about the impending dangers of climate change or vociferously argue that vaccines save lives do not simply represent "one side" of the controversy. Rather, one "side" of those debates is simply incorrect—climate change is occurring, and vaccines work to eradicate or control communicative diseases. Think-tank scholar Brynn Tannehill argues that the logic of "both-sideism" encourages media outlets to "feel obligated to present both sides in situations where truth has only one face."[30] For her, "both-sideism not only makes things worse by further obscuring truth, but it widens the Overton Window a bit further each time, eventually making political positions that would have been unthinkable a few years ago part of the mainstream conversation."[31] By refusing to claim which side is "right," mainstream journalists not only cede their epistemic authority and create an ambiguous epistemological terrain in which contrived controversies continue to circulate but also open up discourse to extreme political positions under the auspices of balance. If the media are biased toward anything, they are biased toward controversy, which invigorates consumers of media and encourages them to continue to engage the media.

Writing specifically about television media, political scientist Diana Mutz maintains that contemporary media are increasingly driven by an "in-your-face" politics characterized by "considerable (if not incessant) political disagreement, and the opinion holders we see and hear are often chosen specifically as examples of extremely divergent, highly polarized positions."[32] Because media are invested in providing a space for cacophonous debate, their bias leans toward disagreement, provocation, and scintillating takes; however, these values are not necessarily amenable to an epistemology that promotes a healthy civil society. As someone who enthusiastically embraces provocation and "in-your-face" politics, Trump emerges as a figure of epistemic authority not because his ideas are the most correct or compelling but because they are the most shocking and divisive.

## Distrust in Media and Conservative Anti-Intellectualism

Before Trump's political ascendance, journalistic institutions that he describes as the "fake news media" were already a source of considerable distrust. Trump luxuriates in the myriad distrusting and anti-intellectual discourses that already circulated about public institutions and the establishment media before his entrance into the political arena. Journalism studies scholar Nikki Usher outlines the importance of trust in journalism's ostensible goal of serving the public good. She asserts that "if news consumers don't trust professional journalism, journalists can't properly act as watchdogs or as conveners of shared experiences."[33] Further, a loss of trust between journalists and their audiences can have deleterious effects as "greater media cynicism and media skepticism have been shown to lead consumption of non-mainstream sources and to undermine journalists' efforts at public service."[34] In her schema, if consumers do not trust mainstream media, they will seek out other sources that are less reliable and more amenable to positions that are beyond the Overton window of mainstream journalism and mainstream politics. The norms and unwritten rules that undergird mainstream journalism, politics, and indeed liberal democracy bend toward the status quo. Journalists and politicians have enjoyed tremendous power by maintaining a symbiotic relationship, and those who question long-standing norms are inherently dangerous to their sustained power. When those institutions lose the trust of the people for whom they ostensibly work, many will turn to alternative journalists and politicians with whom they can develop a more trusting relationship—even if those journalists and politicians are selling the public a bill of goods.

Journalism historian Michael Schudson advocates for trust in experts as a necessary condition in a healthy democracy. For him, experts are important because they are able to "speak truth to power" and they "can clarify the grounds of public debate and so improve the capacity of both legislators and the general public to engage effectively in democratic decision-making."[35] Further, they are able to "diagnose opportunity and diagnose injustice," which "empowers the general public that might be perfectly capable of discerning a problem or trouble without being qualified to translate that general trouble into a legislatively or administratively decidable."[36] In other words, if democracy is built upon the assumption that "the people" should be involved with making important policy decisions, they should be accurately informed by entities that are not invested in maintaining their own power. Schudson notes that "none of us is well enough informed to make judgements about every important issue before the public."[37] For example, the average voter may not have enough knowledge of macroeconomics to ascertain whether the Federal Reserve should raise or lower interest rates; thus, the role of the expert should be to translate the meaning of complex economic issues into language that can empower a well-informed public to make a choice. While this idea is, of course, idealistic, the basic premise that voters should be informed about the candidates and their issues before making a choice at the ballot box is a prevalent theme in narratives about how a healthy democracy should function.

Conservatives have been successful in mobilizing their disdain for expertise politically. In *The Death of Expertise*, international affairs scholar Tom Nichols addresses the anger in people's distaste for experts, contending that "we do not have a healthy skepticism about experts; instead, we actively resent them, with many people assuming that experts are wrong simply by virtue of being experts."[38] In the 1960s, historian Richard Hofstadter famously outlined an anti-intellectual trend in conservative politics. He isolates a particularly American trend that characterizes intellectuals as "pretentious, conceited, effeminate, and snobbish; and very likely immoral, dangerous, and subversive."[39] In contrast, those who view intellectuals in this way prefer the "plain sense of the common man," which to those invested in anti-intellectualism is "an altogether adequate substitute for, if not actually much superior to, formal knowledge and expertise acquired in schools."[40] Politically, an anti-intellectual sensibility has become a trait that voters, particularly conservatives, value in a candidate.

As president, George W. Bush embodied the anti-intellectual sensibility. Many pundits suggested that he won the 2000 and 2004 elections over Al Gore and John Kerry because he was the type of guy people "wanted to have a beer with," whereas Gore and Kerry were overly stiff, wonky, and indeed intellectual. Journalist Seth Stevenson explains this dominant frame in which "uptight Al Gore and pinot-sipping John Kerry just weren't desirable barstool neighbors, the now-cemented conventional wisdom holds, while Bush could sell himself as someone whom you'd like to sip a Coors adjacent to."[41] Many conservatives admired Bush because he was "just like us" in that he did not present himself as having any expertise gained from his Ivy League education. Bush's self-proclaimed decision-making style accentuated his anti-intellectual bona fides as he described himself as a "gut player" rather than one who overthinks a situation.[42] David Frum, Bush's own speech writer, describes the president as "often uncurious and as a result ill informed, more conventional in his thinking than a leader probably should be."[43] Bush's anti-intellectual qualities left him vulnerable to critiques by members of the media who often characterized him as stupid.

Donald Trump builds upon the fantasy in which people desire to have a beer with their political heroes—though like Bush, Trump is Ivy League educated and a teetotaler. Writing in the run-up to the 2016 election, journalist Seth Stevenson opines that "for a certain swath of voters, there has never been and perhaps never will be a candidate you'd be more eager to have a beer with than Donald Trump."[44] Writing at a similar point in time, journalist Phillip Elliott contrasts Trump's "shoot from the hip" style in which he "trusts his gut" to Hillary Clinton's ethos as a "thoughtful, cautious leader."[45] These journalists frame Trump as a new version of George W. Bush—Bush 2.0. However, Trump takes the anti-intellectual discourse that characterizes Bush to a new level as he asserts himself as an extraordinarily intelligent person who is an expert at nearly everything. Trump famously quipped on Twitter that he was "like, really smart," and then escalated his boast by asserting that he "would qualify as not smart, but genius."[46] Unlike Bush, Trump does not just claim that he makes decisions as leader based on his "gut"; instead, he positions himself as an expert of all things.

An example of Trump's extraordinary confidence in his own intelligence occurred at the beginning of the Covid-19 pandemic when Trump met with epidemiologists from the Centers for Disease Control and Prevention. After his meeting, Trump addressed the media and proclaimed that after the short interaction that he had with the experts, he was now indeed an expert about the situation. Trump bragged: "People are really surprised I understand this stuff. Every one of these doctors said, 'How do you know so much about this?' Maybe I have a natural ability."[47] When a reporter tried to ask a follow-up question, directed to Trump's Secretary of Health and Human Services Alex Azar, "Trump, without looking at Azar, raised his right hand and waved him off."[48] Despite Azar being an expert in the field, Trump felt that after his short meeting with the Centers for Disease Control (CDC), he was better suited to answer a question about the forthcoming pandemic than Azar.

Unlike Bush, who often dismissed the idea of intellectual expertise altogether by relying on his instincts, Trump imbues himself with a superhuman ability to absorb information and transform himself immediately into an expert. On another occasion, when the hosts of *Morning Joe* (2007–) asked Trump who was advising him about foreign policy in advance of the 2016 debate, Trump named himself, stating, "I'm speaking with myself, number one, because I have a very good brain and I've said a lot of things... my primary consultant is myself and I have a good instinct for this stuff."[49] Trump challenges the epistemic authority of experts and positions himself as the sole arbiter of truth.

Journalism scholars Michael McDevitt and Patrick Ferrucci maintain that the populist inclination of journalists to provide a voice for "the people" undermines journalists' expertise, which is a necessary condition for them to successfully function in the aid of democracy. They maintain that "populist anti-elitism is rationalized (so to speak) in journalism's view of itself as tribune of the people... The demos is portrayed as holding intellect accountable, and journalism's complicity remains muddled in an imagined public."[50] For McDevitt and Ferrucci, the tension between journalists' conflicting desires to be experts and populists destabilizes the authority of journalism. They contend that "a disregard for intellect, experts, and expertise is... antithetical to journalism's understanding of its contribution to an informed electorate," and they maintain a distinction between the "emotions" of the public and the rationality of "reasoned-based reporting."[51] In their schema, by providing a voice to the emotional populace that competes with the rational expert, they create the conditions in which a politician like Trump can thrive, as he maintains his popularity by arousing the emotions of the people.

## Populism and Anti-Intellectualism

The anti-intellectual qualities that characterize or caricaturize politicians such as George W. Bush, Sarah Palin, and Donald Trump leave them ripe for criticism by the mainstream media. However, they also provide an opportunity for them to make a populist appeal by critiquing those liberal elites and members of the "lamestream media" who supposedly look down upon "real Americans." In the 1952 and 1956 presidential elections, Adlai Stevenson lost to Dwight Eisenhower, and pundits maintained that Stevenson lost because he was an "egghead," who was overly intellectual, especially in comparison to Eisenhower, the decorated war hero. While it has fallen somewhat out of use, "egghead" is a derisive term for an overly educated person; the moniker stuck to Stevenson because journalists considered him to be aloof. According to journalist Kevin Mattson, the nickname resonated by "solidifying the perception that the candidate was too intellectual to connect to ordinary Americans."[52] Being perceived as an egghead has been a detriment to political ambitions since.

As a vice-presidential candidate for Eisenhower, Richard Nixon contributed to the perception that Stevenson was overly intellectual. Nearly two decades later, when Nixon was president, he often deployed Vice President Agnew to attack the liberal elite. Agnew opined that "in the United States today, we have more than our share of the nattering nabobs of negativism."[53] He understood that the media would find themselves implicated in the attack and would subsequently report it. According to historian Rick Perlstein, "Agnew knew that the scribes would write about it, if only to mock him. That was good; let the elites mock patriotism."[54] The practice of demonizing elitist intellectuals has been a feature of Republican campaigns since Agnew dropped his famous quote. Ronald Reagan deployed the strategy against Jimmy Carter and Walter Mondale, and George W. Bush, the product of two Ivy League universities, sold himself as a "man of the people" in his campaigns against two eggheads—Al Gore and John Kerry.

In the anti-egghead model, true patriotic Americans are averse to too much education and "book learning" and politicians are subsequently careful not to seem "out of touch" with everyday Americans. These so-called everyday Americans ostensibly maintain a deep distrust in the institution of academia and have come to associate mainstream journalism with these educated elite. In 2009, Rush Limbaugh lumped several institutions together, citing "corruption that exists between government and academia and science and the media," which he identified as the "Four Corners of Deceit."[55] This provides room for epistemic authority to emerge in new spaces.

In the contemporary media environment, these new spaces include cable news channels that cater to tastes of these everyday Americans, conspiratorial radio hosts such as Alex Jones who appeals to cultural fears and anxiety, and podcast hosts such as Joe Rogan, who markets himself as an intellectual for the everyman. Journalist Justin Peters snarkily describes *The Joe Rogan Experience* (2009–) as "one of the most popular podcasts in the world, where shaky premises inevitably lead to sweeping conclusions, where there's always time for endless discussions of truly exasperating ideas, and where the worst thing that you can do is not give a white guy a second chance."[56] Rogan serves as a vox populi and provides a platform for populist discourses to emerge and circulate.

Sociologist Ronald Jacobs contends that before the 2016 election, mainstream media aligned against Donald Trump because they understood that he posed a threat to establishment institutions, which included the mainstream media. He maintains that "when reporters and columnists finally realized that Trump was a formidable and serious candidate, they mobilized against him, in a manner that violated normative principles of journalistic detachment and that reinforced conservative narratives of mainstream press bias and undermined the legitimacy of the press itself."[57] In his schema, because the media positioned themselves against Trump, he was able to amplify an already existing populist sentiment that was sceptical of or hostile to mainstream journalism. Within the populist framework, the media are the enemy in a Manichean struggle between good and evil. Jacobs continues by arguing that populist discourses help "to mobilize large masses of people against traditional political leaders and traditional forms of expertise, and it encourages them to dismiss elite criticisms of populist leaders."[58] In other words, these populist discourses work to situate mainstream media as enemies of the people.

The term "enemy of the people" evokes totalitarian regimes that sought to quell all journalism besides that which the government produces or journalists who parrot the dominant discourses of that government. Journalist Emma Graham-Harrison explains that the term "became well known in the 20th century when it was adopted by dictators from Stalin to Mao, and Nazi propagandists, to justify their murderous purges of millions."[59] Trump's populist tendencies position him as a synecdoche for "the people"; as such, any attacks on Trump become attacks on "the people" and consequently on the "real Americans" who constitute that group. Carlson, Robinson, and Lewis claim that Trump "shifts attention away from himself as an individual being victimized by the news media to instead situate the press as an implacable foe of the country as a whole—indeed *the* 'enemy of the American people.'"[60] They go further and argue that this type of Manichean distinction justifies potential violence because it constructs political disagreement in martial terms. "Identifying the press as an enemy justifies all sorts of retribution against journalists. It uses the language of war, and places the press against the rest of the population."[61] By denigrating mainstream media as "enemies of the people," Trump aligns himself with monstrous historical authoritarians and amplifies the anti-democratic potential of populist anger.

## Strategies for Journalists in the Trump and Post-Trump Era

Trump's refusal to adhere to the norms of the presidency is deeply imbricated with the assemblage of right-wing media platforms that do not adhere to the norms of professional journalism in a liberal democracy. Emily Bazelon argues that "the conservative and far-right media are eroding the norms of the fourth estate to aid Trump in eroding the norms of the presidency."[62] Writing over three years before Trump refused to concede the election and the insurgency at the Capitol building on January 6, 2021, Bazelon worries that it "seems like an act of collective faith that our norms of government—including the most precious ones—will hold at all."[63] Her worries proved to be prescient as the most essential norm of electoral democracy—the peaceful exchange of power—was pushed to its limit. Journalists and scholars of journalism are mostly united in believing that the professional norms of journalism that provided a procedural framework during the century preceding Donald Trump's ascension to power are in crisis. However, they disagree as to what the path forward for collective journalists should be.

Historian Gregory Shaya explains that "the faith in the press as the guardian of truth, the watchdog of power, the foundation of democracy—in brief, the fourth estate—lies at the heart of the liberal imagination of the west. It is the principle enshrined in the First Amendment, nestled in between freedom of religion and the freedom of assembly."[64] Although writing in the 2000s, Shaya was already questioning the value of treating the press as a reliable watchdog. He positions the so-called fourth estate as a myth—not a myth in the sense of it being necessarily false but rather as a story that is "selective and obscuring, a sacred story that embodies higher values and ignores so much in the history of the modern world."[65] For him, the function of journalism should be simply to observe and report; journalists should "stand as witness to the unfolding of events and to tell it like it is"[66] By insisting upon a "just the facts" model of journalism, Shay dismisses the "watchdog" model for journalists and seeks to distance the press from any ethical responsibilities beyond maintaining a dogged commitment to the invaluable nature of objective facts.

Many journalists seem eager to double down on those norms and processes that peaked in the 1970s when journalism was able to upend a presidency and end an unpopular war. Carlson, Robinson, and Lewis aver that when journalistic authority comes under attack, journalists often default to the professional norms of objectivity and balance from which they believe they derive their authority. They state that "feeling untrusted, journalists tell us they fall back to norms and routines of the standard model of journalism to distinguish themselves and to preserve the sense of authority they have spent more than a century cultivating, brandishing objectivity as their main weapon."[67] Journalists have endorsed several ways to reaffirm the commitment to norms as a way to position themselves as the standard bearers of authentic news, rather than the pernicious "fake news."

One of the ways that journalists have countered accusations of "fake news" and reinforced their commitment to normative journalistic practices is by creating "fact-checking" institutions that work to certify the validity of claims made by politicians and journalists. The contemporary practice of fact-checking emerged in the first decade of the twenty-first century in both paper and online journalistic platforms.[68] Perhaps the most famous of these fact-checking organizations is PolitiFact, run by the Poynter Institute, which ranks statements on a truth-o-meter, deeming them to be true, mostly true, half true, mostly false, false, or "pants on fire." For example, as of December 2021, Donald Trump had been fact-checked 943 times; 348 of those had resulted in a "false" claim, while 167 earned a "pants on fire." In fact, Trump produced PolitiFact's "lie of the year" five of the six years between 2015 and 2020.

Jane Singer explains the difference between traditional journalistic practices and fact-checking: "Although both fact-checkers and journalists value truthfulness, journalists tend to focus on accurately reporting what was said, while fact-checkers are more interested in judging the veracity of the statement."[69] For journalism scholar Lucas Graves, the practice of fact-checking reflects a new style of journalism. In his account, "a group of journalists [invented] a new style of political news, one that seeks to revitalize the 'truth-seeking' tradition in journalism by holding public figures to account for the things they say."[70] In his schema, the practice of fact-checking does not comport with the journalistic norm of objectivity because it refuses to take politicians at their word, which leads them to "take sides" in a way that is antithetical to traditional journalistic norms. He suggests that fact-checking is not a corrective to journalistic practices run amok; instead, "fact-checkers are the product of the same fractured and fragmented media world they seek to repair. Their work shows every day how the facts in political life depend on institutional knowledge-building regimes and how difficult public reasoning becomes when those regimes lose authority."[71] In a media environment in which epistemic authority is up for grabs, fact-checkers assert themselves as a foundation for such authority.

Journalism scholar Michelle Amazeen similarly suggests that fact-checking is filling a void left by the disruption of journalistic epistemic authority. She holds that "fact-checking may be understood as a democracy-building tool that emerges where democratic institutions are perceived to be weak or are under threat."[72] For Amazeen, the practice of fact-checking comes about when foundations of liberal democracy are weak. If traditional journalism is one of those institutions undergirding a weakening liberal democracy, then fact-checking ostensibly provides a corrective. Singer explains that "fact-checkers, then, believe they fill the normative role of providing the kind of civically important, trustworthy information that legacy news outlets should be providing but, in their view, largely are not."[73] The practice of fact-checking aligns with the journalistic ideal of providing a "watchdog" service for the public or serving as a "fourth estate" by providing an additional place for "checks and balances" to transpire, limiting the powers of government in a republican democracy.

Though writing three years before the election of Donald Trump, political scientists Joseph Uscinski and Ryden Butler offer a harsh critique of fact-checking as a journalistic practice. They argue that "fact checkers often attempt to check statements that are not facts and cannot be verified as true or false. In other instances, the typical tools of journalism available to most fact checkers are not adequate for investigating the statements in question."[74] In their estimation, fact-checking offers to locate the "real truth" beneath the layers of spin that characterize political discourse, but the practice does not deliver on its promise. For them, political discourse is inherently ambiguous, so any attempt to bring clarity to bear on the discourse will produce misleading results.

Uscinski and Butler are critical not only of the practice of fact-checking but also of the entire profession of journalism and its institutional norms. They contend that

> in reality, the meaning of political talk is sometimes opaque and interpretation is in the eye of the beholder. This ambiguity, however, never seems to make fact checkers question the adequacy of their implicit epistemology. This may be due to the fact that fact checking is conducted by journalists, and journalism is inherently selective and, arguably, naïve in reporting "the facts."[75]

If the journalistic practice of searching to identify "the facts" is inherently problematic, perhaps journalists can provide more useful functions in a Trumpist media environment.

One of the journalistic functions that journalists and scholars tout about the profession is the press's ability to provide a "watchdog function" and protect against governmental abuses of power in its role as the "fourth estate." Writing for *The New York Times* in the aftermath of Trump clinching the Republican primaries, media pundit Nicholas Kristof asserts that "despite some outstanding coverage of Trump, on the whole we in the media empowered a demagogue and failed the country. We were lap dogs, not watchdogs."[76] Several months later, after Trump won the general election, Kyle Pope, writing for the *Columbia Journalism Review*, proclaimed that the election of Donald Trump reflected an "anti-Watergate" moment for journalists.[77] In his lament, he challenges journalism to return to its "oppositional roots" and "embrace, even relish, our legacy as malcontents and troublemakers, people who are willing to say the thing that makes everyone else uncomfortable."[78] For Kristof and Pope, journalism needs to return to its status as essential watchdogs of corruption and malfeasance—a status it enjoyed in the aftermath of Watergate.

Michael Schudson similarly believes that journalism should embrace its watchdog function. He deploys the term "accountability journalism," which he argues serves a valuable function by "asserting itself in the face of the powerful persons and institutions it covers—all in the interest of helping make a democratic government more fully accountable to the public. Democracy cannot truly exist if accountability journalism does not."[79] According to Schudson, the type of journalism in which the profession serves as a "fourth estate" is a necessary component of democracy. As the public has lost its faith in journalistic expertise and discourses of post-truth circulate freely, the field of journalism needs to regain its epistemic authority and assume its rightful place as a pillar of liberal democracy. In this framework, "journalism monitors the work of elected and appointed public servants and turns its searchlight on the achievements and the failures and the corruptions of these men and women in public office."[80] Schudson confidently declares that "no other institution does this work so consistently and with such independence of mind as the professional press, and that, in a nutshell, is why journalism matters."[81] This argument reflects a common current among journalistic thought that the weakness in journalistic institutions that Trump exploited and continues to exploit reflects a need for those institutions to shore up its professional norms. Schudson does not entertain the possibility that those journalistic practices elevating the profession as a safeguard for liberal democracy are vulnerable to exploitation or deserving of reconsideration. The possibility that critiques of long-held journalistic norms might rupture the foundation of the profession is terrifying to those whose epistemic authority as journalists or journalism scholars relies upon those very foundations.

Some scholars are working to destabilize what Ronald Jacobs terms "the sacred discourse of journalism" which elevates the importance of the profession by insisting that it is an indispensable institution in a liberal democracy. Jacobs explains that this "sacred discourse" proscribes that "journalists serve democracy by being objective, independent, and critical seekers of truth" and "understands the press as the 'fourth estate,' charged with carefully watching state actors and publicizing instances when those actors abuse their power or act against the interests of democracy."[82] He astutely shows the ways in which the established norms of journalism are not, in fact, sacred discourses handed down from above but are rather in need of consistent reinforcement and rearticulation as the profession of journalism faces new challenges in the political landscape and media ecology.

Jacobs is clearly skeptical of any entrenched journalistic processes wherein following the correct procedure and employing the appropriate methodology will necessarily produce an estimable product that is integral to a functioning liberal democracy. Unfortunately, Jacobs does not offer any advice as to how journalists should proceed in light of the current epistemological crisis. From his 2017 vantage point, he felt that it was "too early to tell what journalism after Trump will look like" and that journalists and critics would have to contextualize and interpret the conditions of Trumpism and update "the sacred discourse of journalism and its associated crisis narratives."[83] One component of the sacred discourse of journalism is an instance upon objectivity and rationality—concepts that are contextual and contingent rather than inherent truisms.

Employing a skepticism similar to that of Jacobs, journalism studies scholars Carlson, Robinson, and Lewis aver that journalists should work to destabilize norms of objectivity and rationality by examining those concepts within larger political and cultural contexts while supplementing them with a deeper understanding of emotionality and affect. They expand upon the notion that journalistic norms are deeply imbricated with democratic norms and maintain that "democratic norms need to account for sociality, identity, and emotionality without denigrating these attributes as inferior to the rational individual model."[84] Because of the connection between democratic norms and journalistic norms, professional journalists should situate their epistemological approach within a democratic context that is constantly in flux. They advocate for a set of journalistic practices that draw "on an epistemological approach that recognizes that facts are never isolated, free-floating things but rather are socially produced and embedded in complex systems. This recognition does not prevent factual claims from being scrutinized, but instead casts suspicion on any view of facts as existing apart from the systems that produce and circulate them."[85] Their framework provides a radically contingent version of journalism that does not inherently revere a set of norms and practices that are nearly a century old; rather, their model expands upon the journalistic charge to be an important institution in liberal democracies by rethinking the foundations of both democracy and journalism.

One foundational norm that scholars have begun to problematize is the notion of the press serving as a "fourth estate" by keeping the three branches of US government in check. Robert Gutsche specifically addresses educators in the field of journalism studies who "refuse to see that the Fourth Estate is neither accessible nor practical in our part of the system. In an age of populism and rampant racism, the fallibility of our democracy is clear, and educators should emphasize the role of power in journalism and prepare students and future journalists in ways of radicalizing the industry."[86] He believes that journalists and journalistic scholars need to recognize their own implication in a democratic system that is not adept at serving its citizenry well. He asserts that "journalism studies scholars should use this moment of contestation to go deeper, to position themselves as constituents of a power system, to redesign how we think about integration of news, politics, behavior and power."[87] A focus on the complicated relationships of power that journalists maintain with the sphere of politics and the liberal democratic state throws the concept of epistemological authority into sharp relief.

Troubling established assumptions about journalistic epistemology is especially crucial in the "post-truth" media environment in which citizens are skeptical of anyone claiming to be an absolute arbiter of truth. A self-reflexive journalistic practice that understands its relationship to democracy and does not blindly adhere to any "sacred discourse" is crucial at an historical and political moment when right-wing extremists are mobilizing discourses of post-truth for political gain and are espousing views that are neither liberal nor democratic. Journalism cannot act as a foundation for a liberal democracy if the profession and the academics who study it fail to evaluate and reconsider an epistemological model that is ill-equipped to challenge anti-democratic right-wing extremism.

## Notes

1 Emily Stewart, "Trump Calls Media the 'True Enemy of the People' the Same Day a Bomb Is Sent to CNN," *Vox*, October 29, 2018, https://www.vox.com/policy-and-politics/2018/10/29/18037894/donald-trump-twitter-media-enemy-pittsburgh
2 Michael Schudson, *Journalism: Why It Matters* (Malden, MA: Polity Press, 2000), 37–8.
3 Clifford Christians et al., *Normative Theories of the Media: Journalism in Democratic Societies* (Urbana, IL: University of Illinois Press, 2009), 29.
4 Mats Extröm, "Epistemologies of TV Journalism," *Journalism* 3, no. 3 (2002): 260.
5 Ibid.
6 Matt Carlson, Sue Robinson, and Seth C. Lewis, *News after Trump: Journalism's Crisis of Relevance in a Changed Media Culture* (New York: Oxford University Press, 2021), 9.
7 Margaret Sullivan, "More Facts, Fewer Pundits: Here's How the Media Can Regain the Public's Trust," *The Washington Post*, January 29, 2017, https://www.washingtonpost.com/lifestyle/style/more-facts-fewer-pundits-heres-how-the-media-can-regain-the-publics-trust/2017/01/29/9c0232ba-e4a7-11e6-a453-19ec4b3d09ba_story.html
8 Carlson, Robinson, and Lewis, 13.
9 Emily Bazelon, "How Do We Contend with Trump's Defiance of 'Norms'?" *The New York Times Magazine*, July 11, 2017, https://www.nytimes.com/2017/07/11/magazine/how-do-we-contend-with-trumps-defiance-of-norms.html
10 Robert E. Gutsche, Jr., *Media Control: News as an Institution of Power and Social Control* (New York: Bloomsbury, 2017), 36.
11 Jon Marshall, "Nixon Is Gone but His Media Strategy Lives On," *The Atlantic*, August 4, 2014, https://www.theatlantic.com/politics/archive/2014/08/nixons-revenge-his-media-strategy-triumphs-40-years-after-resignation/375274/
12 Ibid.
13 Agnew, Spiro Theodore, "Television News Coverage," *American Rhetoric*, November 13, 1969, https://www.americanrhetoric.com/speeches/spiroagnewtvnewscoverage.html

14  Ibid.
15  Prashanth Bhat, "Advertisements in the Age of Hyper-Partisan Media: Breitbart's #DumpKellogs Campaign," in *The Trump Presidency, Journalism, and Democracy*, ed. Robert E. Gutsche Jr. (New York: Routledge, 2018), 196.
16  Ben Adler, "Palin Pushes Back against 'Lamestream Media' over Video," *Newsweek*, August 10, 2010, https://www.newsweek.com/palin-pushes-back-against-lamestream-media-over-video-213776
17  Rosa Brooks, "The 'Real' America, Really," *The Los Angeles Times*, October 23, 2008, https://www.latimes.com/archives/la-xpm-2008-oct-23-oe-brooks23-story.html
18  Marc Tracy and Rachel Abrams, "Police Target Journalists as Trump Blames 'Lamestream Media' for Protests," *The New York Times*, June 1, 2020, https://www.nytimes.com/2020/06/01/business/media/reporters-protests-george-floyd.html
19  Nadine White, "Trump Lashes Out at 'Lamestream' Media as He Still Refuses to Concede," *Huffington Post*, November 9, 2020, https://www.huffingtonpost.co.uk/entry/trump-lashes-lamestream-media-refuse-concede_uk_5fa8f536c5b6f21920ddaa37
20  Christopher Hayes, *Twilight of the Elites: America After Meritocracy* (New York: Crown Publishers, 2012), 4.
21  Hayes, 12–13.
22  Zvi Reich, "Journalism as Bipolar Interactional Expertise," *Communication Theory* 22, no. 4 (2012): 339.
23  Zvi Reich and Hagar Lahav, "What on Earth Do Journalists Know? A New Model of Knowledge Brokers' Expertise," *Communication Theory* 31, no. 1 (2021): 64.
24  Ibid.
25  Nilay Patel, "Chuck Todd on Why *Meet The Press* Can't Survive on Just One Platform," *The Verge*, July 27, 2021, https://www.theverge.com/22594290/chuck-todd-meet-the-press-decoder-interview-nbc-news
26  Ibid.
27  Natasha Rietdijk and Alfred Archer, "Post Truth, False Balance, and Virtuous Gatekeeping," in *Virtues. Democracy, and Online Media: Ethical and Epistemic Issues*, eds. Nancy Snow and Mary Silvia Vacarezza (New York: Routledge, 2021), 66.
28  Rietdijk and Archer, 69.
29  Ibid., 66.
30  Brynn Tannehill, *American Fascism: How the GOP Is Subverting Democracy* (Oakland, CA: Transgress Press, 2021), 72.
31  Tannehill, 86.
32  Diana C. Mutz, *In-Your-Face Politics: The Consequences of Uncivil Media* (Princeton, NJ: Princeton University Press, 2015), 3.
33  Nikki Usher, "Rethinking Trust in the News: A Materialist Approach through 'Objects of Journalism'," *Journalism Studies* 19, no. 4 (2018): 565.

34  Ibid.
35  Michael Schudson, "The Trouble with Experts—And Why Democracies Need Them," *Theory & Society* 35, no. 5–6 (2006): 500.
36  Schudson, "The Trouble with Experts," 502.
37  Ibid., 505.
38  Tom Nichols, *The Death of Expertise: The Campaign against Established Knowledge and Why It Matters* (New York: Oxford University Press, 2018), xiii.
39  Richard Hofstadter, *Anti-Intellectualism in American Life* (New York: Vintage Books, 1963), 19.
40  Ibid.
41  Seth Stevenson, "A Cold One with Donald," *Slate*, February 11, 2016, https://slate.com/news-and-politics/2016/02/trump-is-winning-the-guy-youd-want-to-have-a-beer-with-election.html
42  "43rd President Is a 'Gut Player' Who Eschews Personal Change," *NBC News*, August 28, 2004, https://www.nbcnews.com/id/wbna5762240
43  Ibid.
44  Stevenson.
45  Phillip Elliott, "What Caused Orlando? Hillary Clinton Blames Guns. Donald Trump Blames Immigration," *Time*, June 13, 2016, https://time.com/4367193/orlando-shooting-hillary-clinton-donald-trump-speeches/
46  Daniella Diaz, "Trump: I'm a 'Very Stable Genius,'" *CNN*, January 6, 2018, https://www.cnn.com/2018/01/06/politics/donald-trump-white-house-fitness-very-stable-genius/index.html
47  David Nakamura, "'Maybe I Have a Natural Ability?': Trump Plays Medical Expert on Coronavirus by Second-Guessing the Experts," *The Washington Post*, March 7, 2020, https://www.washingtonpost.com/politics/maybe-i-have-a-natural-ability-trump-plays-medical-expert-on-coronavirus-by-second-guessing-the-professionals/2020/03/06/3ee0574c-5ffb-11ea-9055-5fa12981bbbf_story.html
48  Ibid.
49  Eliza Collins, "Trump: I Consult Myself on Foreign Policy," *Politico*, March 16, 2016, https://www.politico.com/blogs/2016-gop-primary-live-updates-and-results/2016/03/trump-foreign-policy-adviser–220853
50  Michael McDevitt and Patrick Ferrucci, "Populism, Journalism, and the Limits of Reflexivity: The Case of Donald Trump," *Journalism Studies* 19, no. 4 (2018): 513.
51  Ibid.
52  Kevin Mattson, "Obama's 'Egghead Problem,'" *Salon*, October 4, 2012.
53  Rick Perlstein, *Nixonland: The Rise of a Presidency and the Fracturing of America* (New York: Scribner Books, 2008), 525–6.
54  Perlstein, 526.

55 David Roberts, "Donald Trump and the Rise of Tribal Epistemology," *Vox*, May 19, 2007, https://www.vox.com/policy-and-politics/2017/3/22/14762030/donald-trump-tribal-epistemology

56 Justin Peters, "Joe Rogan's Galaxy Brain," *Slate*, March 21, 2019, https://slate.com/culture/2019/03/joe-rogans-podcast-is-an-essential-platform-for-freethinkers-who-hate-the-left.html

57 Ronald Jacobs, "Journalism after Trump," *American Journal of Cultural Sociology* 5, no. 3 (2017): 415.

58 Ibid.

59 Emma Graham-Harrison, "'Enemy of the People': Trump's Phrase and Its Echoes of Totalitarianism," *The Guardian*, August 3, 2018, https://www.theguardian.com/us-news/2018/aug/03/trump-enemy-of-the-peop e-meaning-history

60 Carlson, Robinson, and Lewis, 89.

61 Ibid.

62 Bazelon.

63 Ibid.

64 Gegory Shaya, "The Myth of the Fourth Estate," *Lapham's Quarterly*, April 3, 2012, https://www.laphamsquarterly.org/roundtable/myth-fourth-estate

65 Ibid.

66 Ibid.

67 Carlson, Robinson, and Lewis, 173.

68 Michelle M. Amazeen, "Journalistic Interventions: The Structural Factors Affecting the Global Emergence of Fact-checking," *Journalism* 21, no. 1 (2020): 97.

69 Jane B. Singer, "Border Patrol: The Rise and Role of Fact-Checkers and Their Challenge to Journalists" Normative Boundaries,' *Journalism* 22, no. 8 (2001): 1930.

70 Lucas Graves, *Deciding What's True: The Rise of Political Fact-Checking in American Journalism* (New York: Columbia University Press, 2016), 6.

71 Graves, 9–10.

72 Amazeen, 99.

73 Singer, 1938.

74 Joseph E. Uscinski and Ryden W. Butler, "The Epistemology of Fact Checking," *Critical Review* 25, no. 2 (2013): 163.

75 Uscinski and Butler, 175.

76 Nicholas Kristof, "My Shared Shame: The Media Helped Make Trump," *The New York Times*, March 27, 2016, https://www.nytimes.com/2016/03/27/opinion/sunday/my-shared-shame-the-media-helped-make-trump.html

77 Kyle Pope, "Here's to the Return of the Journalist as Malcontent," *Columbia Journalism Review*, November 9, 2016, https://www.cjr.org/criticism/journalist_election_trump_failure.php?link

78 Ibid.
79 Shudson, *Journalism*, 34.
80 Ibid., 49.
81 Ibid.
82 Jacobs, 410.
83 Jacobs, 422–3.
84 Carlson, Robinson, and Lewis, 188.
85 Ibid.
86 Robert E. Gutsche, Jr., "Epilogue: Facing Tomorrow in an Age of Trump," in *The Trump Presidency, Journalism, and Democracy*, ed. Robert E. Gutsche Jr. (New York: Routledge, 2018), 320.
87 Gutsche, Jr., "Epilogue," 323.

# 7

# Post-Truth, Fake News, and Postmodernism

The *Oxford Dictionary*'s Word of the Year for 2016 was "post-truth," an adjective the dictionary defined as "relating to or denoting circumstances in which objective facts are less influential in shaping public opinion than appeals to emotion and personal belief."[1] Upon the announcement that post-truth was indeed the Word of the Year, comedian Stephen Colbert called shenanigans and accused the dictionary of copying his neologism, "truthiness," *Merriam-Webster*'s 2006 Word of the Year.[2] In a November 17, 2016, episode of *The Late Show with Stephen Colbert* (2015–), Colbert notes that "post-truth is clearly just a rip-off of my 2006 word of the year, truthiness," which he defines as "the belief in what you feel to be true, rather than what the facts will support."[3] In an article following Colbert's outrage about the striking similarities between "truthiness" and "post-truth," Jack Holmes attempts to parse the difference between the two terms. Specifically, he locates "truthiness" within the context of the George W. Bush administration. He argues, "The question is whether today's 'post-truth' is the same as the 'truthiness' of a decade ago. While it's the same notion—that people are disregarding facts in favor of whatever backs up their pre-existing viewpoint—things seem to have… escalated." He goes on to state, "In the age of Bush, there was at least the veneer of engaging with reality… 'Post-Truth' is apt for this new era because it indicates a wholesale departure from facts and reality."[4] For Holmes, the "truthiness" era of the Bush administration held that facts were malleable, but were still important, whereas in the age of Trump, facts were completely divorced from any underlying reality. In this chapter, I engage the notion of post-truth that has emerged in myriad discourses surrounding Trump and Trumpism. Specifically, I look at the ways that scholars and journalists have looked to blame postmodernism for the epistemological orientation of the

Trump years. I examine the ways in which discourses of post-truth, fake news, and postmodernism have circulated during the Trump years and ultimately look for strategies to challenge a Trumpist epistemology based around post-truth.

## Post-Truth

The day after Trump's 2017 inauguration, pictures circulated showing that the crowds for the inauguration were significantly smaller than those that had attended Obama's, eight years prior. In his first public statements after being sworn in as president, Trump claimed that 1.5 million people attended the event—a number that was verifiably false.[5] At a press conference later in the day, Trump's press secretary Sean Spicer vehemently asserted that Trump's "was the largest audience to ever witness an inauguration, period, both in-person and around the globe."[6] He also told the press corps that "sometimes we can disagree with the facts," suggesting that facts were fluid and subject to interpretation.[7] Spokeswoman Kellyanne Conway supported the press secretary the next morning on *Meet the Press* (1947–). Chuck Todd, the program's host, called Spicer's characterization of the crowd size a "falsehood," and Conway responded, "you're saying it's a falsehood... Sean Spicer, our press secretary—gave alternative facts."[8] The Spicer press conference and Conway's neologism "alternative facts" set the tone for an administration that was unconcerned with sharing a fact-based reality with the mainstream media. In the interview, Chuck Todd pushed back against Conway and asserted that "alternative facts aren't facts, they're falsehoods."[9] Conway retorted by noting that Trump and his administration were more popular than the mainstream media. She snapped back: "you want to talk provable facts... Look—you've got a 14 percent approval rating in the media, that you've earned. You want to push back on us?"[10] For her, the credibility gap between the president and the national media meant that they did not have to share the same mediated factual reality. They had run a campaign by constructing their own version of reality and planned to continue to do so now that they were in the White House. The kerfuffle over the crowd size was simply a demonstration of the force of the post-truth strategy that the administration was employing.

Writing a few months after the election of Donald Trump, historian Gleb Tsipursky asserted, "Donald Trump is our first post-truth president. And he may well be the first of many."[11] Even before Trump won the election, *New York Times* columnist Timothy Egan penned an article titled "The Post-Truth Presidency."[12] Egan claims that every presidential election features lies, but that because of Trump, the 2016 election featured lies that were different in kind. For him, the election would portend a post-truth presidency because "the lies that many Americans now believe, and that make it so difficult to move the country on the big issues, go to existential facts."[13] Both Tsipursky and Egan believed that Trump's relation to truth was unique in presidential politics.

In his book simply titled *Post-Truth*, Lee McIntyre provides a cogent definition of post-truth. For him, it "mounts to a form of ideological supremacy, whereby its practitioners are trying to compel someone to believe in something whether there is good evidence for it or not. And this is a recipe for political domination."[14] In this schema, truth takes on an ideological function rather than existing as a given; to know the truth is to believe the same way about something that others do. An example that McIntyre provides is an interview that former Speaker of the House Newt Gingrich gave while he was working for the Trump campaign in 2016. Gingrich is sparring with CNN reporter Alisyn Camerota, who makes the claim that violent crime rates are down. Gingrich notes, "The Average American, I will bet you this morning, does not think crime is down, does not think we are safer." Camerota insists that "it's a fact. These are the national FBI facts." Gingrich makes the pivotal move when he states that "liberals have a whole set of statistics that theoretically may be right, but is not where human beings are... what I said is equally true. People feel more threatened." When Camerota explains the difference between objective facts and subjective feelings, Gingrich retorts that "as a political candidate, I'll go with how people feel and let you go with the theoreticians."[15] In Gingrich's framework, liberals have their facts, which may indeed be true in a traditional sense, but that truth does not resonate with a large section of the public. He seems to be evoking Stephen Colbert's mocking 2006 claim that "reality has a well-known liberal bias."[16] However, Gingrich is dead serious and revealing a strategy for the Right, which is much less concerned with being technically correct than with winning and being popular. In a post-truth world, the objective facts are less important than how one can use people's perceptions to mobilize them politically. If people feel that crime is on the rise, they can be persuaded to vote for a candidate who purports to be "tough on crime," regardless of what the actual crime statistics are.

For McIntyre, this move from motivating people with facts to motivating people based upon their feelings or perceptions is problematic because he worries that people might become untethered from reality. He asserts that "the danger of post-truth is not just that we allow our opinions and feelings to play a role in shaping what we think of as facts and truth, but that by doing so we take the risk of being estranged from reality itself."[17] In a Trumpian framework, reality does not exist on its own, waiting to be discovered; rather, Trump and his supporters construct the very contours of reality itself. The facts may demonstrate that crime rates are down but Trump plays on his supporters' fears by claiming that crime is rampant, creating a reality that is extraordinarily compelling for his supporters, if empirically untrue. Education scholar Nesta Devine shows that Trump's deployment of alternative facts is a more complicated strategy than simply lying or dissembling. She avers that "the insistence on the validity of 'alternative facts' can be seen as simply lying, and lying in the support of a particular form of interest—or it can be seen as a more significant reflection on the status of truth in a world that is neither entirely modern, nor entirely post-modern."[18] She goes on to note that "one-third of the US voting public find his 'alternative facts' more cogent than 'mainstream facts' aka 'fake news.'"[19] In her framework, Trump supporters feel let down by traditional media and consequently find the truths enumerated by Trump to be more compelling than those put forth by conventional sources. In a similar way that people might become supporters of QAnon because the stories on alternative media sources resonate with their own lived experiences, alternative facts become a source of pride for Trump supporters. By not believing their lying eyes (and consequently the lying press), they can give a middle finger to the mainstream media and show their devotion to Trump.

While Trump based his presidency upon a logic of post-truth, the idea predates Trump; Trump is simply the apotheosis of post-truth media figures, as he had no regard for a shared version of reality and utter contempt for traditional media. The first known use of the term "post-truth" was by Steve Tesich, writing for *The Nation* in 1992. Tesich was flabbergasted that the American public could find out about lies the government admitted to regarding the Iran-Contra Affair and the first Gulf War, and seemingly not care enough to hold its leaders accountable. In "A Government of Lies," he writes, "we are rapidly becoming prototypes of a people that totalitarian monsters could only drool about in their dreams. All the dictators up to now have had to work hard at suppressing the truth... In a very fundamental way we, as a free people, have freely decided that we want to live in some post-truth world."[20] Tesich was not worried that the public's shared version of reality was bifurcating; rather, he was concerned about the public not being engaged enough with political affairs to care whether the government was lying or not. The post-truth environment in which Trump thrives is not based on apathy but is rather based on a deep commitment to personal and political convictions.

Writing at the end of the George W. Bush administration, journalist Farhad Manjoo was already arguing that a version of reality shared by everyone was fracturing. He explains that the proliferation of new media technologies and sites of media production occurred concomitantly with the increasing bifurcation of the United States along lines of politics and culture. Manjoo holds that "in a world that lacks real gatekeepers and authority figures, and in which digital manipulation is so effortless, spin, conspiracy theories, myths, and outright lies may get the better of many of us."[21] He describes the famous "Swift Boat" ads that attacked John Kerry in the 2004 election cycle as promoting "two competing *versions of reality.*"[22] The erstwhile senator Daniel Patrick Moynihan famously quipped that "everyone is entitled to his opinion, but not to his own facts."[23] Manjoo describes a shift from a moment when politicians, journalists, and everyday people agreed on basic objective facts, but disagreed on the politics that emerged from those facts. In a post-fact society, people maintain a commitment to competing versions of reality that are seemingly incompatible. Those who listen to NPR, read *The New York Times*, and watch MSNBC have entirely different views of reality than those who listened to the now-deceased Rush Limbaugh, read *The New York Post*, and watch Fox News. This bifurcation that Manjoo describes has only intensified since the Bush administration, and the famous Moynihan quote seems downright quaint. The proliferation of social media has amplified and accelerated the processes through which people receive information and process truth.

A memorable example of the George W. Bush administration employing a post-truth epistemological strategy that demonstrates the bifurcation between the official media version of truth and the administration's version comes from a Bush aide, later confirmed to be chief advisor Karl Rove. Rove enters into a conversation with *New York Times* reporter Ron Suskind, in which he asserts that guys like Suskind were "in what we call the reality-based community" comprised of people who "'believe that solutions emerge from your judicious study of discernible reality.'" Rove continues, claiming that "we're an empire now, and when we act, we create our own reality. And while you're studying that reality—judiciously, as you will—we'll act again, creating other new realities, which you can study too, and that's how things will sort out."[24] Here, Rove demonstrates the epistemological gap between the establishment media and those who hold power in the administration, and suggests that the media will always be chasing the truth constructed by those who have the real power, those in positions of political power. Rove proved to be overly ambitious about his administration's ability to create a reality more appealing than that constructed by the media; by the end of Bush's second term in office, his war in Iraq had proved to be built upon a series of lies, and the forty-third president left office with incredibly low approval ratings. However, Trump learned from Rove's claims and built an administration determined to construct an empire completely disentangled from the "reality-based community," one in which any opposition to the president became "fake news," and in which his supporters would believe any claim the president made, regardless of its mendacity.

While Manjoo describes a process whereby multiple truths thrive in isolation from one another, journalist Ralph Keyes describes the post-truth society as one built upon the propensity for deception. Writing in 2004, Ralph Keyes contends that folks living in contemporary society are more wont to lie or dissemble than those who lived previously. He writes that "we live in a post-truth era. Post-truthfulness exists in an ethical twilight zone. It allows us to dissemble without considering ourselves dishonest... This term refers to ethical systems in which dissembling is considered ok. Not necessarily wrong, therefore not really 'dishonest' in the negative sense of the word."[25] Though writing twelve years before Trump's rise to political prominence, Keyes uses Trump as an exemplar of a post-truth way of thinking. In the wake of the release of *The Art of the Deal*, Trump made several false claims about the sales of his book. According to Keyes, after the businessman was called out for making false claims about the number of copies that *The Art of the Deal* was selling, Trump "called this kind of braggadocio 'truthful hyperbole.'... Trump's boasts about himself were, at best, 'loosely truth-based.'"[26] Trump has been honing his post-factual self at least since the 1980s, and his ability to massage or ignore the truth makes him the perfect person to succeed in a post-truth environment. Keyes goes on to argue that society in general has become more dishonest, and that this is detrimental to society. He writes, "I think it's fair to say that honesty is on the ropes. Deception has become commonplace at all levels of contemporary life."[27] His assessment of why this is bad rests on an argument in which honesty is one of the qualities that holds society together. He maintains that "civilization would crumble if we assumed others were as likely to lie as to tell the truth. Our social contract cannot survive lying so routine that citizens consider it normal. One sign of a healthy democracy is its citizens' capacity for outrage when they are deceived."[28] Keyes rests his argument on a stable version of truth rather than on a constructed version of truth. To him, lying is willfully obfuscating a truth shared by all.

The logic of Trumpism does not hold that truth is a stable identifiable reality, and as such the notions of lying and truth-telling are more complicated in a post-truth era. To claim that Trump and his surrogates are lying is to engage them on the wrong register. They are instead providing alternative constructed narratives that stand in for truth. This is more than a semantic claim; Kellyanne Conway's assertion of alternative facts has been fully ridiculed by mainstream media and liberal pundits, but the underlying assertion that facts are malleable reflects a profound change in epistemology.

The claim that lying for its own sake is problematic does not register for the Trump supporter, for they are in a war against what they perceive to be an evil enemy in the mainstream media. In their ethical framework, if Trump is indeed lying (though I'm not sure that lying/truth-telling binary holds sway), he is doing so for the greater good of "draining the swamp" and fighting the real enemy of the corrupt media and the Washington establishment. For communication scholar Giovanni Gobber, challenging the authority of the official outlets of truth—the mainstream or "lamestream" media—is as important in constructing truth as any objective reality. The pleasure of a post-truth media environment is being able to challenge those who continue to adhere to traditional assumptions about truth and reality. He identifies "post-truthers" who refuse to believe factual claims, such as the fact that Biden won the 2020 presidential election. Post-truthers "choose the clash, in which they deny validity to the statements of others."[29] For those invested in a more traditional epistemological project, "these statements refer to facts; for post-truthers, they refer to lies."[30] Thus, in a post-truth environment, truth becomes a struggle over ideas and a struggle to decide what is the truth. By the 2020 election, the public had become so bifurcated that different sectors of the public used different epistemological systems to make up their mind about the truth of the election. For the majority of Biden supporters, the traditional election system worked as it always had, and the establishment media reported the truth as it had always done; by these standards, he indeed had won the election. However, looking at the world through a post-truth lens, the majority of Trump supporters felt that the election had been rigged and that the establishment media could not be trusted; the only reliable source for the truth of the election was Trump himself, who had for years been warning of the prospect of a rigged election and who had admonished the established media at every term, claiming that they were "fake news."

## Fake News

One of the terms that entered popular discourse conterminously with post-truth is that of "fake news." In the weeks following the 2016 election, media studies scholar Melissa Zimdars posted a list of sources, intended for an undergraduate classroom, which her students should be wary of if using them as sources. She published the list online as a Google Doc, and it ultimately went viral. In a follow-up piece in *The Washington Post*, Zimdars notes thus: "that a list of sources you should be skeptical of when you encounter their stories on social media would go viral on social media might be a sign that the problem goes deeper than just the fake news."[31] However, her list did go viral at a particular moment when discourses of fake news were circulating wildly around the election. Zimdars argues that "there is evidence that fake news drew more engagement on Facebook than real news did during the closing weeks of the election." Her list goes further than simply listing fake news sites; she also includes satirical sites and sites that "publish news that exists in a liminal area."[32] For her, the proliferation of sites that muddy the waters between real and fake news is a call for more media literacy education so that users can be better equipped to differentiate between different types of news stories. The idea that certain news exists in a "liminal area" offers a useful point of departure for thinking about discourses of fake news in the contemporary media environment. During the course of the Trump presidency, the term "fake news" moved from being a descriptor of news that was satirical or constructed out of whole cloth to be misleading, to one co-opted by Trump to refer to information that he did not agree with or that did not comport with his worldview.

Before the 2016 election cycle, fake news was a self-deprecating term, which Jon Stewart used to describe his satirical comedy program and other similar programs. Writing in 2007, media scholars Sandra Borden and Chad Tew suggest that fake news programs like *The Daily Show* with Jon Stewart and *The Colbert Report* with Stephen Colbert destabilized the journalistic practices of established news organizations. "Borden and Two parse different types of fake news, arguing that within discourses of fake news "the same set of 'facts' can be interpreted differently and contextualized more thoroughly."[33] For them, what distinguished Colbert and Stewart from previous satires of the news is that they often started with real journalism and "they parody the news while simultaneously presenting and criticizing it—hence the term 'fake' news."[34] Because Colbert and Stewart relied upon actual news as the fodder for their programs while not being required to adhere to any journalistic standards, they achieved a freedom to critique the news that would not be possible within the world of traditional journalism. While the notion of fake news has shifted in the decade since Borden and Tew took up the idea in the 2000s, the concept holds a potential to reconfigure the terrain of the journalistic establishment and the stable notion of truth that accompanies traditional journalistic discourses.

For Zimdars, satirical news was only one of several stumbling blocks for her students to get real news as she was writing in 2016. A new conception of fake news had emerged in dominant discourses and circulated widely through news media, think pieces, and academic writing. Journalist Kalev Leetaru connected the rise in chatter about fake news to Facebook's CEO Mark Zuckerberg's announcement the week following the 2016 election that he doubted "that fake news on Facebook, of which it's a very small amount of the content, influenced the election in any way is a pretty crazy idea."[35] Leetaru notes that the day after Zuckerberg made that pronouncement, widespread use of the term "fake news" "appears to have burst into popularity."[36] In this instance, Zuckerberg is referring to news stories that are completely fabricated, usually overseas, and promoted on social media sites such as Facebook. During the 2016 election, Russia created millions of fake accounts or "bots" on Facebook and Twitter that would spread stories—usually in support of Donald Trump—many of which were created entirely out of thin air.[37] Not long after Zuckerberg's statement, the term seems to have become a signifier unmoored from any version of reality, as fake news became any news that existed within a different news ecosystem from the one making the claim that the news was fake.

Donald Trump took up the notion of "fake news" as any news that he disagreed with or that did not align with his political agenda. In a 2017 tweet, Trump wrote that "The FAKE NEWS media (failing @nytimes, @NBCNews, @ABC, @CBS, @CNN) is not my enemy, it is the enemy of the American People!"[38] By characterizing the mainstream media as "fake," he is able to validate his preferred sources as providing the true version of the facts and to suggest to his followers that he is the ultimate judge as to the distinction between what is real and what is fake. Journalist Alex Woodward notes that Trump used the phrase "fake news" nearly 2,000 times between 2016 and 2020.[39] Woodward juxtaposes that with a fact-checker who observed that during the same period, Trump made over 20,000 false or misleading claims, including falsely claiming that he coined the term "fake news."[40] Trump worked hard to create a divide between the epistemological circuits through which his supporters understood the truth and through which the mainstream media covered the truth. This process had its roots in a conservative media ecosystem that predated Trump and accelerated rapidly with a president who refused to participate in the rituals of the mainstream media. By the time of the 2020 election, Trump's supporters were ready to accept the "big lie" that he had actually won the election instead of Joe Biden. Trump supporters even turned their back on reliably conservative Fox News when they called Arizona for Biden before other networks, with protesters outside a Phoenix election facility chanting, "Fox News sucks."[41] Fox News had dared to challenge the "big lie" that the election was rigged, and regardless of any facts they might have to support their claims, the network was now on the side of fake news.

Communication scholars Johan Farkas and Jannick Schou argue that fake news has thus become a floating signifier in that its meaning can be taken up within various discursive frameworks for different political ends. For traditional media and scholars invested in the tradition of journalism based on objective facts, as traditionally understood, fake news is news that does not meet the criteria for that level of journalism, either because it is engaging in satire or because it is constructing its facts from thin air. For Trump and his followers, the term means the exact opposite, and fake news comes from exactly those news outlets who value the ideals of traditional journalistic integrity. Farkas and Schou maintain that

> instead of entering the terrain of what defines "truthfulness" or "falsehood," a battleground in which a multiplicity of agents struggle to define what counts as valid or deceitful, we seek to understand "fake news" as a discursive signifier that is part of political struggles. We take a step back and look at how different conceptions of "fake news" serve to produce and articulate political battlegrounds over social reality.[42]

For them, Trump is engaging in a hegemonic struggle with mainstream media over who gets to decide truth and whose version of truth should have legitimacy, and ultimately who should be able to construct the parameters of reality. They aver that "what is ultimately at stake within this struggle is who obtains the power to define what is deemed as truthful, who can portray social reality accurately, and in what ways."[43] By the end of Trump's presidency, the struggle over versions of reality had become so bifurcated that large swathes of the country could not even agree on who had won the 2020 presidential election. Repurposing the notion of fake news for his own political goals was one of the ways that Trump was able to constitute a version of reality that made this possible.

## Post-Truth, Postmodernism, Poststructuralism

Postmodernism is a set of ideas about truth, self, aesthetics, and meaning that have circulated in the academy and beyond since the late 1970s. While its roots go back further, the 1980s and 1990s roiled with academic debates that ultimately coalesced around the meanings of truth and self. For those invested in the Enlightenment project of modernity, truth is an ontologically stable singular phenomenon that exists outside of human culture and society. In the modernist framework, the goal of academics is subsequently to try to discover the truth or get as close as possible to it through a serious of methodological practices, including the scientific method, peer review, historical archives, and journalistic objectivity. All of these practices rely upon a stable singular version truth that is objectively verifiable and relies upon facts for verification. Postmodernists challenged the notion that truth was singular, and that objectivity and unbiased inquiry could even exist outside of the myriad cultural institutions and practices that ultimately informed that objectivity and supported its preeminent position as a means of discovering truth. In fact the postmodernists challenged the idea of a singular truth, and instead suggested that multiple truths might exist simultaneously and that these truths can at times be contradictory. In this model, truth is an effect of discourses and institutions that produce truths.

In a similar way, postmodernists challenged the notion of a stable self whose existence was ontologically prior to culture, discourse, and ideology. In the European tradition since the Enlightenment, the self was a unique autonomous entity; the entire system of representative democracy is based upon the uniqueness of individuals and the certain inalienable rights that accompanied selfhood. Postmodernists challenged the notion of the stable unique self, and instead saw the self as an effect of discourses and ideologies. Indeed, for postmodernists the notion of a singular truth and a unique individual self are social and cultural constructions—effects of discursive practices that seem natural but are instead deeply intertwined with culture, politics, economics, and power.

In a 1993 article in *The Atlantic*, Steven Stark described the Clinton administration as "The First Postmodern Presidency." Stark specifically points to a dispersed media environment as providing an environment in which postmodern ideas can thrive For many years, three major broadcast television networks and a handful of national newspapers produced the news, and they created an ideological consensus that promoted the idea of a singular version of objective truth. When a US president wanted to address the public, he could count on the major networks to provide him a platform and could assume a large audience. Stark explains that "that era may be drawing to a close. The ability of a President to draw the mass audience that broadcasting once afforded has been dramatically diminished by the rise of cable television."[44] Stark is writing before the proliferation of the internet through the World Wide Web, but already he sees a fragmented media environment creating a new version of a mediated presidency.

Twenty-three years after Stark claimed that Clinton was the first postmodern president, pundit Max de Haldevang declared that Donald Trump was the "ultimate postmodern presidential candidate." He credits the fragmented media environment with creating confusion between truth and fiction. For him, in a postmodernism environment, "the growth of mass media has blurred all lines between truth and fiction. As a result of the vast number of conflicting stories presented in the media's different mediums, we have begun to confuse our sense of truth and reality making everything seem subjective."[45] In other words, the sheer number of media discourses in postmodern society allows multiple truths to proliferate. During his presidency, Trump was able to borrow from his reality TV past and his history with conservative talk radio; he was able to draw from outside of the mainstream from the depths of the internet on sites like reddit and 4chan, while setting the agenda for Fox News, all from his Twitter account. He did not need to adhere to an objectively verifiable version of the truth; rather, his truth was a Trumpian one that aligned with his particular way of viewing the world.

Max de Haldevang uses the term "pastiche," a tenet of many postmodern discourses, to describe the ways in which Trump is able to construct his self/persona from myriad existing discourses. In his canonical *Postmodernism: Or, the Cultural Logic of Late Capitalism*, Fredric Jameson defines pastiche as "the imitation of a peculiar or idiosyncratic style, the wearing of a linguistic mask, speech in a dead language."[46] De Haldevang contends that Trump displays characteristics of pastiche as he performs the character of Trump. He writes that "as he shape-shifts across roles of businessman, TV star, race-baiter, statesman, stand-up comedian, and his campaign's claim of 'blue collar billionaire,' all social roles and concrete identities come to seem like masks he can put on and take off at will."[47] In a fractured media environment in which postmodern notions of truth and identity proliferate, all politicians ultimately inhabit multiple masks and emerge as a pastiche of different selves designed to appeal to a variety of constituencies. However, most politicians try to present themselves as a unified self at all times; commonsense holds that voters value consistency, and consequently most politicians work hard to avoid contradicting themselves, "flip-flopping," or other gaffes that might reveal the multiplicities that constitute their selves. Trump does not seem to mind inconsistencies and luxuriates in the multiplicities that his performance allows. In a frustrating irony for those set in the framework of rationalist discourse, Trump succeeds because he lies so much. Hillary Clinton lies very little, but when she does, her lies stand out because they are juxtaposed against a personality that purports to be honest and forthright. By lying, she highlights the fact that she is a mere politician. Trump's entire framework is based on dissembling and deconstructing any notion of truth in a postmodern world. By lying, he confirms what people already believe about him rather than revealing a character flaw. For Trump, lying is not a bug but a feature of the postmodern version of truth and self that Trump performs.

## *Is Postmodernism to Blame for Trump?*

Many journalists and academics have made the connection between the proliferation of discourses of post-truth in the Trump era and the critiques of truth as a singular concept that emerged through academic discourses of postmodernism that emerged at the end of the 1960s and have retained currency in some academic circles since then. Many have gone so far as to argue that high academic theory was the root cause of the conditions that allowed Trump to rise to power. British journalism scholar Andrew Calcutt muses that "more than 30 years ago, academics started to discredit 'truth' as one of the 'grand narratives' which clever people could no longer bring themselves to believe in. Instead of 'the truth,' which was to be rejected as naïve and/or repressive, a new intellectual orthodoxy permitted only 'truths'— always plural, frequently personalised, inevitably relativised."[48] Calcutt offers a simplistic version of postmodernism that insists upon modernist notions of a singular truth as the only possible epistemological framework. He does not defend his modernist point of view, except to say that the alternative is relativist and is susceptible to cooption by the likes of post-truth. He cites Jean-Francois Lyotard's famous 1979 book *The Postmodern Condition* as the point when these dangerous discourses of postmodernism seeped into everyday use in the academy and the literary Left. For him, "as long as we have been postmodern, we have been setting the scene for a 'post-truth' era." To that end, he chastises those liberal journalists and academics who subscribed to any version of postmodernism, including himself, noting that "it would be better to acknowledge our own shameful part in it."[49] Rather than offer a strong defense of modernism or its supposed monopolistic epistemology, Calcutt suggests that anyone who doubted the inherent superiority of modernism ought to feel shame in their complicity with the proliferation of post-truth discourses in the Trump era.

Already in 2004, French theorist Bruno Latour was concerned about the postmodern turn in academia that he helped to promote being used by right-wing opportunists. Latour worries that contemporary academics are being trained in programs "that facts are made up that there is no such thing as natural, unmediated, unbiased access to truth, that we are always prisoners of language, that we always speak from a particular standpoint, and so on, while dangerous extremists are using the very same argument of social construction to destroy hard-won evidence that could save our lives."[50] Latour laments that the very arguments used to promote postmodernism have been taken up by extremist and conspiracy theorists, and consequently the postmodern line of thought is dangerous. Literary critic Michiko Kakutani makes an argument that Trump supporters specifically took advantage of ideas forwarded by postmodern scholars to promote their political agenda. She argues that Trump "presided over an administration that became, in its first year, the very embodiment of anti-Enlightenment principles, repudiating the values of rationalism, tolerance, and empiricism in both its policies and its modus operandi."[51] She goes on to assert that "postmodernists are hardly to blame for all the free-floating nihilism abroad in the land. But some dumbed-down corollaries of their thinking have seeped into popular culture and been hijacked by the president's defenders, who want to use its relativistic arguments to excuse his lies."[52] In a remarkably postmodern move, Kakutani suggests that the authors of postmodern scholarship are not responsible for the theories that eventually found their way into right-wing political politics; those discourses took on a life of their own and were taken up for different purposes.

Alt-lite conservative Mike Cernovich specifically names postmodern as one of the theoretical tools that he uses to construct a conservative discourse that challenges the mainstream. In a 2016 interview with Andrew Marantz from *The New Yorker*, Cernovich explains that he "read postmodernist theory in college. If everything is a narrative, then we need alternatives to the dominant narrative."[53] Cernovich and the far right create narratives that often include "alternative facts" that run counter to dominant narratives from the mainstream media. The academic press, which includes many scholars who have long been skeptical of postmodernism, used Cernovich's interview as an opportunity to discredit the postmodern line of thinking. In a 2017 article for the *Chronicle of Higher Education*, Alan Lavinovitz cites the Cernovich interview and makes the claim between Trumpism and postmodernism explicit. He writes that "Trump and much of his base reject the truth-making mechanisms of academic culture by appealing to anti-elitism, and sow uncertainty via indignation and cultural pride. Why should pompous experts get the last word on the truth when working-class folk have their own ideas about it?"[54] Lavinovitz's assertion, especially his snarky rhetorical question, reveals an implied hierarchy between the academy and working-class folk. The latter in his estimation should not have a stake in the construction of truth. He shows a keen ability to critique the truth claims of the working class and Trump voters, but he holds as self-evident the academy's claim to authoritative truth. Lavinovitz should look to ascertain why those alternative narratives are so powerful. If a singular truth's power was indeed so evident, its grasp on power should not be so tenuous as to wither before these alternative narratives. Lavinovitz's demonstration of the power of alternative narratives should not reflect a call to limit narratives and insist upon a singular version of truth but rather should encourage scholars and activists on the Left to construct compelling narratives to counter those produced by the alt-right and Trump. A facile dismissal of a set of truths that resonate deeply with a large swath of the population seems less useful than a critical analysis of why those narratives resonate and how to construct compelling narratives and competing truths.

Two years before Lavinovitz's article, Lee McIntyre had already connected the anti-science narratives of climate denial and vaccination skepticism to left-wing postmodernists who dared to challenge any existing epistemological frameworks. In "The Attack on Truth," McIntyre adopts a sanctimonious paternalistic voice to chastise leftists in the humanities for the tenacity to question the notion of a singular truth. For him, climate denial and vaccination skepticism are "the price one pays for playing with ideas as if doing so has no consequences, imagining that they will only be used for the political purposes one intended."[55] In this schema, ideas that radical leftists in the humanities "play with" are so powerful as to be able to challenge 500 years of scientific scrutiny. Again, McIntyre does not question why these narratives are compelling or why many people have lost faith in the idea that a singular truth is conserved through the academy and judiciously imparted onto the public at large.

Rather than exist only in the ivory towers of the academy, the debate about postmodernism proliferated more widely in popular discourses. Writing for the liberal Christian blog *Mere Orthodoxy*, S. D. Kelly penned an article titled "Blame Jacques Derrida for Donald Trump." Kelly contends that the notion of deconstruction, central to many versions of postmodernism, has fanned out from the academy and proliferates within the culture at large. She maintains that "the ideas emanating from deconstructionism have long since escaped the laboratory of the university. College graduates, people who now comprise nearly 40% of working-aged Americans... have carried and spread the spores over the last several decades."[56] These spores have so thoroughly scattered in contemporary political and social discourses that "Americans no longer share a reality, culturally speaking. They don't even believe in reality, except in an individual sense—the sense of personal narrative."[57] The reason that Trump supporters do not care if he is telling the truth is that in the contemporary cultural context, there is not a singular truth that holds for the entire population. Even Trump supporters, many of whom have not had the advantages of a college education, "have come to implicitly understand that words themselves no longer signify any kind of objective reality." In Kelly's reading of deconstruction, once words are disassociated from having a singular meaning, they no longer have any meaning, and thus any truth claim is just as legitimate as any other. Kelly is correct in linking Trump and his popularity to discourses of postmodernism, but such a connection needs a more nuanced account. She writes that "Trump is everything and he is nothing. What Trump says, the words he uses, are made significant only in terms of the signified, which has been reduced to Trump himself" Rather than lament the reduction of Trump to a signifier, I suggest thinking about Trump as a nodal point for a complex web of media systems that have been circulating and gaining power since the 1980s.

By thinking of Trump as a nodal point for a system that has been gaining momentum for forty years, Trump becomes the mouthpiece for an epistemological media ecosystem that circulates as an alternative to the mainstream media. Communication scholar Grant Kien notes that "no one person can own a discourse, so even though it is tempting to credit Trump with the ownership of post-truth politics, he is, rather, a skilled conductor within the discourse, manipulating the pieces together like a constantly changing rubrics [sic] cube."[58] The diversification of media that began with the rise of cable news and the proliferation of talk radio in the 1980s and continued through the development of the internet and social media in the twenty-first century laid the groundwork for multiple epistemological channels to circulate conterminously. This process has only accelerated as social media have become among the dominant ways that people engage with news and politics. Literary scholar Amina Hussain explains that "post-truth flourishes as people cherry pick only those facts which suits their beliefs, generating information silos. News silos are created on social media not only with the sharing of the stories but also with the 'trending stories' phenomenon which will display only those stories that one is more inclined to watch, according to its recorded history of likes and shares."[59] Moreover, within the postmodern environment in which post-truth discourses flow, those facts need not have any grounding in a material reality. A salient example of this is the "PizzaGate" claim that liberals, including Hillary Clinton, were running a child trafficking center out of the basement of a pizza shop in Washington, DC. Not only was this verifiably false but the pizza joint did also not even have a basement. Nevertheless, the discourse circulated throughout enough right-wing media circuits, including those of avowed postmodernist Michael Cernovich, that it called an armed person to action. Moreover, many still believe that something nefarious is still going on with the Clintons, pedophilia, and a pizza shop in DC; no evidence will convince them otherwise.

## *How to Fight Trump*

Some scholars on the Left insist that the only way to fight Trumpism is to provide facts that are more grounded in a modernist epistemology or "real facts." For example, Grant Kien advocates for a resuscitation of "logic, rediscovery of 'capital T' Truth, verifying 'capital F' Facts, applying rigorous critical methods, and the ruthless rejection of nostalgia. Method may be the only thing that can rescue us in the longer term from this postmodern limbo we created for ourselves."[60] For Kien, a return to modernist principles of Truth, with a "capital T," will provide firm ground for the Left to challenge Trump and the Right. Writing for the Marxist publication *Jacobin*, Harrison Fluss and Landon Frim agree, suggesting that when the Right is able to hijack postmodern notions of Truth, the darkest ideas of the alt-right are able to take hold. They isolate "one of the Alt-Right's primary tactics: adopting leftist rhetoric as cover for its racialist, nativist, and often misogynistic agendas."[61] They go on to claim that the Right's "appropriation of identity politics for its own chauvinist brand of white identity politics attests to this strategy's success. If the Left wants to resist the alt-right's growing power, it needs to return to the roots of Enlightenment rationality."[62] For them, where the Left went astray was when they began to focus on identity politics, which requires an understanding of subject positions and subjectivity in considering epistemology, rather than maintaining a cool and detached rationality, which is the foundation of Enlightenment epistemology. Once identity politics were able to gain a foothold, the Right was able to flip the script and focus on white, male, and straight identity politics.

In her jeremiad "How French 'Intellectuals' Ruined the West,' humanities scholar Helen Pluckrose offers her critique of the postmodern notions that truth is complicated, multiple, contingent, and deeply related to structures of power. For her, postmodernism's insistence on multiplicities, fragments, and intersectional identity politics is antithetical to a liberal modernist project that should focus on establishing a single universal truth to combat the deluge of deception and dissembling that characterize Trumpism. She holds that "in order to regain credibility, the Left needs to recover a strong, coherent and reasonable liberalism... We need to meet their oppositions, divisions and hierarchies with universal principles of freedom, equality and justice. There must be a consistency of liberal principles in opposition to all attempts to evaluate or limit people by race, gender or sexuality."[63] In other words, any version of identity politics only serves to divide people, and any appeals to contested or multiple understandings of freedom, equality, and justice run counter to the modernist version of liberalism, and consequently to any notion of leftist politics in contemporary culture. All of these arguments represent a nostalgia for a twentieth-century version of journalism that was steeped in Enlightenment principles of truth. They demonstrate a desire to make American great again by returning to the days when establishment media would keep politicians honest by holding their feet to the fire through traditional journalistic practices. They also work to silence the voices of women, BIPOC, LBGTQ+ people, and others who have struggled against a univocal version of truth that has been decidedly white, patriarchal, homophobic, and transphobic. Illuminating intersectional and identity politics because the theories that undergird them might be co-opted by the Right seems to be a steep price to pay for a reversion to Enlightenment ideals.

In an effort to promote Enlightenment ideals of objective truth during the Trump presidency, numerous journalistic outlets were dedicated to "fact-checking" the President and trying to call him out on his numerous lies. However, Trump's supporters do not care if he is called out by the media for telling lies; the dishonest media are the ones calling him out, so they are the enemy. Journalist David Graham notes that "the president's extremely loose regard for the truth, even for a politician, has produced a surfeit of fresh grist to verify—or more often, debunk. Yet it doesn't seem to make a great deal of difference... They know he's wrong, and they don't care."[64] In fact, his supporters may luxuriate in Trump being able to lie to the mainstream media and get away with it, maintaining his approval ratings. They enjoy being in on the lie, even if all evidence points in a different direction. An April 2021 poll showed that a majority of Republican voters thought that the 2020 presidential election was rigged or illegitimate.[65] Regardless of the objective truthfulness of this claim, those polled knew that this was the version of truth circulating in the Trump ecosystem and responded accordingly.

Rhetorical scholar Dana Cloud argues that a strict adherence to fact-checking as well as an unflappable devotion to objective truth is a flawed strategy for the Left. For her, "a section of the Left has defined the problem as a problem of truth rather than of power. Instead of responding with fact-checking, we should speak and write in ways that motivate resistance in the full acceptance that knowledge is partial and partisan."[66] She goes on to assert that "the truth does not necessarily set us free; indeed the powerful often control the circulation and authority of what counts as truth."[67] Rather than trying to parse exactly which words Trump spouts are true and which are false, scholars should look for the ways in which power circulates in contemporary discursive frameworks. The different media networks through which Trump speaks and which Trump's supporters connect allow for truth claims to circulate that differ from those in mainstream media. Whether those claims are objectively true or false is less important than how those claims circulate in ways that impact contemporary political discourse.

In a *New York Times* op-ed, literary scholar Casey Williams offers a mode for critique of the discursive strategies of Trump. He writes that "even in a 'post-truth era,' a critical attitude allows us to question dominant systems of thought, whether they derive authority from an appearance of neutrality, objectivity or inevitability or from a more Trumpian appeal to alternative facts that dispense with empirical evidence."[68] Williams offers a strategy for deploying a critical lens of engagement that eschews simply fact-checking the President and his surrogates, and instead asks for what purpose the statement was made and to what effect. For Williams, "we can ask not whether a statement is true or false, but how and why it was made and what effects it produces when people feel it to be true. Paying attention to how knowledge is created and used can help us hold leaders like Trump accountable for what they say."⁶⁹ Williams' model comports with a version of truth-making that sees the production of truth as an act of political force rather than an undisputable given. Thus, for Trump's supporters, something becomes true simply by dint of Trump's endorsement. When he claimed that the 2020 election was rigged, he did not need to provide evidence or use the traditional truth-producing methods of the Enlightenment; rather, he just had to repeat his claim with authority and his followers took him at his word. Supplying more empirical evidence to counter Trump's claims would not persuade his followers to change their minds about the truth of the election, because empirical evidence was not the grounds on which they had made up their minds in the first place. The political force of Trump and the media that allowed him to attain and sustain power produced the truth of the election results for the Trump supporter.

Thinking about the political effects of truth claims rather than their empirical verifiability provides a way to think about how to offer a challenge to Trumpism and its reliance upon postmodern notions of post-truth. Education scholar David Backer offers a useful framework for thinking about post-truth as a possibility for political activism rather than an inherently detrimental to a shared public sphere. Backer argues that statements that truth claims ought not necessarily to be tethered to empirical reality but rather should relate to those statements that have a political force or that come to be understood as commonsensical or part of everyday political discourse. Backer provocatively asserts that "it could be that, in political contexts, one must 'untether' oneself from the notion that true statements correspond to a reality in order to vindicate one's position through discourse."⁷⁰ Rather than dismiss a postmodern notion of truth, Backer explains how it can be useful politically. He goes on to explain that "a correct statement—like a slogan—names the present conjuncture (a Gramscian term) and condenses it in such a way as to vindicate an ideological position."⁷¹ For example, Trump's campaign slogan "Make America Great Again" is able to name the present conjuncture and to allow a political idea— the United States is in decline, and needs to reassert itself as a preeminent power—and tie it to a political movement. In this framework, no political position has a monopoly over the production of correct statements, which Backer aligns with political truth, and most conjunctures feature competing claims to correct statement. He highlights the populist notion of "The 99%," which was mobilized by progressives and Occupy Wall Street and provided the conditions upon which left-leaning populism could find a foothold at that particular conjuncture. He also demonstrates the ways in which competing sides of the abortion debate have been able to produce correct statements by highlighting the abstract notions of "life" and "choice" and mobilizing them toward political ends. Trump has political goals, and his statements are true insofar as he succeeds at articulating a set of statements that resonate at this particular historical conjuncture.

In general, the Right has done a better job of framing truth in ways that comport with the popular sentiment of voters because they have been less tethered to truth grounded in empirical reality. Cultural studies scholar Lawrence Grossberg argues that if scholars want to combat Trumpism, they need to rethink traditional academic approaches to culture, politics, and truth as particular manifestations at this historic conjuncture. He writes that "we need to offer something other than the stories we have been telling for decades, which have, in case you have not noticed, largely failed."[72] In Grossberg's schema, Trump's post-truth discourses do not reflect a difference in kind, but rather of scale. Politicians have always lied, but what Trump and the media apparatuses behind him have done is amplified the level of mendacity. For him, "what is being produced is a field of discourse and epistemological chaos, in which statements and contradictions endlessly multiply and change. Statements, whether truths or lies, begin to take on a strange, almost eerie quality, as if they have a kind of autonomy and singularity, as if they were free-floating, not connected to anything."[73] The epistemology and politics of Trumpism is based on chaos; trying to rein in that chaos by a return to an enlightenment epistemology is understandable, but has proven to be useless in the face of the chaos constructed by Trump. Regardless of how many experts and analysts show that Joe Biden won the 2020 election, Trump's supporters will never be convinced. Even if the day of reckoning does not manifest for QAnon supporters, they will find clues that they simply had the date wrong, and Trump will rise to rid the world of the pedophiles any day now. Like Backer, Grossberg is interested in the Left constructing better narratives to counter the truth claims that the Right presents.

Critics of postmodernism will suggest that abandoning a faith in Enlightenment devotion to facts and objectivity is dangerous and argue that the reason Trump has succeeded as a politician is because certain scholars challenged a stable notion of truth in the first place. While some on the Left cling to an ideology in which the best way to combat the post-truth discourses that characterize the current political conjuncture is by pointing out that Trump and his ilk are lying and dissembling, those on the Right continue to deploy successfully the strategy of constructing their own version of truth. The notion of constructing truth contradicts a traditional Marxist framework in which truth and reality are grounded in an economic base while culture, language, and politics exist in a superstructure determined by that economic base. In his famous work from the 1960s, French theorist Guy Debord worried that a grounded material reality was evaporating and being replaced by a "society of the spectacle." In his manifesto of the same name, Debord writes that "the whole life of those societies in which modern conditions of production prevail presents itself as an immense accumulation of spectacles. All that was once directly lived has become mere representation."[74] Debord was terrified by his proposition, and progressives have traditionally maintained a belief that truth and rationality will be the cure for an artificial society increasingly dominated by spectacle. In his 2007 book, media and culture scholar Stephen Duncombe offers a desperate plea for progressives to embrace the politics of the spectacle that so frightened Debord. For Duncombe, progressives have relied much too heavily on a commitment to rationality and truth, and an incorrect belief in "an Enlightenment faith that somehow, if reasoning people have access to the Truth, the scales will fall from their eyes and they will see reality as it truly is and, of course, agree with us."[75] Duncombe foreshadowed the logic of post-truth that characterizes the contemporary political moment, noting that the kind of truth produced by logic and rationality is not necessarily the regime of truth that holds the most sway in the spectacular contemporary media environment, and the traditional version of truth may not hold much purchase with potential voters.

Writing in the middle of the George W. Bush administration, Duncombe believed that Bush and his handlers understood the power of a media-induced fantasy and its profound power in a way that the Democrats fundamentally did not. For him, the Bush administration "understood that people often prefer a simple, dramatic story to the complicated truth."[76] For Duncombe, Democrats and Progressives were mistaken in their myriad attempts to demonstrate that Bush was mistaken, wrong-headed, or even mendacious. Duncombe insisted that instead of basing their campaign on appeals to rationality and truth, "Progressives should have learned to build a politics that embraces the dreams of people and fashions spectacles which give these fantasies form—a politics that understands desire and speaks to the irrational; a politics that employs symbols and associations; a politics that tells good stories."[77] In the face of a politician who won the presidency by employing these strategies, the Left still relies too often on complicated truths rather than simple, dramatic stories. They have doubled down on a traditional notion of truth and rationality, while Trump prevailed by completely severing himself from traditional understandings of truth.

The realm of the spectacle is where Trump thrives; freed from any coherent ideology, he luxuriates in fantasy, and deftly negotiates the terrain of what Duncombe describes as the "spectacular vernacular." Trump built his entire career, campaign, and presidency upon his ability to manipulate the media and to present himself and his supporters as a spectacle that resembles a reality show or a Barnumian carnival. Duncombe is writing for an audience of progressives when he argues that "if progressives are going to engage, rather than ignore, the phantasmagoric terrain of politics, we need to learn from those who do spectacle best: the architects of Las Vegas, video game designers, advertising's creative directors, and the producers and editors of celebrity media."[78] Trump is the ultimate personification of the notion of politics that Duncombe describes. He literally has a hand in Vegas architecture, advertising, and producing celebrity media, and even had a 2002 video game titled *Donald Trump's Real Estate Tycoon*. To embrace Duncombe's political strategy, progressives need to rethink politics in ways that sever it from modernist understandings of truth and rationality. This does not necessarily mean that progressive scholars, politicians, and pundits need to abandon any notion of truth; rather, they need also to embrace the spectacular and understand that in the contemporary postmodern political moment, embracing the spectacle is one way to attain power and voice, and subsequently to have a say in the terms upon which truth is produced. Tom Syverson agrees with this strategy, suggesting that "contrary to many liberal critiques of so-called post-truth politics, our ability to construct and narrativize social reality need not be a dangerous anarchy. Rather it can be a wellspring of human creativity and progress."[79] For him, "it's precisely within the context of a postmodern blurring of fact and fantasy that we can open up a dialectical space of meaning, taking control of both the facts we encounter and the stories we wish to tell about them."[80] The goal of the Left should be to take advantage of the blurring of facts and fantasy in the way that Trump does—to use the ability to "construct and narrativize social reality" in ways that tell compelling stories that appeal to broad swaths of the population. Trump and the Right have indeed figured out how to tell these stories, and in order to counter them, the Left ought to use the available tools provided in the given media environment to construct counternarratives that challenge the Right's stories and new narratives that create their own political force.

## A Post-Truth Media Environment

When Donald Trump entered the political media landscape in the 2010s, the mediascape was already primed for a candidate who would embrace a post-truth political strategy. The rise of conservative talk radio in the 1980s and 1990s, and the right-wing ecosystem that it portended, cleared the path for a bifurcated political landscape and a populace that failed to unite around a single epistemological strategy. The popularity of reality television in the 2000s challenged the distinction between "true" events that occurred in the world of documentary and politics and "scripted" events that happened in the world of entertainment. The genre purported to be presenting true events, but the viewers knew that the truth on offer was constructed and manipulated by those who held power in the media apparatus. The rise of social media in the 2000s and 2010s challenged the authority of traditional gatekeepers and institutions who had traditionally wielded power and subsequently confirmed a consensual version of truth for a mostly coherent public. Twitter provided a platform for successful users to create what Oborne and Roberts describe as a "personal epistemology," which allows versions of truth to circulate that circumvent those traditional gatekeepers. Social media also created a mechanism from which ideas that percolated in the deeper realms of the internet could travel into mainstream media, thus creating the possibility for darker ideologies and conspiratorial discourses to challenge dominant versions of truth. Donald Trump was able to take advantage of all of these shifts in the media landscape, and to employ a political strategy devoid of any fact-based relationship to truth. He leaves behind a nation that is unable to agree upon seemingly basic political facts—such as who won the 2020 presidential election.

The goal for scholars, activists, and others committed to a Leftist politics should be to consider what democratic politics looks like in an era of post-truth. Political theorist Jodi Dean explains that "most politica discussion (as well as political theory) takes for granted the existence of a consensus regarding the rules and conditions for establishing truth and falsity, not to menton a shared notion of reality."[81] Consensus and a shared notion of reality no longer seem operable in a country divided by its leaders and its mediated environment. To use Arendt's phrase, a "hole in the fabric of factuality" has emerged, and scholars and activists need to grapple with the implications of a democratic society that no longer maintains a common conception of truth.

Political theorist Ari-Elmeri Hyvönen suggests that those interesting in constructively struggling with this issue need to take on the project of "world building" and need to combat what he dubs "careless speech." For Hyvönen, post-truth "emerges from several economic, media-related, and cultural factors that erode the 'common world' and make truth increasingly irrelevant in public discourse."[82] He derives his notion of careless speech as contrasting with Michel Foucault's notion of "fearless speech," in which one takes great risk in truth-telling.[83] In contrast, careless speech is "unconcerned not only with truth but also with the world as a common space in which things become public. It means an unwillingness to engage with other perspectives, a reluctance to accept that speech has repercussions and words matter. It involves creating uncertainty over whether what is said aloud is actually meant; it means believing that anything can be unsaid.'[84]

Thus, to combat a world in which careless speech abounds, those interested in constructing a democratic society need to imagine a world built around discourses of care that create the conditions of possibility for thinking about the world as a common space. Merely fact-checking or correcting people who are factually incorrect or who are engaging truth through different registers does not work to rebuild the bonds of a society whose shared fabric of reality has been torn. Hyvönen argues that facts "become a collection of irrelevant, unrelated, inconsequential statements without public spaces that would allow us to place them into context, have a debate about them, and acknowledge their weight" and suggests that "it is crucial to engage in practices of world-building that address the deeper socio-political problems in play."[85] The goal of future scholarship on post-truth should work to conceptualize new worlds that embrace new epistemological frameworks, rather than revert to modernist strategies that have failed to curtail the politics of Trumpism. Acknowledging a multiplicity of epistemological frameworks does not necessitate a vulgar relativism, and scholars and activists on the Left should be at least as creative as their counterparts on the Right, who have proven to be quite deft at utilizing a post-truth media landscape for their political advantage.

## Notes

1. "Word of the Year 2016," *Oxford Languages*, 2016, https://languages.oup.com/word-of-the-year/2016/
2. "Words of the Year: A Decade in Review," *Merriam-Webster*, https://www.merriam-webster.com/words-at-play/words-of-the-year-decade-in-review/2010-word-of-the-year-austerity
3. "Stephen Colbert Used to Weaponize Truth as Satire. Now It's Reality," *Esquire*, November 18, 2016, https://www.esquire.com/news-politics/videos/a50815/stephen-colbert-post-truth-truthiness/#:~:text=Stephen%20Colbert%20Used%20to%20Weaponize%20'Truthiness'%20as%20Satire.&text=But%20as%20Colbert%20pointed%20out,content%20is%20imported%20from%20YouTube
4. Ibid.
5. Julie Hirschfeld Davis and Matthew Rosenberg, "With False Media Claims, Trump Attacks Media on Turnout and Intelligence Rift," *The New York Times*, January 21, 2017, https://www.nytimes.com/2017/01/21/us/politics/trump-white-house-briefing-inauguration-crowd-size.html
6. "Transcript of White House Press Secretary Statement to the Media," *Politico*, January 21, 2017, https://www.politico.com/story/2017/01/transcript-press-secretary-sean-spicer-media-233979

7   David Smith, "Sean Spicer Defends Inauguration Claims: 'Sometimes We Can Disagree with Facts,'" *The Guardian*, January 23, 2017, https://www.theguardian.com/us-news/2017/jan/23/sean-spicer-white-house-press-briefing-inauguration-alternative-facts

8   Eric Bradner, "Conway: White House Offered 'Alternative Facts' on Crowd Size," *CNN*, January 23, 2017, https://www.cnn.com/2017/01/22/politics/kellyanne-conway-alternative-facts/index.html

9   Ibid.

10  Jim Rutenberg, "'Alternative Facts' and the Costs of Trump-Branded Reality," *The New York Times*, January 22, 2017, https://www.nytimes.com/2017/01/22/business/media/alternative-facts-trump-brand.html

11  Gleb Tsipursky, "A Post-Lies Future: Fighting 'Alternative Facts' and 'Post-Truth' Politics," *The Humanist*, February 21, 2017, https://thehumanist.com/magazine/march-april-2017/features/towards-post-lies-future/

12  Timothy Egan, "The Post Truth Presidency," *The New York Times*, November 4, 2016, https://www.nytimes.com/2016/11/04/opinion/campaign-stops/the-post-truth-presidency.html

13  Ibid.

14  Lee McIntyre, *Post-Truth* (Cambridge, MA: The MIT Press, 2018), 13.

15  McIntyre, 3–4.

16  Jacques Steinberg, "After Press Dinner, the Blogosphere Is Alive with the Sound of Colbert Chatter," *The New York Times*, May 3, 2006, https://www.nytimes.com/2006/05/03/arts/03colb.html

17  McIntyre, 172.

18  Nesta Devine, "Beyond Truth and Post-Truth," in *Post-Truth, Fake News: Viral Modernity & Higher Education*, eds. Michael A. Peters, Sharon Rider, Mats Hyvönen, and Tina Besley (Singapore: Springer, 2018), 161.

19  Devine, 165.

20  Steve Tesich, "A Government of Lies," *The Nation*, January 6/13, 1992, https://www.thefreelibrary.com/A+government+of+lies.-a011665982

21  Farhad Manjoo, *True Enough: Learning to Live in a Post-Fact Society* (New York: John Wiley & Sons, 2008), 18.

22  Manjoo, 21.

23  Stephen R. Weisman, "An American Original," *Vanity Fair*, October 6, 2010, https://www.vanityfair.com/news/2010/11/moynihan-letters-201011

24  Ron Suskind, "Faith, Certainty, and the Presidency of George W. Bush," *The New York Times Magazine*, October 17, 2004, https://www.nytimes.com/2004/10/17/magazine/faith-certainty-and-the-presidency-of-george-w-bush.html

25  Ralph Keyes, *The Post-Truth Era: Dishonesty and Deception in Contemporary Life* (New York: St. Martin's Press, 2004), 13.

26  Keyes, 15.

27. Ibid., 5.
28. Ibid., 228.
29. Giovanni Gobber, "The Scarlet Letter of 'Post-Truth': The Scarlet Letter of Communication," *Church, Communication, & Culture* 4, no. 3 (2019): 292.
30. Ibid.
31. Melissa Zimdars," My 'Fake News List' Went Viral, but Made-Up Stories Are Only Part of the Problem," *The Washington Post*, November 18, 2016, https://www.washingtonpost.com/posteverything/wp/2016/11/18/my-fake-news-list-went-viral-but-made-up-stories-are-only-part-of-the-problem/
32. Ibid.
33. Sandra Borden and Chad Tew, "The Role of Journalist and the Performance of Journalism: Ethical Lessons from 'Fake' News (Seriously)," *Journal of Mass Media Ethics* 22, no. 4 (2007): 305.
34. Borden and Chew, 306.
35. Kalev Leetaru, "Did Facebook's Mark Zuckerberg Coin the Phrase Fake News?" *Forbes*, February 17, 2017, https://www.forbes.com/sites/kalevleetaru/2017/02/17/did-facebooks-mark-zuckerberg-coin-the-phrase-fake-news/#3adc70866bc4
36. Ibid.
37. Scott Shane, "The Fake Americans Russia Created to Influence the Election," *The New York Times*, September 7, 2017, https://www.nytimes.com/2017/09/07/us/politics/russia-facebook-twitter-election.html
38. Jim Acosta, "How Trump's 'Fake News' Rhetoric Has Gotten out of Control," *CNN*, June 11, 2019, https://www.cnn.com/2019/06/11/politics/enemy-of-the-people-jim-acosta-donald-trump/index.html
39. Alex Woodward, "'Fake News': A Guide to Trump's Favorite Phrase—And the Dangers It Obscures," *The Independent*, October 20, 2020, https://www.independent.co.uk/news/world/americas/us-election/trump-fake-news-counter-history-b732873.html
40. Ibid.
41. Lois Beckett, "'Fox News Sucks!: Trump Supporters Decry Channel as It Declares Biden Wins," *The Guardian*, November 5, 2020, https://www.theguardian.com/media/2020/nov/05/fox-news-sucks-trump-supporters
42. Johan Farkas and Jannick Schou, "Fake News as a Floating Signifier: Hegemony, Antagonism, and the Politics of Falsehood," *Javnost: The Public* 25, no. 3 (2018): 300.
43. Farkas and Schou, 308.
44. Steven Stark, "The First Postmodern President," *The Atlantic*, April 1993, https://www.theatlantic.com/past/docs/politics/polibig/postmod.html
45. Max de Haldevang, "Trump Is the Ultimate Postmodern Presidential Candidate—And He's Been a Long Time Coming," *Quartz*, September 23, 2016, https://qz.com/781798/trump-is-the-ultimate-postmodern-presidential-candidate-and-hes-been-a-long-time-coming/

46  Fredric Jameson, *Postmodernism: Or, the Cultural Logic of Late Capitalism* (Durham, NC: Duke University Press, 1992), 17.

47  de Haldevang.

48  Andrew Calcutt, "The Surprising Origins of 'Post-Truth'—And How It Was Spawned by the Liberal Left," *The Conversation*, November 18, 2016, https://theconversation.com/the-surprising-origins-of-post-truth-and-how-it-was-spawned-by-the-liberal-left–68929

49  Ibid.

50  Bruno Latour, "Why Has Critique Run Out of Steam?: From Matters of Fact to Matters of Concern," *Critical Inquiry* 30, no. 2 (2004): 227.

51  Michiko Kakutani, *The Death of Truth: Notes on Falsehood in the Age of Trump* (New York: Tim Duggan Books, 2018), 27.

52  Kakutani, 45–6.

53  Andrew Marantz, "Trolls for Trump," *The New Yorker* October 24, 2016, https://www.newyorker.com/magazine/2016/10/31/trolls-for-trump

54  Alan Jay Levinovitz, "It's Not All Relative," *The Chronicle of Higher Education*, March 5, 2017, https://www.chronicle.com/article/Its-Not-All-Relative/239356

55  Lee McIntyre, "The Attack on Truth," *The Chronicle of Higher Education*, June 8, 2015, https://www.chronicle.com/article/The-Attack-on-Truth/230631

56  S.D. Kelley, "Blame Jacques Derrida for Donald Trump," *Mere Orthodoxy*, March 31, 2016, https://mereorthodoxy.com/blame-jacques-derrida-for-donald-trump/

57  Ibid.

58  Grant Kien, "Postmodernism Trumps All: The World without Facts," *Qualitative Inquiry* 27, no. 3–4 (2021): 378.

59  Amina Hussain, "Theorising Post-Truth: A Postmodern Phenomenon," *Journal of Comparative Literature and Aesthetics* 42, no. 1 (2019): 152.

60  Kien, 379–80.

61  Harrison Fluss and Landon Frim, "Aliens, Antisemitism, and Academia," *Jacobin*, March 11, 2017, https://www.jacobinmag.com/2017/03/jason-reza-jorjani-stony-brook-alt-right-arktos-continental-philosophy-modernity-enlightenment/

62  Ibid.

63  Helen Pluckrose, "How French 'Intellectuals' Ruined the West: Postmodernism and Its Impact, Explained," *Areo*, March 27, 2017, https://areomagazine.com/2017/03/27/how-french-intellectuals-ruined-the-west-postmodernism-and-its-impact-explained/

64  David A. Graham, "Why Fact-Checking Doesn't Faze Trump Fans," *The Atlantic*, July 5, 2017, https://www.theatlantic.com/politics/archive/2017/07/the-strange-effect-fact-checking-has-on-trump-supporters/532701/

65  Harry Enten, "Polls Show Majority of Republicans Mistakenly Think the 2020 Election Wasn't Legitimate," *CNN*, April 11, 2021, https://www.cnn.com/2021/04/11/politics/voting-restrictions-analysis/index.html

66 Dana Cloud, *Reality Bites: Rhetoric and the Circulation of Truth Claims in U.S. Political Culture* (Columbus, OH: The University of Ohio Press, 2018), xii.
67 Cloud, 1.
68 Ibid.
69 Ibid.
70 David I. Backer, "Towards an Activist Theory of Language," in *Truth in the Public Sphere*, ed. Jason Hannon (Lanham, MD: Lexington Books, 2016), 4.
71 Ibid.
72 Lawrence Grossberg, *Under the Cover of Chaos: Trump and the Battle for the American Right* (London: Pluto Press, 2018), 145.
73 Grossberg, 126.
74 Guy Debord, *Society of the Spectacle* (Detroit: Black & Red Books, 2000), 1.
75 Stephen Duncombe, *Dream: Re-Imagining Progressive Politics in an Age of Fantasy* (New York: The New Press, 2007), 7.
76 Ibid.
77 Duncombe, 9.
78 Ibid., 14.
79 Tom Syverson, *Reality Squared: On Reality TV and Left Politics* (Washington, DC: Zero Books, 2021), 14.
80 Syverson, 12.
81 Jodi Dean, *Democracy and Other Neoliberal Fantasies: Communicative Capitalism and Left Politics* (Durham, NC: Duke University Press, 2009), 147.
82 Ari-Elmeri Hyvönen, "Careless Speech: Conceptualizing Post-Truth Politics," *New Perspectives* 26, no. 3 (2018): 33.
83 Michel Foucault, *Fearless Speech* (Los Angeles: Semiotext(e), 2001).
84 Ibid.
85 Hyvönen, 48.

# Conclusion

On November 7, the major networks called the 2020 presidential campaign for Joe Biden. The announcement came as Trump surrogate Rudy Giuliani was giving a press conference at the Four Seasons in Philadelphia—not the famous Four Seasons hotel chain, but a local landscaping business that was on the same strip of businesses as a crematorium and a store selling sex toys. Early in the morning, Trump tweeted, "Lawyers News Conference Four Seasons, Philadelphia. 11:00 a.m." Worried that it might somehow become involved, the Four Seasons hotel chain issued its own tweet: "To clarify, President Trump's press conference will NOT be held at Four Seasons Hotel Philadelphia. It will be held at Four Seasons Total Landscaping— no relation with the hotel."[1] The reporters who were covering the event actually packed up their equipment and started heading out once they realized that Biden had been declared the winner of the election. The mix-up was blamed on a "garbled game of telephone," and the incident provided fodder for numerous jokes on the internet and late-night comics.[2] Journalist Katelyn Burns characterizes the incident as a metaphor for the Trump presidency. She writes:

> The president and the right-wing media apparatus in the US spent the past four years constructing an alternate reality... And the Four Seasons press conference was a real emperor-has-no-clothes moment: A presidency that began with Trump's descent into a golden lobby ended in a landscaping company's parking lot, with the press packing up and leaving instead of staying and listening to nonsense.[3]

Trump and his followers had worked so hard to construct a reality, and on this day, the lack of substance behind the apparatus became apparent. Trump himself was unable to confront the reality that he had lost the election, and he was losing the ability to maintain the attention of the mainstream media; he simply walked away from an absurd press conference at a landscaping business in the outskirts of Philadelphia.

Trump was, however, able to maintain the attention of the mainstream media through the insurgency at the Capitol, but when his Twitter account went dark on January 8, 2021, Trump lost his biggest tool with which to communicate to his supporters. Mainstream news coverage of Trump decreased dramatically, and the new president, Joe Biden, did not indulge in the excessive use of social media in the way that his predecessor had. In the four months after Trump's Twitter account was turned off, his mentions declined by about 90 percent on both Facebook and Twitter.[4] In May 2021, Trump launched a website called "From the Desk of Donald J. Trump," from which he offered his opinions on the news of the day in an effort to stay relevant politically without Twitter or Facebook at his disposal.[5] By June, he had shut down the website, which was essentially a blog, citing poor traffic and the fact that people were mocking the site for its lack of readership and its overall absurdity.[6]

The celebrity-cum-president who had demanded so much attention from the media and from individuals was no longer constantly the center of the media's attention. For over five years from the time that he descended the escalator in Trump Tower to the day that his Twitter account was disconnected, Trump was able to dominate media coverage from the depths of 4chan and Reddit to mainstream news outlets like the *New York Times*. Whether people loved him or hated him, Donald Trump was an unavoidable part of people's everyday lives in a way that no other president had been because of his ubiquitous presence across all forms of media. Many in the mainstream media observed the shift from Trump to Biden as a return to normalcy. Writing for *The Guardian*, David Smith notes, "Americans no longer dread awakening to all caps tweets that run the gamut from threatening war to insulting some celebrity's looks. Journalists express gratitude for getting their weekends back. Cable news has returned to its old drumbeat of hurricanes, mass shootings and the British royal family soap opera."[7] *New York Times* journalist Sarah Lyall writes that "to many of the former president's detractors, the absence of a daily barrage of anxiety-provoking presidential verbiage feels closer to a return to normalcy than anything else (so far) in 2021."[8] These discourses suggesting that the Biden presidency represents a return to normalcy highlight the extraordinary phenomenon that was Trump and his rise to power. On the one hand, Trump was unique in his ability to command attention across media and to be able to thrive politically while taking advantage of different media and cultivating his own post-truth epistemology for his followers to embrace. On the other hand, once he was no longer at the center of national media attention, many of the cultural and political structures that brought him into power and that he magnified continued to circulate in the contemporary media environment.

The year 2020 was an incredibly tumultuous year, culminating in the inauguration of Biden on January 20, 2021. In addition to the contentious elections and Trump's refusal to concede, the year featured a global pandemic, with many people locked inside their homes, and the most widespread protests since the 1960s in the wake of the murder of George Floyd by a Minneapolis police officer. Some people did indeed experience a desire to return to normalcy, and Joe Biden was the old, white, male establishment embodiment of that normalcy. However, many on the Left experienced a profound ambivalence toward the Biden victory in November. On the one hand, Biden did not present the clear and present danger that Trump did, as Biden did not actively encourage and activate the alt-right and white nationalist wings of the conservative movement. On the other hand, Biden was a decidedly milquetoast centrist who only begrudgingly and partially accepted the agenda of the Black Lives Matter movement, which had been the inspiration and the organization for the 2020 protests. For activists on the Left, a return to normal meant a return to the racist, sexist, homophobic, transphobic status quo that they had been protesting, which was thrown into stark relief by the pandemic. Journalists Daniel Dawes and Brian Castrucci argue that "the 'normal' to which many are so eager to return was the normal that helped pave the path for this devastation. Before Covid-19, normal meant widening racial gaps in income and wealth, higher rates of food insecurity among Black and Latinx households, and less than half of low-wage workers with access to paid sick leave."[9] While Biden might indeed represent a return to normalcy in that he is the sine qua non of the Washington establishment, for many on the Left, that normalcy was less than appealing.

For some in the mainstream media, Biden's normalcy seemed downright boring. An *L.A. Times* headline reads, "100 Days Into Biden's Presidency, Boring is Biden's Superpower."[10] Journalist Amanda Marcotte writes that

> after years of relentless reality show antics caused by Donald Trump, the latest word in the cable news discourse is that President Joe Biden is *boring*. He spends all his time doing policy work and his press engagement is a total snoozefest, with nary a single unhinged rant in front of buzzing helicopter blades. And the mainstream press is starting to get annoyed by it.[11]

Marcotte shows the strange relationship that the mainstream media maintained with Trump. Trump loathed and berated the mainstream press, but he always provided entertaining fodder for stories, and ratings were always high on cable news stations. Meanwhile, Biden is an affable man, who maintains a cordial relationship with the mainstream media, but they become annoyed when he does not perform the same litany of hijinks as his predecessor. The same deliberate, predictable qualities that make Biden a frustrating president for some on the Left make him a frustrating figure for the mainstream media; they may enjoy not being called the "enemy of the people," but they miss the pizazz that came with Trump and his administration.

For Trump supporters, Biden is anything but normal and boring; in the world they inhabit, he is a hardline communist. On the day of Biden's inauguration, QAnon believer and US Congressperson Marjorie Taylor Greene referred to Biden as the president of "Communist China."[12] In a 2021 interview with Fox News' Sean Hannity, Wisconsin senator Ron Johnson referred to Biden as a "liberal, progressive, social, Marxist."[13] An open letter from over 100 retired military generals and flag officers claimed that Biden was working to create "a Marxist form of tyrannical government."[14] Despite Biden's relatively centrist politics and his decidedly establishment position in Washington, DC, the Right views him as a committed Leftist and as an existential threat to the republic. The seeming return to normalcy after the barrage of chaos that characterized the Trump administration looks to many on the Right like a kind of tyrannical rule. The bifurcation of the country is so drastic that the septuagenarian centrist Biden can seem like a Marxist tyrant to a substantial sector of the American public.

## Right-Wing News Media in a Post-Trump World

One development in the media environment in the final days of the Trump administration and the beginning of the post-Trump era was the increased visibility of two right-wing news channels, Newsmax and One America News (OAN), which positioned themselves to the right of Fox News. Newsmax began as a conservative website in the 1990s and launched as a cable channel in 2014. It had very little following before the 2020 election, but it has found an audience with die-hard Trump supporters who refused to believe the election results that the other mainstream news networks, including Fox News, reported. A *New York Times* journalist showed that the network grew from an audience of about 58,000 viewers for its top shows before the 2020 election to an audience topping one million viewers afterward.[15] Following a similar path to Newsmax, OAN launched in 2013 and became increasingly popular during the Trump presidency. Because of its ardent sycophancy toward the forty-fifth president, Trump adored the network and it gained notoriety as Trump would call on reporters for the network disproportionately during press conferences. Writing during the Trump presidency, Devin Gordon observes that "to watch OAN is to experience the Trump presidency the way Trump himself would cover it, if he built a network from the ground up and then, as he did with his administration, hired amateurs to run it."[16] While Fox News was reliably conservative, though not always in complete lock-step with Trump, OAN always presented news the way that Trump wanted it to be portrayed. There was no gap between the truth that existed in Trump's head and the truth presented to him on OAN. The network gained a considerable number of viewers during the 2020 election when Fox News called Arizona for Joe Biden before the other major networks, essentially assuring a Biden victory. OAN was careful to leave the results of the 2020 election in doubt well into Biden's presidency in order to placate Trump and his supporters. After his Twitter account was suspended, Trump no longer had social media as a way to communicate with his most devout followers; subsequently, these networks have picked up the slack and have become organizations dedicated to presenting a Trumpian version of truth. Over two months after Biden was sworn in as president, an OAN correspondent claimed that there was "still serious doubt about who's actually president."[17] Journalist Rachel Abrams notes that OAN "has become a kind of Trump TV for the post-Trump age, an outlet whose reporting has aligned with the former president's grievances at a time when he is barred from major social media platforms."[18]

The increased popularity of Newsmax and OAN provides spaces where right-wing versions of truth can circulate without contamination from mainstream media. In these media pockets, the outcome of the 2020 election is still in doubt and Trump might rise to power any day; at the very least he will run for president in 2024 and win in a landslide. These networks put pressure on Fox News—which has already moved considerably rightward and maintains a solid reverence toward Trump—and work to move the Overton window of acceptable content. They are free to indulge in conspiracy theories that come from the likes of QAnon, such as the theory that Dominion Voting (a company who made voting machines for the 2020 election) erased millions of votes for Trump, swinging the election for Biden.[19]

Perhaps sensing competition from these networks, Tucker Carlson, one of Fox News' popular primetime commentators, has moved decidedly into alt-right territory on his news and opinion show *Tucker Carlson Tonight* (2016–). On an April 2021 episode of the show, Carlson endorsed a "great replacement theory" of immigration, which is one of the popular talking points of the alt-right. The great replacement theory suggests that birthrates among white women are lower than birthrates among women of color, and countries that have majority white populations should discourage any immigration, legal or otherwise, lest the white population be completely replaced by people of color.[20] The theory found its way into mainstream media when the gunman for the El Paso Walmart shootings cited the theory in a manifesto he left behind before he went on his race-based shooting spree.[21] The ideas of the great replacement theory and its fear of a "white genocide" had previously tended to reside in the far reaches of the alt-right and the darker corners of the internet. However, by 2021, Tucker Carlson felt comfortable espousing the ideas on one of the most watched shows on basic cable. He suggested that Democrats were trying to "replace" the electorate through immigration, strongly implying that they were replacing a majority white electorate with a majority non-white electorate. Journalist Zachary Petrizzo notes that after Carlson's comments about replacement, "white nationalists and other denizens of the far right have offered the Fox News host praise for his 'great replacement' commentary. Carlson's remarks strongly echo rhetoric pushed by overt white supremacists, who have suggested that white Christians in English-speaking countries are becoming endangered by immigration and growing demographic diversity."[22] In the post-Trump era, decidedly white nationalist voices have a home on basic cable; they no longer need to lurk on the imageboards of 4chan or the message boards of Reddit. The Overton Window has shifted to such an extent that Fox News is carrying alt-right content, perhaps in an effort to compete with the increasingly radical content provided on OAN and Newsmax.

In June 2021, Facebook upheld a ban on Donald Trump's account until at least 2023; because Instagram is part of the Facebook empire, Trump is also unable to post there.[23] As of that time, Trump was still locked out of his Twitter account, and thus is unable to maintain a visible presence on the three largest social media sites. He and other members of the far right have been searching for a platform that will allow them to post anything—some haven for absolute free speech, even if that free speech might include hate speech or calls to violent insurrection. Parler and Gab seem to offer a space between the mainstream sites and the darker corners of the web, such as 4chan and alt-right subreddits, where far-right extremists can mix with a broader public for the purposes of political action. Politics and technology scholar Luke Munn argues that Parler and Gab "mobilize users by marking out a position halfway between the mainstream Web and what we might term the sewer Web. The mainstream Web is composed of the social media behemoths of Facebook, Instagram, Twitter, and others. This bright arena is highly accessible and widely used but also highly controlled in policing behaviors and language that are allowed. The sewer Web, by contrast, is made up of legacy hate havens like 4chan and 8kun as the 'cesspools of the Internet.'"[24]

Trump succeeded in moving the Overton window of acceptable conservative politics by providing legitimate platforms for ideas that might otherwise have resided in the cesspools of the internet. For Trumpism to continue in the future, these lines of contact need to remain open so that mainstream conservatism and the alt-right are able to comingle. For a time, the microblogging app Parler seemed to be the platform of choice for conservatives who felt that Twitter and Facebook were too quick to ban people who might express ideas that might fall within the realm of hate speech or violent speech. Parler was indeed the app of choice for those who were involved in organizing the January 6 insurrection, as the site had increased its membership numbers exponentially as members of the far right felt that Facebook and Twitter had become too restrictive. Following the insurrection, Apple, Google, and Amazon no longer allowed users to download the app from their sites, "saying it had not sufficiently policed posts that incited violence and crime"; within a few days the site went dark.[25] As of June 2021, Parler was active, but not available on the Apple or Android stores, and its impact was greatly diminished. Journalist Abram Brown suggests that the Trump team may be working on developing their own social media platform, which would allow them to circumvent the free speech issues that plagued them on Facebook and Twitter.[26] However, without a social media presence, Trump is unable to maintain momentum in the day-to-day media repertoire and is no longer able to dominate the political conversation.

## Comeback?

In an effort to bring himself back to the center of the national conversation, Trump began holding rallies again in June 2021. On June 26 in Ohio, Trump held a "Save America" rally in which he continued to claim that he was the actual winner of the 2020 election and that Biden was only sitting in the office because of unprecedented fraud. He appeared at the rally with QAnon-believer Representative Marjorie Taylor Greene, giving a nod to the conspiratorial minded members of his base.[27] Journalist David Smith argues that "the rally was a vivid demonstration of how distortions of the rightwing political and media ecosystem seep down into the grassroots with real world consequences."[28] Even though he was out of office, did not have a major social media platform, and was not front-and-center in mainstream media coverage, Trump still commanded great political force, and had millions of followers who were eager to devour the truth according to Trump. While the media mechanisms may not be fully operational, the cult-like adoration for Trump allows him to hold considerable force in right-wing politics and indeed the Republican Party. On display at the rally was the boorish masculinity that Trump favors, with rally-goers donning T-shirts emblazoned with "Fuck Joe and The Hoe" on the front and "Biden Sucks and Kamala Swallows" on the back; such shirts were readily available for purchase at the rally.[29] The anger and hatred toward Trump's political foes still pervaded among the Trump crowd, and many erroneously believed that he would reclaim his rightful position as president in August 2021, based upon several conspiracy theories circulating at the time of the rally.[30]

While Trump somehow ascending to the office of president in the middle of the summer in 2021 is far-fetched, he does have the political support for him to make a comeback, whether through another presidential run or through controlling a media platform. Writing the day after the first rally after his presidency, journalist Meredith McGraw worries that "Trump's reemergence on the political scene is promising to spark a seismic disruption to America's political system bigger than the one he caused when he came down his gilded escalator six years ago. Where once his supporters were hopeful, they now seemed aggrieved. The crowds are more frenzied, the conspiracies more fantastical, the cast of characters more outlandish."[31] She notes that the crowd at the Trump event was darker and less optimistic than the ones that characterized the rallies during the 2016 and 2020 campaigns; its participants felt aggrieved and angry. One attendee at the event was convinced that if Trump was not reinstated as president in August 2021, "we're going to be in a civil war because the militia will be taking over."[32] Donald Trump's true believers are so invested in the "big lie" that circulates in the alternative media spaces that they are convinced that a civil war may be drawing nigh.

While the question of whether Trump is able to pull off a political comeback is unknowable in 2022, the political and media landscape from which Trump emerged is at least as fertile as when he announced his candidacy for president in 2015. Subsequent politicians might not be as deft as Trump at using various media to their advantage, though they might have more ideological convictions, political savvy, or determined work ethic. Future politicians will look to emulate Trump's complete embrace of the post-truth environment of contemporary media and his uncanny ability to capture the attention of all media at every turn. Those who see the presidency of Joe Biden as a breath of fresh air and a return to normalcy should recognize that a sizable portion of the population is seething with contempt that this ostensibly "normal" president has stolen the office. Journalists and pundits committed to a politics of bipartisanship should realize the flaw in that discourse when a populace is so bifurcated that a civil war seems to be a viable solution for perceived differences, and when the versions of truth on different sides of the political schism are incompatible. Scholars and activists should look for ways to mobilize a new politics in a post-truth environment that is consistent with the goals of equity and inclusion that the Left proffers; tyrants and demagogues should not hold a monopoly on post-truth politics. Those invested in a leftist politics should work toward world building and challenging careless speech, while not ceding ground to authoritarians and bigots in the name of bipartisanship or compromise. Similarly new media technologies and practices should not be summarily dismissed because of their potential to be used for hate and demagoguery. Further activism and scholarship should work toward mobilizing new media technologies and exploring the creative potentialities of post-truth discourses while being acutely aware of their potential use in the production of hatred and harm. Donald Trump may have been the first president who took full advantage of the political opportunities of the contemporary media environment, but he will not be the last. Scholars and activists need to work arduously to ensure that subsequent political figures who travel similar routes are able to enact less harm and unleash less hatred.

## Notes

1. Annie Karni and Nick Corasaniti, "Which Four Seasons? Oh, Not That One," *The New York Times*, November 7, 2020, https://www.nytimes.com/2020/11/07/us/politics/trump-books-four-seasons.html
2. Ibid.
3. Katelyn Burns, "The Trump Legal Team's Failed Four Seasons Press Conference Explained," *Vox*, November 8, 2020, https //www.vox.com/policy-and-politics/2020/11/8/21535022/four-seasons-landscaping-trump-giuliani-philadelphia-press-conference
4. Shirin Ghaffary and Rani Molla, "Here's Just How Much People Have Stopped Talking about Trump on Facebook and Twitter," *Vox*, May 3, 2021, https://www.vox.com/recode/22421396/donald-trump-social-media-ban-facebook-twitter-decrease-drop-impact-youtube
5. Kevin Breuninger, "Trump Blog Page Shuts Down for Good," *CNBC*, June 2, 2021, https://www.cnbc.com/2021/06/02/trump-blog-page-shuts-down-for-good.html
6. Sara Morrison, "Donald Trump's New Blog Lasted Less than a Month," *Vox*, June 2, 2021, https://www.vox.com/recode/2021/6/2/22465127/trump-desk-blog-gone
7. David Smith, "Biden Presidency": Return to 'Normal' Belies an Audacious Agenda," *The Guardian*, April 26, 2021, https://www.theguardian.com/us-news/2021/apr/26/biden-presidency-100-days-return-to-normal
8. Sarah Lyall, "100 Days without Trump on Twitter: A Nation Scrolls More Calmly," *The New York Times*, April 17, 2021, https://www.nytimes.com/2021/04/17/us/politics/trump-twitter.html
9. Daniel E. Dawes and Brian C. Castrucci, "Back to 'Normal' Isn't Good Enough," *Stat*, February 10, 2021, https://www.statnews.com/2021/02/10/back-to-normal-isnt-good-enough/

10  Jonah Goldberg, "100 Days into Biden's Presidency, Boring Is Biden's Superpower," *The Los Angeles Times*, April 27, 2020, https://www.latimes.com/opinion/story/2021-04-27/joe-biden-100-days-politics-ratings

11  Amanda Marcotte, "Joe Biden Is Boring—And It's Driving the Media Crazy," *Salon*, March 15, 2021, https://www.salon.com/2021/03/15/joe-biden-is-boring--and-its-driving-the-media-crazy/

12  Jeffery Martin, "Marjorie Taylor Greene Faces Backlash Online for Calling Biden President of Communist China," *Newsweek*, January 20, 2021, https://www.newsweek.com/marjorie-taylor-greene-faces-backlash-online-calling-biden-president-communist-china–1563207

13  Bill Glauber, "Ron Johnson Called Biden 'a Liberal, Progressive, Socialist, Marxist.' Can Someone Be All of Those Things? *Milwaukee Journal Sentinel*, June 11, 2021, https://www.jsonline.com/story/news/politics/2021/06/11/ron-johnson-joe-biden-a-liberal-progressive-socialist-marxist/7655294002/

14  Peter Feaver, "The Military Revolt against Joe Biden," *Foreign Policy*, May 12, 2021, https://foreignpolicy.com/2021/05/12/joe-biden-military-revolt-liz-cheney/

15  Michael M. Grynbaum and John Koblin, "Newsmax, Once a Right-Wing Also-Ran, Is Rising, and Trump Approves," *The New York Times*, November 22, 2020, https://www.nytimes.com/2020/11/22/business/media/newsmax-trump-fox-news.html

16  Devin Gordon, "Trump's Favorite TV Network Is Post-Parody," *The Atlantic*, May 19, 2020, https://www.theatlantic.com/politics/archive/2020/05/trumps-favorite-tv-network-post-parody/611353/

17  Rachel Abrams, "One America News Network Stays True to Trump." *The New York Times*, April 18, 2021, https://www.nytimes.com/2021/04/18/business/media/oan-trump.html

18  Ibid.

19  Ben Collins, "QAnon's Dominion Voter Fraud Conspiracy Reaches the President," *NBC News*, November 13, 2020, https://www.nbcnews.com/tech/tech-news/q-fades-qanon-s-dominion-voter-fraud-conspiracy-theory-reaches-n1247780

20  Nellie Bowles, "'Replacement Theory,' a Racist, Sexist Doctrine, Spreads in Far-Right Circles," *The New York Times*, March 18, 2019.

21  Lauretta Charlton, "What Is The Great Replacement?" *The New York Times*, August 6, 2019, https://www.nytimes.com/2019/08/06/us/politics/grand-replacement-explainer.html

22  Zachary Petrizzo, "White Nationalists Go Wild for Tucker Carlson's 'Great Replacement' Theory," *Salon*, April 14, 2021, https://www.salon.com/2021/04/14/white-nationalists-go-wild-for-tucker-carlsons-great-replacement-theory/

23  Mike Isaac and Sheera Frenkel, "Facebook Says Trump's Ban Will Last at Least 2 Years," *The New York Times*, June 4, 2021, https://www.nytimes.com/2021/06/04/technology/facebook-trump-ban.html

24. Luke Munn, "More Than a Mob: Parler as Preparatory Media for the Capitol Storming," *First Monday* 26, no. 3 (2021).
25. Jack Nicas and Davey Alba, "How Parler, a Chosen App of Trump Fans, Became a Test of Free Speech," *The New York Times*, January 10, 2021, https://www.nytimes.com/2021/01/10/technology/parler-app-trump-free-speech.html
26. Abram Brown, "Dumped By Twitter, Trump Looks to Build or Buy His Way Back onto Social Media," *Forbes*, March 23, 2021, https://www.forbes.com/sites/abrambrown/2021/03/23/trump-gab-parler-social-media-app-network/?sh=f09aaf01107
27. Jeremy W. Peters, "Trump, Seeking to Hold G.O.P. Sway, Holds First Rally Since Jan. 6," *The New York Times*, https://www.nytimes.com/2021/06/26/us/politics/trump-rally-ohio.html
28. David Smith, "'He's Not a Quitter': Faithful Out In Force as Trump Back to the Campaign Trail," *The Guardian*, June 27, 2021, https://www.theguardian.com/us-news/2021/jun/27/hes-not-a-quitter-faithful-out-in-force-as-trump-gets-back-to-the-campaign-trai
29. Kadia Goba, "The People Still Going to Trump Rallies Are Committed to Trump's Fantasy: 'He's Our True President,'" *Buzzfeed*, June 27, 2021, https://www.buzzfeednews.com/amphtml/kadiagoba/trump-rally-ohio-election-fantasy?__twitter_impression=true
30. Teri Kanefield, "Trump, Mike Lindell and Why the August Election Theory Should Worry Republicans," *NBC News*, June 8, 2021, https://www.nbcnews.com/think/opinion/trump-mike-lindell-why-august-election-conspiracy-should-worry-republicans-ncna1269912
31. Meredith McGraw, "A New Darkness Falls on the Trump Movement," *Politico*, June 29, 2021, https://www.politico.com/news/magazine/2021/06/29/trump-movement-new-darkness-future-496991
32. Graeme Massie, "Trump Supporter Warns Civil War Is Coming in Alarming Live Segment," *The Independent*, June 29, 2021, https://www.independent.co.uk/news/world/americas/us-politics/trump-supporters-rally-ohio-cnn-b1875064.html

# References

Abramowitz, Alan I. *The Great Alignment: Race, Party Transformation, and the Rise of Donald Trump*. New Haven, CT: Yale University Press, 2018.
Alterman, Eric. *What Liberal Media?: The Truth about Bias in the News*. New York: Basic Books, 2003.
Amazeen, Michelle M. "Journalistic Interventions: The Structural Factors Affecting the Global Emergence of Fact-checking." *Journalism* 21, no. 1 (2020): 95–111.
Anderson, Carol. *White Rage: The Unspoken Truth of Our Racial Divide*. New York: Bloomsbury Press, 2016.
Andrejevic, Mark. "The *Jouissance* of Trump." *New Media and Society* 17, no. 7 (2016): 651–5.
Andrejevic, Mark. *Reality TV: The Work of Being Watched*. Landham, MD: Roman & Littlefield, 2004.
Arendt, Hannah. *Between Past and Future: Eight Exercises in Political Thought*. New York: Penguin Books, 1968.
Banet-Weiser, Sarah, Cynthia Chris, and Anthony Freitas, eds. *Cable Visions: Television beyond Broadcasting*. New York: New York University Press, 2007.
Barthes, Roland. *Mythologies*. New York: Hill & Wang, 1972.
Baudrillard, Jean. *Simulation and Simulacra*. Ann Arbor: University of Michigan Press, 1994.
Benoit, William L. and K. Kerby Anderson. "Blending Politics and Entertainment: Dan Quayle versus Murphy Brown." *Southern Journal of Communication* 62, no. 1 (1996): 73–85.
Biressi, Anita and Heather Nunn. *Reality TV: Realism and Revelation*. London: Wallflower Press, 2005.
Bissonette, Devon. "'Modern Day Presidential': Donald Trump and American Politics in the Age of Twitter." *The Journal of Social Media in Society* 9, no. 1 (2020): 180–206.
Bloom, Mia and Sophia Moskaleno. *Pastels and Pedophiles: Inside the Mind of QAnon*. Sanford, CA: Redwood Press, 2021.
Boczkowski, Pablo J. and Zizi Papcharissi, eds. *Trump and the Media*. Cambridge, MA: The MIT Press, 2018.
Booker, Sara and Bradley M. Waite. "Humilitainment? Lessons from *The Apprentice*: A Reality Television Content Analysis." In *17th Annual Convention of the American Psychological Society*, Los Angeles. 2005.
Borden, Sandra and Chad Tew. "The Role of Journalist and the Performance of Journalism: Ethical Lessons from 'Fake' News (Seriously)." *Journal of Mass Media Ethics* 22, no. 4 (2007): 300–14.

Brownell, Kathryn Cramer. *Showbiz Politics: Hollywood in American Political Life.* Chapel Hill, NC: University of North Carolina Press, 2014.
Campbell, John L. *American Discontent: The Rise of Donald Trump and Decline of the Golden Age.* New York: Oxford University Press, 2018.
Carlson, Matt, Sue Robinson, and Seth C. Lewis. *News after Trump: Journalism's Crisis of Relevance in a Changed Media Culture.* New York: Oxford University Press, 2021.
Christians, Clifford et al. *Normative Theories of the Media. Journalism in Democratic Societies.* Urbana, IL: University of Illinois Press, 2009.
Cloud, Dana L. *Reality Bites: Rhetoric and the Circulation of Truth Claims in U.S. Political Culture.* Columbus, OH: The University of Ohio Press, 2018.
Compton, Josh. "Live from DC: Saturday Night Live Political Parody References in Presidential Rhetoric." *Comedy Studies* 7, no. 1 (2016): 62–78.
Dean, Jodi. *Democracy and Other Neoliberal Fantasies: Communicative Capitalism and Left Politics.* Durham, NC: Duke University Press, 2009.
Debord, Guy. *Society of the Spectacle.* Detroit: Black & Red Books, 2000.
DeCook, Julia R. "Memes and Symbolic Violence: #proudboys and the Use of Memes for Propaganda and Construction of Collective Identity." *Learning, Media, & Technology* 43, no. 4 (2018): 485–504.
Douglas, Susan. *Listening In: Radio and the American Imagination from Amos "N" Andy and Edward R. Murrow to Wolfman Jack and Howard Stern.* New York: Times Books, 1999.
Duncombe, Stephen. *Dream: Re-Imagining Progressive Politics in an Age of Fantasy.* New York: The New Press, 2007.
Dunn, Jennifer C. "Critical Rhetoric in the Age of the First Reality TV President: A Critique of Freedom and Domination." *International Journal of Communication* 14 (2020): 813–30.
Edwards, Brian T. "Trump from Reality TV to Twitter, or the Selfie-Determination of Nations." *Arizona Quarterly: A Journal of American Literature, Culture, and Theory* 74, no. 3 (2018): 25–45.
Enli, Gunn. "Twitter as an Arena for the Authentic Outsider: Exploring the Social Media Campaigns of Trump and Clinton in the 2016 Presidential Election." *The European Journal of Communication* 32, no. 1 (2017): 50–61.
Escoffery, David S., ed. *How Real Is Reality TV?: Essays on Representation and Truth.* Jefferson, NC: McFarland & Company, 2006.
Extröm, Mats "Epistemologies of TV Journalism." *Journalism* 3, no. 3 (2002): 259–82.
Farkas, Johan and Jannick Schou. "Fake News as a Floating Signifier: Hegemony, Antagonism, and the Politics of Falsehood." *Javnost: The Public* 25, no. 3 (2018): 298–314.
Foucault, Michel. *Fearless Speech.* Los Angeles: Semiotext(e), 2001.
Gobber, Giovanni. "The Scarlet Letter of 'Post-Truth': The Scarlet Letter of Communication." *Church, Communication, & Culture* 4, no. 3 (2019): 287–304.
Goffman, Erving. *The Presentation of Self in Everyday Life.* New York: Anchor Books, 1959.
Graves, Lucas. *Deciding What's True: The Rise of Political Fact-Checking in American Journalism.* New York: Columbia University Press, 2016.

Gray, Jonathan, Jeffrey P. Jones, and Ethan Thompson. *Satire TV: Politics and Comedy in the Post-Network Era*. New York: New York University Press, 2009.
Grossberg, Lawrence. *Under the Cover of Chaos: Trump and the Battle for the American Right*. London: Pluto Press, 2018.
Grusin, Richard A. "Donald Trump's Evil Mediation." *Theory and Event* 20, no. 1 (2017): S-86–99.
Gutsche, Jr., Robert E. *Media Control: News as an Institution of Power and Social Control*. New York: Bloomsbury, 2017.
Gutsche Jr., Robert E., ed. *The Trump Presidency, Journalism, and Democracy*. New York: Routledge, 2018.
Hall, Kira, Donna M. Goldstein, and Matthew Bruce Ingram. "The Hands of Donald Trump: Entertainment, Gesture, Spectacle." *Hau: Journal of Ethnographic Theory* 6, no. 2 (2016): 71–100.
Hanan, Jason, ed. *Truth in the Public Sphere*. Lanham, MD: Lexington Books, 2016.
Happer, Catherine, Andrew Hoskins, and William Merrin, eds. *Trump's Media War*. Cham, CH: Palgrave Macmillan, 2019.
Hayes, Christopher. *Twilight of the Elites: America after Meritocracy*. New York: Crown Publishers, 2012.
Hofstadter, Richard. *Anti-Intellectualism in American Life*. New York: Vintage Books, 1963.
Hofstadter, Richard. *The Paranoid Style in American Politics and Other Essays*. New York: Vintage Books, 2008.
Hussain, Amina. "Theorising Post-Truth: A Postmodern Phenomenon." *Journal of Comparative Literature and Aesthetics* 42, no. 1 (2019): 150–62.
Hyvönen, Ari-Elmeri. "Careless Speech: Conceptualizing Post-Truth Politics." *New Perspectives* 26, no. 3 (2018): 31–55.
Jacobs, Ronald. "Journalism after Trump." *American Journal of Cultural Sociology* 5, no. 3 (2017): 409–25.
Jameson, Fredric. *Postmodernism: Or, the Cultural Logic of Late Capitalism*. Durham, NC: Duke University Press, 1992.
Janack, James. "The Rhetoric of 'The Body': Jesse Venture and Bakhtin's Carnival." *Communication Studies* 57, no. 2 (2006): 197–214.
Jeffords, Susan. *Hard Bodies: Hollywood Masculinity in the Regan Era*. New Brunswick, NJ: Rutgers University Press, 1994.
Kakutani, Michiko. *The Death of Truth: Notes on Falsehood in the Age of Trump*. New York: Tim Duggan Books, 2018.
Katz, Jackson. *Man Enough?: Donald Trump, Hillary Clinton, and the Politics of Presidential Masculinity*. Northampton, MA: Interlink Books, 2016.
Kazin, Michael. *The Populist Persuasion: An American History*. Ithaca, NY: Cornell University Press, 1998.
Keyes, Ralph. *The Post-Truth Era: Dishonesty and Deception in Contemporary Life*. New York: St. Martin's Press, 2004.
Kien, Grant. "Postmodernism Trumps All: The World Without Facts." *Qualitative Inquiry* 27, no. 3–4 (2021): 374–80.
Kruse, Kevin M. and Julian E. Zelizer. *Fault Lines: A History of the United States since 1974*. New York: W. W. Norton & Company, 2019.

Latour, Bruno. "Why Has Critique Run out of Steam?: From Matters of Fact to Matters of Concern." *Critical Inquiry* 30, no. 2 (2004): 225–48.

Litherland, Benjamin. "Breaking Kayfabe Is Easy, Cheap, and Never Entertaining: Twitter Rivalries in Professional Wrestling." *Celebrity Studies* 5, no. 4 (2014): 531–3.

Lockhart, Michelle. *President Donald Trump and His Political Discourse: Ramifications of Rhetoric via Twitter*, ed. New York: Routledge, 2019.

Manjoo, Farhad. *True Enough: Learning to Live in a Post-Fact Society*. New York: John Wiley & Sons, 2008.

Marwick, Alice E. and Danah Boyd. "I Tweet Honestly, I Tweet Passionately: Twitter Users, Context Collapse, and the Imagined Audience." *Media & Society* 13, no. 1 (2011): 114–33.

Mayer, William G. "Why Talk Radio Is Conservative." *Public Interest* 156 (2004): 86–103.

McChesney, Robert. "The Problem of Journalism: A Political Economic Contribution to an Explanation of the Crisis in Contemporary US Journalism." *Journalism Studies* 4, no. 3 (2003): 299–329.

McDevitt, Michael and Patrick Ferrucci. "Populism, Journalism, and the Limits of Reflexivity: The Case of Donald Trump." *Journalism Studies* 19, no. 4 (2018): 512–26.

McIntosh, Dawn Mari D., Dreama G. Moon, and Thomas K. Nakayama, eds. *Interrogating the Communicative Power of Whiteness*. New York: Routledge, 2019.

McIntyre, Lee. *Post-Truth*. Cambridge, MA: The MIT Press, 2018.

McLuhan, Marshall. *Understanding Media: The Extensions of Man*. Cambridge, MA: The MIT Press, 2001.

Mello, Joseph. "Free Speech from Left to Right: Exploring How Liberals and Conservatives Conceptualize Speech Rights through the Works of Lenny Bruce and Milo Yiannopoulos" *Law, Culture, & the Humanities* 17, no. 2 (2021): 1–20.

Mercieca, Jennifer. *Demagogue for President: The Rhetorical Genius of Donald Trump*. College Station, TX: Texas A&M University Press, 2020.

Meyers, Marian, ed. *Neoliberalism in the Media*. New York: Routledge, 2019.

Miles, Matthew R. and Donald P. Haider-Markel. "Polls and Elections. Trump, Twitter, and Public Dissuasion: A Natural Experiment in Presidential Rhetoric." *Presidential Studies Quarterly* 50, no. 2 (2020): 436–50.

Milosavljević, Marko and Sally Broughton Micova. "Banning, Blocking and Boosting: Twitter's Solo-Regulation of Expression." *Media Studies* 7, no. 13 (2016): 43–58.

Mittell, Jason. *Television and American Culture*. New York: Oxford University Press, 2010.

Momen, Mehnaaz. *Political Satire, Postmodern Reality, and the Trump Presidency: Who Are We Laughing at*. Landham, MD: Lexington Books, 2019.

Mondak, Jeffery J. "The Politics of Professional Wrestling." *Journal of Popular Culture* 23, no. 2 (1989): 139–49.

Moskalenko, Sophia and Clark McCauley. "QAnon: Radical Opinion versus Radical Action." *Perspectives on Terrorism* 15, no. 2 (2021): 142–6.

Munn, Luke. "More Than a Mob: Parler as Preparatory Media for the Capitol Storming." *First Monday* 26, no. 3 (2021).
Murray, Susan and Laurie Ouellette, eds. *Reality TV: Remaking Television Culture*. New York: New York University Press, 2004.
Murray, Susan and Laurie Ouellette, eds. *Reality TV: Remaking Television Culture*, 2nd ed. New York: New York University Press, 2009.
Mutz, Diana C. *In-Your-Face Politics: The Consequences of Uncivil Media*. Princeton, NJ: Princeton University Press, 2015.
Nagle, Angela. *Kill All Normies: The Online Culture Wars from Tumblr and 4chan to the Alt-Right and Trump*. Washington, DC: Zero Books, 2017.
Nichols, Tom. *The Death of Expertise: The Campaign against Established Knowledge and Why It Matters*. New York: Oxford University Press, 2018.
Oborne, Peter and Tom Roberts. *How Trump Thinks: His Tweets and the Birth of a New Political Language*. London: Head of Zeus Publishing, 2017.
O'Brien, Shannon Bow. *Donald Trump and the Kayfabe Presidency: Professional Wrestling Rhetoric in the White House*. Cham, CH: Palgrave MacMillan, 2020.
Ott, Brian and Greg Dickenson. *The Twitter Presidency: Donald J. Trump and the Politics of White Rage*. New York: Routledge, 2019.
Perlman, Allison. "Rush Limbaugh and the Problem of the Color Line." *Cinema Journal* 51, no. 4 (2012): 198–204.
Perlstein, Rick. *The Invisible Bridge: The Fall of Nixon and the Rise of Reagan*. New York: Simon and Schuster, 2014.
Perlstein, Rick. *Nixonland: The Rise of a President and the Fracturing of America*. New York: Scribner Books, 2008.
Peters, Michael A. Sharon Rider, Mats Hyvönen, and Tina Besley, eds. *Post-Truth, Fake News: Viral Modernity & Higher Education*. Singapore: Springer, 2018.
Pomerantsev, Peter. *Nothing Is True and Everything Is Possible: The Surreal Heart of the New Russia*. New York: Public Affairs Books, 2014.
Poniewozik, James. *Audience of One: Donald Trump, Television, and the Fracturing of America*. New York: W.W. Norton & Company, 2019.
Postman, Neil. *Amusing Ourselves to Death: Public Discourse in the Age of Show Business*. New York: Penguin Books, 1985.
Reich, Zvi. "Journalism as Bipolar Interactional Expertise." *Communication Theory* 22, no. 4 (2012): 339–58.
Reich, Zvi and Hagar Lahav. "What on Earth Do Journalists Know? A New Model of Knowledge Brokers' Expertise." *Communication Theory* 31, no. 1 (2021): 62–81.
Richards, Steve. *The Rise of the Outsiders: How Mainstream Politics Lost its Way*. London: Atlantic Books, 2017.
Rosenwald, Brian. *Talk Radio's America: How an Industry Took Over a Political Party That Took Over the United States*. Cambridge, MA: Harvard University Press, 2019.
Sammond, Nicholas, ed. *Steel Chair to the Head: The Pleasure and Pain of Professional Wrestling*. Durham, NC: Duke University Press, 2005.
Schudson, Michael. *Journalism: Why It Matters*. Malden, MA: Polity Press, 2000.
Schudson, Michael. "The Trouble with Experts—And Why Democracies Need Them." *Theory & Society* 35, no. 5–6 (2006): 491–506.
Serfaty, Viviane. "Passionate Intensity: Political Blogs and the American Journalistic Tradition." *Journal of American Studies* 45, no. 2 (2011): 303–16.

Shafer, Jessica Gantt. "Donald Trump's 'Political Incorrectness': Neoliberalism as Frontstage Racism on Social Media." *Social Media & Society* 3, no. 3 (2017): 1–10.
Singer, Jane B. "Border Patro: The Rise and Role of Fact-Checkers and Their Challenge to Journalists' Normative Boundaries." *Journalism* 22, no. 8 (2001): 1929–46.
Smith, Tyson. "Wrestling With 'Kayfabe'." *Contexts* 5, no. 2 (2006): 54–5.
Snow, Nancy and Mary Sivia Vacerreza, eds. *Virtues, Democracy, and Online Media: Ethical and Epistemic Issues*. New York: Routledge, 2021.
Stern, Alexandra Minna. *Proud Boys and the White Ethnostate: How the Alt-Right Is Warping the American Imagination*. Boston: Beacon Press, 2019.
Stiegler, Zack. "Michael Savage and the Political Transformation of Shock Jock." *Journal of Radio & Audio Media* 21, no. 2 (2014): 230–46.
Stolee, Galen and Steve Caton. "Twitter, Trump, and The Ease: A Shift to a New Form of Presidential Talk?" *Signs & Society* 6, no. 1 (2018): 147–65.
Syverson, Tom. *Reality Squared: On Reality TV and Left Politics*. Washington, DC: Zero Books, 2021.
Tannehill, Brynn. *American Fascism: How the GOP Is Subverting Democracy*. Oakland, CA: Transgress Press, 2021.
Trump, Donald J. and Tony Schwartz. *Trump: The Art of the Deal*. New York: Random House, 1987.
Tuters, Marc and Sal Hagen. "( (They))) Rule: Memetic Antagonism and Nebulous Othering on 4chan." *New Media & Society* 22, no. 12 (2020): 2218–37.
Tuters, Marc, Emilija Jokubauskaité, and Daniel Bach. "Post-Truth Protest: How 4chan Cooked Up the Pizzagate Bullshit." *M/C Journal: A Journal of Media and Culture* 21, no. 3 (2018).
Uscinski, Joseph E. and Ryden W. Butler. "The Epistemology of Fact Checking." *Critical Review* 25, no. 2 (2013): 162–80.
Usher, Nikki. "Rethinking Trust in the News: A Materialist Approach through 'Objects of Journalism.'" *Journalism Studies* 19, no. 4 (2018): 564–78.
Vancil, David L. and Sue D. Pendell. "The Myth of Viewer-Listener Disagreement in the First Kennedy-Nixon Debate." *Central States Speech Journal* 38, no. 1 (1987): 16–27.
Van, Den Bulk and A Hyzen. "Of Lizards and Ideological Entrepreneurs: Alex Jones and Infowars in the Relationship between Populist Nationalism and the Post-Global Media Ecology." *The International Communication Gazette* 82, no. 1 (2020): 42–59.
Wendling, Mike. *Alt Right: From 4chan to the White House*. London: Pluto Press, 2018.
Wiggins, Bradley E. "Boogaloo and Civil War 2: Memetic Antagonism in Expressions of Covert Activism." *New Media & Society* (2020): 1–27.
Wild, Nickie Michaud. "Dumb vs. Fake: Representations of Bush and Palin on Saturday Night Live and Their Effects on the Journalistic Public Sphere." *Journal of Broadcasting & Electronic Media* 59, no. 2 (2015): 494–508.
Winberg, Oscar. "Insult Politics: Donald Trump, Right-Wing Populism, and Incendiary Language." *European Journal of American Studies* 22, no. 2 (2017): 1–15.
Woods, Heather Suzanne and Leslie A. Hahner. *Make America Meme Again: The Rhetoric of the Alt-Right*. New York: Peter Lang Publishing, 2019.

# Index

4chan 2, 10, 34–5, 91–2, 113–14, 116–25, 128, 131, 134–5, 178, 196, 200
1952 election 15
1992 election 23, 26
1996 election 26
2000 election 27
2004 election 30, 171
2012 election 33
2016 election 15, 18, 24–7, 32–3, 42, 45, 48–50, 52–3, 57, 63, 69, 73, 77, 83, 91–2, 94–6, 101, 113–15, 119, 122–4, 133–4, 153, 155, 168–9, 173–5, 202

ABC News 20, 32, 97, 120, 129, 175
Agnew, Spiro 145–6, 154–5
Ailes, Roger 25, 56–7
alternative facts 28, 81, 168, 170, 172, 180, 184
America First 22, 79
Anderson, Carol 53–4
Andrejevic, Mark 72, 74
Anglin, Andrew 115–16
Antifa 129–30
anti-intellectualism 32, 151–2, 154
anti-vaccine movement 48, 149
*The Apprentice* 2, 9, 29, 57, 63–4, 67, 71
*The Art of the Deal* 66–7, 172
*Associated Press* 93
*The Atlantic* 52, 55, 68, 70, 177
authenticity 27, 31, 48, 70, 80, 82, 95, 99–100, 146
autism 48, 149

Beck, Glenn 56
bias (in media) 18, 56, 102, 141, 146, 149–50, 155, 169

Biden, Joseph R. 1, 6, 81, 108, 130, 133, 146, 173, 175, 186, 195–9, 201–2
birther movement 34, 101
blogosphere 31
Boogaloo Bois 35, 114, 124–8, 131–3
Breitbart News 123–4, 133–4
broadcast networks 7, 103
Burnett, Mark 29, 67
Bush, Billy 45, 73–4
Bush, George H.W. 22
Bush, George W. 27, 31, 33, 152–5, 167, 170–1, 187
Bush, Jeb 69, 91

cable news 2, 24–5, 28, 56–7, 144, 155, 182, 196–7
capitalism 21, 83, 147, 178
Carlson, Matt 143–4, 156–7, 161
Carlson, Tucker 199–200
CBS News 3, 20, 31–2, 97, 175
censorship 89, 102, 106, 121
Cernovich, Michael 123, 134, 180, 182
Charlottesville (VA) 129
Checkers (Nixon) 15–16
civil rights 55
civil rights movement 39, 54
civil society 150
civil unrest 126
climate change 148–50
climate denial 180–1
Clinton, Bill 23–5, 118
Clinton, Hillary 24, 31–3, 41, 50, 52, 57, 70, 79, 92, 95–7, 118–19, 131, 134, 153, 177–8, 182
CNN 3, 20, 25, 56, 92, 98, 125, 169, 175
*The Colbert Report* (2005–14) 28, 174
Colbert, Stephen 28, 167, 169, 174

# INDEX

conservative talk radio 2, 8–9, 22, 25, 39–51, 53–4, 56–8, 89–90, 97–8, 146, 177, 182, 188
conspiracy theories 7, 10, 34–5, 48–50, 69, 94, 101, 118, 123–4, 132–4, 147, 171, 179, 199 202
Conway, Kellyanne 28, 168, 172
Couric, Katie 32–3
Covid-19 pandemic 5, 153, 197

*The Daily Show* (1996–) 27–8, 174
dark web 35
democratic norms 48, 161
Democratic Party 8, 25, 30–1, 51, 91–2, 102, 107, 187, 200
democratic system 8, 81, 83, 143, 147, 151, 158–9, 161–2, 177, 189–90
Dickenson, Greg 55, 89–90, 96
Douglas, Susan 15, 40, 43, 53
Duncombe, Stephen 187–8

Elliott, Phillip 153
Enlightenment epistemology 183, 186
entertainment sphere 17, 24
epistemic authority 10, 141–5, 147–50, 153, 155, 158, 160
epistemological ecosystem 64, 173
establishment media 2, 4, 7, 28, 31, 48–9, 98, 103, 151, 171, 173–4, 183
expertise 31, 148–50, 152–5, 160

Facebook 30, 32, 49, 102, 113, 125, 128–9, 133, 173–5, 196, 200–1
fact-checkers 76, 158–9
fake news 27–8, 64, 98, 134, 141, 151, 157, 167–8, 170–1, 173–6
feminism 39–41, 55, 114–15, 122–3
Fey, Tina 33
Ford, Gerald 17–18
*Fox and Friends* 57
Fox News 14, 24–5, 40–1, 56–8 90, 98, 104, 129, 133, 146, 171, 175, 178, 198–200
freedom of speech 103, 121–2
free-market capitalism 7, 121

Gab 200
#Gamergate 121–3

gatekeepers (of media) 2–4, 7, 9–10, 15, 30, 48, 97–9, 104, 107, 170, 189
Greene, Marjorie Taylor 131, 198, 201

Hannity, Sean 40, 56, 198
Hayes, Chris 147–8
Hirschorn, Michael 70
Hollywood 19, 23, 72–3, 79, 124, 131, 133

incivility 89–90
Ingraham, Laura 56
internet technology 30

Jackson, Michael 21
January 6 insurrection 1, 3 6, 10, 35, 83, 108, 113–14, 124–7, 130–4, 156, 201
Jeffords, Susan 19
Johnson, Dwayne 75
Johnson, Jenna 79, 94
Johnson, Ron 198
Jones, Alex 48–50, 119, 155
Jones, Hannah 26
Jones, Leslie 102–3
journalism 3, 7, 10, 28, 31, 48, 103, 134, 141–5, 148–9, 151, 153–62, 174–5, 179, 183
 epistemology 143, 150, 159, 161, 172

kayfabe 64, 74, 80–1
Keller, Jason 129
Kennedy, John F. 16–17, 65, 69
Kharakh, Ben 94
knowledge-accumulation 118, 134, 152, 184
knowledge brokers 148
knowledge building regimes 158
knowledge claims 143–4

"lamestream media" 146, 154, 173
Lewis, Justin 71
Lewis, Seth 143–4, 156–7, 161
liberal democracy 7, 9–10, 103, 141–2, 144, 151, 156, 158, 160, 162
liberal talk radio 46

Limbaugh, Rush 22, 39–41, 43–4, 46–8, 51–6, 89, 155, 171
*Los Angeles Times* 97

Marcotte, Amanda 132, 197
Mathis-Lilley, Ben 92
McCain, John 32
McGahan, Jason 131
McInnes, Gavin 129
McIntyre, Lee 169, 180–1
media environment 2–3, 8, 47–8, 74, 81, 108, 133–5, 155, 158–9, 161, 173–5, 177–8, 181–2, 187–8, 196, 198, 201, 203
media ecosystem, *see* media environment
mediascape 14, 70, 73, 108, 188
meme culture 91–2, 113, 116, 118–20, 124, 127, 132
misogyny 40, 42, 45–6, 73, 78, 103–4, 113–14, 117, 122, 128–9
Mittell, Jason 7
Mooney, Michael 127
MSNBC 24–5, 40, 54, 147, 171
Murray, Mark 30
Murray, Susan 63–5
Muslim ban 117
Muslims 52, 77, 83, 101, 104, 129

nationalism 76, 79, 115, 120, 124, 129
National Public Radio 46–7, 93, 171
Nazi Germany 3, 9
Nazis 114–17, 119, 156
Nazism 102, 115
NBC News 20, 97, 175
neo-Nazi 92
news cycle 10
Newsmax 198–200
New York 42
New York City 15, 17–18, 43
*New York Times* 6, 18, 41, 48–9, 57, 80, 93, 97, 134, 143–4, 159, 168, 171, 184, 196, 198
nihilism 83, 116, 123, 179
*New Yorker* 66–8, 180
Nixon, Richard M. 15–17, 23, 56, 65, 145–6, 154

Obama, Barack 31–4, 48, 51, 54, 70, 72, 78, 96–7, 101, 131, 168
objectivity 80, 97, 142, 157–8, 160–1, 176, 184, 186
oligopolistic system 97
Omar, Ilhan 52
One America News (OAN) 198–200
O'Reilly, Bill 56
Ott, Brian 53, 55, 89–90, 96
Ouellette, Laurie 63, 65

Palin, Sarah 32–3, 146, 154
Parler 130, 200–1
Pepe the Frog 113, 119–20
PizzaGate 118, 131, 134, 182
Poehler, Amy 33
political sphere 17, 24
political system 9, 117, 202
*Politico* 122
Pomerantsev, Peter 82–3
Poniewozik, James 13–14, 16, 21
populism 25, 32–3, 54, 63, 119, 141, 145, 150, 153–6, 185
populist rhetoric 25
postmodernism 11, 28, 83, 167–8, 176–83, 185–6, 188
post-truth 11, 73, 83, 135, 160–2, 167–73, 176, 178–9, 182, 184–90, 196, 202–3
professional wrestling 25–6, 63–5, 74–81
Proud Boys 35, 114, 124, 127–33
public sphere 10, 13, 41, 101–3, 107, 161, 185
punditry 2, 4, 25, 28, 31, 33, 49, 52, 77, 97, 141, 147, 152, 154, 159, 172, 177, 188, 202

QAnon 35, 114, 124, 131–4, 170, 186, 198–9, 201

racial discrimination 18
racism 52, 55–6, 73, 79, 104–5, 115–17, 119, 129, 161
radio 13–16, 19, 22, 46–7, 93
rationality 154, 160–1, 183, 187–8
Reagan, Ronald 8, 18–19, 22, 72–3, 155
Reaganomics 21

reality television 2, 4, 9, 18, 28–30, 33, 63–77, 80–3, 89, 177, 188
Reddit 2, 10, 34, 92, 113–14, 116–18, 120–2, 128, 135, 178, 196, 200
Republican Party 8, 15, 18, 22, 25, 31–2, 51, 69, 77, 93, 99, 101–2, 129, 146, 155, 158–9, 184, 201
rhetoric 41, 53, 93, 95, 104, 120, 183, 200
right-wing ecosystem 188
Robinson, Sue 143–4, 156–7, 161
Rogan, Joe 155
Rosenwald, Brian 46–8, 51, 56
Russia 32–3, 64, 81–3, 175

Sanders, Bernie 50
Savage, Michael 40
satellite technology 21
satire 28, 33, 174–5
*Saturday Night Live* 17–18, 33
second civil war 124–5, 127, 202
self-censorship 99–100
Schwartz, Tony 66–8
Schreckinger, Ben 91, 122
shock jocks 9, 39–41, 43, 45, 47
Spencer, Richard 102, 104, 115, 117, 121, 123–4
Spicer, Sean 78, 168
Stewart, Jon 27–8, 174
*Survivor* (2000–) 28–9, 67–8

troll 14, 103–4, 116–18, 123
Trump, Donald, J.
  agenda 90, 98, 115
  big lie 7
  Brokaw, Tom 18
  celebrity 13–14, 21–2
  Covid-19 pandemic 5
  ecosystem 184
  epistemology 99–101, 104, 168, 186, 189, 196
  image construction 16–17
  impeachment 107–8, 133
  inauguration (2017) vi, 63, 77, 133, 168
  January 6 insurrection 1

  journalistic coverage 10
  mainstream media 2–3, 16
  Make America Great Again 8, 19
  misogyny 14, 34, 42, 45–6, 73, 104
  November 2016 election 4, 13, 15, 24–5
  November 2020 election 7
  Overton window 9
  post-truth 4–5, 9, 11
  rallies 2–3, 42, 47–8, 52–3, 55, 130–1, 134, 201–2
  Republican Party 8
  *Saturday Night Live* 18
  speeches 3
  Trump Tower 18
  Trumpism 4
  *see also* Twitter
  wealth 21–2
  website 24
Trump Jr., Donald 119–20
Twitter
  4chan 113, 118
  Alex Jones 49
  authenticity 95, 99
  Biden, Joseph 196
  censorship 102–4
  community 91–2
  conservative media 133
  launch 30
  political campaign 32
  politics 96
  post-truth 189
  Proud Boys 129
  removal policy 6
  Russia 175
  system 105
  Trump, Donald 1–3, 5, 9–10, 14, 24, 34, 54, 80, 89–91, 95–101, 105–8, 118, 153, 178, 196, 199–201
  white nationalists 94
  Yiannopoulos, Milo 104
Twittersphere 106
"truthiness" 11, 167

United States Congress 1, 40, 51–3, 131

vaccines 5, 48, 147, 149–50
violence 1, 11, 53, 90, 103–4, 124, 126, 128–30, 146, 156, 201

*Wall Street Journal* 55, 97
*Washington Post* 97, 107, 143, 173
white America 8
White House 15, 30, 71, 81, 107, 113, 168
   doctors 5
   reporters 145
white masculinity 39, 41, 45–6, 51
white nationalism 93, 114–17, 120, 122–4, 128–30, 197, 200
white rage 53–6, 90
white supremacy 10, 35, 45, 52–3, 91–4, 120, 126, 129–31, 200
whiteness 51–5, 70, 93–4, 119–20
white working class 14, 52
World War II 7, 15, 19, 50, 54
WWE 26, 75, 80

Yiannopoulos, Milo 102–4, 119, 123
YouTube 30, 33, 48, 102, 123, 133–4

www.ingramcontent.com/pod-product-compliance
Lightning Source LLC
Chambersburg PA
CBHW062223300426
44115CB00012BA/2192